LIVY

HIS HISTORICAL AIMS
AND METHODS

LIVY

HIS HISTORICAL AIMS AND METHODS

BY

P. G. WALSH

*Lecturer in Humanity and Ancient
History in the University of
Edinburgh*

CAMBRIDGE
AT THE UNIVERSITY PRESS
1970

870
Wa ✓

PUBLISHED BY
THE SYNDICS OF THE CAMBRIDGE UNIVERSITY PRESS
Bentley House, 200 Euston Road, London, N.W. 1
American Branch: 32 East 57th Street, New York N.Y. 10022

© CAMBRIDGE UNIVERSITY PRESS 1961

S.B.N. 521 06729 4

First printed 1961
Reprinted 1963
1967
1970

First printed in Great Britain at the University Press, Cambridge
Reprinted by photolithography Unwin Brothers Limited Woking and London

HELENAE
UXORI DILECTISSIMAE

CONTENTS

PREFACE   *page* ix

LIST OF ABBREVIATIONS   xi

   I   THE PERSONAL BACKGROUND:
       PATAVIUM AND AUGUSTAN ROME   1

  II   THE TRADITION OF ANCIENT
       HISTORIOGRAPHY   20

 III   RELIGIOUS, PHILOSOPHICAL AND
       MORAL PRECONCEPTIONS   46

  IV   ROMAN MORALITY HISTORICALLY
       CHARACTERISED   82

   V   LIVY'S HISTORICAL AUTHORITIES   110

  VI   LIVY'S HISTORICAL METHODS   138

 VII   LIVY'S LITERARY METHODS   173

VIII   THE NARRATIVE: LITERARY GENRES   191

  IX   THE SPEECHES   219

   X   LIVY'S LATINITY   245

  XI   CONCLUSION: LIVY AS THE
       HISTORIAN OF ROME   271

SELECT BIBLIOGRAPHY   288

INDEX   293

PREFACE

LIVY is a writer curiously unpopular in the English-speaking world. Every schoolboy imbibes the conventional but erroneous belief that the historian's writing is monotony unrelieved. Professional historians rightly stress his glaring defects: above all, his inability to impose upon the historical material an organised design, a sense of control, and an acutely personal vision such as Polybius and Tacitus manifest. Thus authority reinforces inclination, which explains the neglect but hardly justifies it. For if Livy exhibits grave deficiencies as an historian of events, he has yet a central importance for Roman studies; in the words of a great Livian scholar, R. S. Conway, 'it is to Livy more than any other writer that we owe our conception of the Roman national character'. This importance has been widely recognised in other countries; in particular, French, German, and Italian scholars have composed numerous monographs and articles which testify to not only the value of Livy as interpreter of the Roman civilisation, but also to the several facets of his literary genius. My heavy debt to these critics is sufficiently indicated in the following pages; *et si in tanta scriptorum turba mea fama in obscuro sit, nobilitate ac magnitudine eorum me qui nomini officient meo consoler.*

Livy is unique amongst the greater Roman historians in having no personal experience in politics and warfare. This fact dictates the direction and the limits of a study of the *Ab Urbe Condita*. In his recent brilliant work on Tacitus, Professor Ronald Syme was concerned above all to relate that historian's work to his career and social background as a consular and a senator. For Livy the private citizen such an approach has little relevance; we cannot even be certain where he lived whilst composing his history. To evaluate the book-scholar's achievement it is necessary to study him primarily in relation to the theories of historiography which he adopted and to the sources which he followed.

Such concentration upon the historian's debt to the earlier tradition is rendered more inevitable by the loss of his analysis of events after 167 B.C. 'I should be glad', wrote Bolingbroke, 'to exchange what we have of this History for what we have not.' This critic doubtless perceived that Sallust and Tacitus achieved historical distinction by cogent analysis of contemporary events in which they had themselves been engaged. Our judgement of Livy might well be kinder if we possessed the later section of his history; certainly the criteria would be different.

I owe an especially heavy debt of gratitude to Dr A. H. McDonald, who accorded me courteous advice and criticism at two successive stages of composition. Professor Arnaldo Momigliano also was kind enough to read the typescript and to make several penetrating suggestions. Above all, I must express my thanks to Professor F. W. Walbank for his constant encouragement and unstinting assistance throughout the past ten years; my debt to him is no less than Livy's to Polybius.

I have also profited from the criticisms of Professor J. J. O'Meara, Professor M. J. Boyd, and Dr L. Bieler. Mr R. M. Ogilvie has read the page proofs and made many salutary criticisms of content and style. Miss E. Power and Miss M. Hogan, of University College Dublin, have assisted me in obtaining works not available in Ireland, where this book was written. Finally, I must thank the Syndics and Secretary of the Cambridge University Press for their generosity and courtesy in accepting this book for publication.

P. G.W.

UNIVERSITY OF EDINBURGH

LIST OF ABBREVIATIONS

AJP	*American Journal of Philology*
CAH	*Cambridge Ancient History*
CIL	*Corpus Inscriptionum Latinarum*
CP	*Classical Philology*
CQ	*Classical Quarterly*
CR	*Classical Review*
Ét. Class.	*Les Études classiques*
GR	*Greece and Rome*
HRR	*Historicorum Romanorum Reliquiae*
HSCP	*Harvard Studies in Classical Philology*
JHS	*Journal of Hellenic Studies*
JRS	*Journal of Roman Studies*
MB	*Musée belge*
Mnem.	*Mnemosyne*
OCD	*Oxford Classical Dictionary*
PCA	*Proceedings of the Classical Association*
RE	Pauly–Wissowa–Kroll, *Real-Encyclopädie*
REA	*Revue des études anciennes*
REG	*Revue des études grecques*
REL	*Revue des études latines*
Rev. Phil.	*Revue de philologie*
RFIC	*Rivista di filologia e d'istruzione classica*
RhM	*Rheinisches Museum*
Riv. IGI	*Rivista Indo-Greco-Italica*
RSA	*Rivista di storia antica*
Symb. Osl.	*Symbolae Osloenses*
TAPA	*Transactions and Proceedings of the American Philological Association*
Wien. Stud.	*Wiener Studien*

I

THE PERSONAL BACKGROUND:
PATAVIUM AND AUGUSTAN ROME

THE work of a good historian is unlikely to embrace much autobiographical detail. If he writes of the events of his own time, there may be incidental mention of acquaintances who provide relevant evidence, of the journeys made to investigate a problem at first hand, of the profession which entitles him to give a specialised judgement on a particular question. In Livy's case this is denied to us because his account of his own times has not survived; the last extant book goes no further than 167 B.C., more than a hundred years before he was born. Equally unfortunately, none of his letters has come down to us. And, as we should expect of a man who spent virtually his whole life in literary composition, there is little evidence of his activities in the writings of others. For these reasons Livy remains the most nebulous figure of all the greater historians of the ancient world.

Saint Jerome's evidence suggests, perhaps wrongly, that he was born in 59 B.C., and it is clear from a variety of sources that his birthplace was Patavium (Padova). It would be difficult to overestimate the importance of this early environmental influence in Transpadane Gaul. This region became increasingly the proverbial repository of the ancient Roman virtues, and Patavium, in contrast to Rome, retained much of the strict moral outlook of older days. This conservatism of manners was naturally reflected in its political outlook, and its pro-Senatorial attitude was manifest in the citizens' refusal to admit the legates of Antony when in 43 B.C. the Senate declared him a public enemy. Livy's history is imbued with a traditionally pro-Republican outlook, and with an emphasis on the strict moral code which regulated the lives of the great Republican leaders; it has even been suggested that this is the *patavinitas*, the quality in Livy's writing at which Asinius Pollio jeered.[1]

It must not however be assumed that Livy's early life was spent in a rustic backwater. Patavium was a flourishing commercial city famous for its woollen products, and the home of more wealth than any other city of Italy with the exception of Rome. It had also a venerable history, claiming to rival the capital in the antiquity of its foundation; Livy patriotically mentions at the beginning of his history Antenor's landing at the head of the Adriatic at about the same time as Aeneas was settling in the south. Patavium, then, was an important city with a considerable population, proud of its traditions and with the educational facilities which its wealth would assure.[2]

Livy almost certainly received his education in Patavium and not in Rome. He was only a schoolboy when Julius Caesar precipitated the Civil War by invading Italy; it would have been madness for responsible

[1] The date of birth may well be inaccurate. Jerome's dating (*ad Euseb. Chron. ad ann. Abr. 1958*) links Livy with Messalla Corvinus, whose birth and death are postdated by five years (see R. Syme, *JRS* (1955), 157). Perhaps Jerome confused the consuls of 59 (Caesare et Bibulo) with those of 64 (Caesare et Figulo). A strong case can thus be made for 64 as date of birth. See R. Syme, *Tacitus* (Oxford, 1958), 137 n. 1, and references there.

For evidence of Patavium as birthplace, there is Pollio's epithet of *patavinitas* (Quint. 1, 5, 56); the remark of the Paduan Asconius, *In Corn.* 68, 'Livius noster'; Mart. 1, 61, 3, 'censetur Apona Livio suo tellus', where 'Apona tellus' is Patavium (Weissenborn–Müller, Livy 1, *Einl.* 3).

For the old-time virtues of Patavium see Pliny, *Ep.* 1, 14, 6; for opposition to Antony see Cic. *Phil.* XII, 4, 10. For *patavinitas*, see below, 267 ff.

[2] Strabo, III, 5, 3; V, 1, 7, stresses Patavium's commercial importance; the city had 500 men of equestrian status. For Antenor's landing, see Livy 1, 1,

guardians[1] to expose a young boy to the considerable physical and moral dangers which both the journey and the disordered life in the capital might produce. At the age of twelve, after a preliminary grounding in the basic subjects at home or at the *ludus*, he presumably went to the local secondary school, where the *grammaticus* supervised the reading of the Greek and Roman poets and historians, and gave instruction in the correct use and pronunciation of words. We do not know the identity of this teacher, but he evidently fired the imagination and enthusiasm of his pupil for the study of history, and has thereby earned a reflected immortality. Under normal circumstances, Livy might well have gone to Rome for the final stage of schooling under the *rhetor*—pupils usually received this training from the age of sixteen. But at this time the Civil War was in progress (or, if we accept Jerome's chronology, the disturbances following Caesar's death were spreading northwards). Livy probably remained in his native city. Here again it is evident from his skill at speech-composition that he was soundly trained in the theory of oratory, though we do not know how effective a public speaker he was.[2]

Very often a Roman student rounded off his formal education with a year or two in Athens or Rhodes, where he attended the lectures of the outstanding philosophers and rhetoricians of the day. There is no certainty that Livy did so. The forties were not the most propitious years for study abroad, and sea travel was hazardous in the years following 40 B.C., when Sextus Pompeius held such a grip on Roman waters that Octavian could scarcely obtain sufficient food supplies for the capital. Doubtless this did not prevent all young Romans from crossing to Greece at this time. But Livy certainly makes no claim to have seen

---

[1] There is, however, no concrete evidence to offer on this point.
[2] For the Roman system of education see H. I. Marrou, *A History of Education in Antiquity*, trans. Lamb (London, 1956), 229 ff.

the Greek sites which he describes, and in general his vagueness of geography might suggest that he travelled little in these formative years.[1]

Whether he travelled to Greece or not, he certainly had no military experience; he is so ignorant of the practical aspects of soldiering that he can never have thrown a *pilum* in anger. It seems clear that he stayed at home and read. At this time his interests were divided between history and philosophy, for during this period he wrote dialogues specifically philosophical, and others with a strong historical flavour. Cicero's philosophical dialogues, several of them published as recently as 45–44 B.C., were undoubtedly his models. These years of philosophical study had a considerable effect on the early sections of his historical writing. They provided an impetus and a direction which reflect that Stoic view of the world expounded by Balbus in Cicero's *De Natura Deorum*, which emerges too in the *De Divinatione*, and which is pre-eminently traceable to the influence of the neo-Stoic Posidonius. Livy may have read the philosophical writings of Plato, Xenophon, and others in the original, but the dynamic in his history is above all attributable to the Stoic ethical influence which already held an important place in the tradition of Roman historiography, and which in Livy's case was reinforced by his philosophical studies.[2]

Before he began to compose his massive history, Livy moved to Rome. The exact date is unknown, but two considerations may be of assistance. Livy came to the capital to write his prose epic for a nation at peace, to guide men in their principles of conduct by an appeal to the *mores* of Republican heroes. But if Antony, and not

---

[1] P. Graindor, *MB* (1923), 135 ff., cites possible epigraphical evidence for a sojourn at Athens, but inconclusively. For geographical weaknesses see Ch. VI, 153 ff.

[2] On Livy as philosopher see Sen. *Ep.* 100, 9. I follow Rossbach, *Hermes* (1882), 367, n. 3, in assuming that the philosophical works preceded the history. On the philosophical preconceptions of the *Ab Urbe Condita* see P. G. Walsh, *AJP* (1958), 355 ff.

Octavian, had won the final round at Actium in September 31, the terror in Italy would have been renewed. Livy may have travelled to Rome when it became clear that the threat from Antony and Cleopatra was circumscribed. Secondly, the first book of the *Ab Urbe Condita*, as we shall see, was published between 27 and 25. It must be assumed that Livy came to Rome partly to consult the works of historians which were not available at Patavium, and that he spent a considerable time in preliminary research. If this is the case, Livy was perhaps in Rome to witness the triumphant return of Octavian from the East in the summer of 29 B.C.

Livy thus began his life's work, which eventually filled one hundred and forty-two books in the unfolding of Rome's history from the foundation to the death of Drusus in 9 B.C.—a period of seven hundred and forty-four years. Of these books only thirty-five have survived, I–X and XXI–XLV, which cover the years 753–293 and 219–167 B.C. It has often been suggested, and with some justification, that this young man in his thirties embarked upon his task with a naïve idea of what it entailed, without sufficient preliminary study, and without an overall plan such as Polybius, for example, gives us at the beginning of his *Histories*. Certainly in his remarks prefatory to the fourth decade he implies that he is increasingly appalled by the immensity of his task. None the less, in the extant books there is every indication that he has surveyed the sources with some care, and has chosen the writers most apposite for his purpose; this general survey may well have extended itself to Livy's own times. The more concentrated study which he made immediately prior to composition can be best appreciated by a division of the work into units of five books. Livy's work should be read in pentads, as it was clearly written in pentads. Many scholars, in their criticism of the arrangement of the later books, have failed to appreciate the greater complexity of events described in them; they expect an orderly division of the major campaigns into pentads as in the early books, and when they see the Civil War, for example, described in Books CIX–CXVI, they assume that Livy has abandoned his orderly arrangement in favour of a more *ad hoc* procedure.

The truth is, however, that Livy's annalistic arrangement militates against a simple overall construction. It was easier in the earlier books, where source-information was largely restricted to successive wars. Later, as the extent of Roman territories widens, and increasing information becomes available on civil matters, Livy's history cannot concern itself in any pentad with one particular field of operations. Often completely different wars are being fought simultaneously, and important civil developments are taking place. Even so, the pentads often have an obvious unity which can be demonstrated by detailed analysis. In such a scrutiny one should examine not merely the last book of each section but also the first, because in many cases he postpones the treatment of a major event to have an arresting topic for the beginning of a new section. Thus the capture and destruction of Carthage are described in LI, the capture of Jugurtha in LXVI, and the murder of Julius Caesar in CXVI.

The first decade is a special case. Book I, which embraces the whole of the Regal period (753–510), may have been published separately, for Book II has a new introduction; it may also be significant that Augustus, whilst Livy was composing Book IV, took the trouble to ensure that the historian was informed of an alleged archaeological discovery. Such flattering attention may suggest that Livy had already won as historian a *succès d'estime*, though it is possible that his fame had spread through *recitationes* rather than by publication.[1]

[1] IV, 20, 5 ff. (the passage is discussed below, 14 f.). There is no evidence to support J. Bayet's theory that this is an addition to an earlier edition first published 31–29 B.C. For support of the theory of *recitationes* see C. Cichorius, *Römische Studien* (Leipzig, 1922), 261–9.

Books ii–v, which embrace the events down to the Gallic capture of Rome (509–390), were presumably published together, as the presence of an introduction to Book vi suggests. Livy's main theme in the next pentad is the Samnite Wars, which culminate in the defeat not only of the Samnites but also of the Etruscans, Gauls, and Umbrians. The lost second decade contains the two separate sections of the war with Tarentum and the First Punic War. The Hannibalic War has the whole third decade allotted to it, but it is artistically divided between the rise of Hannibal's star and the Roman counter-attack. Books xxxi–xlv should be seen as three pentads—the first comprising the war with Philip and affairs in Greece prior to the war with Antiochus, the second the struggle with Antiochus in Greece and Asia, and the third taking in the Third Macedonian War and the triumph of Aemilius Paulus over Perseus.

The *Periochae*, or summaries, of the later books suggest how this arrangement in pentads continues. The ninth decade, for example, has the two themes of Sulla's war against Mithridates and his savage behaviour on returning to Italy. In the twelfth, the first pentad covers Caesar's campaigns from Dyrrachium to Munda, and the second the twenty months between Caesar's death and the formation of the Second Triumvirate. These examples may provide a significant clue to the unity of the later pentads; they appear to be constructed not around particular campaigns, but around the dominant Roman of the day. Thus Scipio Aemilianus dominates the sixth decade, beginning with the capture of Carthage in li: Marius begins his career in lxvi, spans three pentads with his achievements, and dies in lxxx; Sulla is conspicuous in the next two pentads, and dies in xc: Pompey first appears in the summary of the following book, xci. Difficulties subsequently arise when the author is confronted with two great figures simultaneously in Pompey and Caesar, but

Caesar's campaigns in the Civil War have been cited as one pentad with a specific unity. Finally, the summaries of the last books are too brief to infer the structure of them, especially as those for CXXXVI–CXXXVII are missing.

There are adequate indications, then, that Livy's history was planned and constructed carefully and artistically, with the pentad as the basic unit. If he wrote continually until his death, he averaged over three books yearly for forty years. In fact his composition was probably still more rapid. We are told that CXXI–CXLII were not published until after Augustus' death; perhaps they had lain completed for years. Significantly CXX contained the execution of Cicero and the condemnation of the conspirators, whom Livy assessed favourably.[1] Was Augustus' reaction one of pained disappointment, and did Livy accordingly postpone publication of his account of 42 to 9 B.C.? Such discretion in launching contemporary history would not be unparalleled in Western letters.

Earlier, Livy may have produced pentads at intervals of little more than a year after publishing Book I in 27–25. Tenuous internal evidence suggests that IX was written before 20, and XXVIII after the 'subjugation of Spain' (26/5 or 19 B.C.?). Long before his death in A.D. 14 Augustus had read the books in which Pompey is prominent, for Tacitus remarks that Livy's pro-Pompeian bias did not forfeit the emperor's affection; now Pompey's death is reported in CXII.[2]

---

[1] The oldest MSS. of the *Periochae* state that CXXI was published after Augustus' death. For Brutus and Cassius see below, 12.

[2] I, 19, 3 refers to Augustus' closing of the temple of Janus. The title Augustus was assumed in 27, and there is no mention of the second closing of 25; Book I was thus composed between those dates. Books VI–X were probably written before the recovery of the standards from Parthia in 20, for Livy does not advert to this at IX, 18, 6. For the reference to the subjugation of Spain see XXVIII, 12, 12. Augustus' comment on the characterisation of Pompey is at Tac. *Ann.* IV, 34. For more cautious suggestions on publication see Weissenborn, *Einl.* 9 f.; H. Bornecque, *Tite-Live* (Paris, 1933), 17 f.

This welter of figures and dates is necessary to demonstrate the historian's phenomenal and unflagging industry. The scrutiny of at least three sources for each book, the attempt to reconcile them, and the translation of their content into the complex medium of Augustan prose, often with a complete rewriting of the speeches—to have worked at this for over forty years at the rate of at least ten books every three years is a programme which leads one to the realisation that Livy led a life of complete dedication to his writing. We are reminded of the Elder Pliny, who took notes of every book read, even at the dinner-table, who composed whilst being scraped and towelled at the bath, and who rebuked his nephew for walking instead of studying inside a conveyance; 'he thought every moment wasted which was not devoted to study'.[1] The *Ab Urbe Condita*, as Livy's work was named, for all its merits contains little personal speculation and must on occasion have become utterly mechanical. It is not surprising to learn that he contemplated abandoning the task when it was well advanced. His mind, however, was too restless to forsake the pen.[2]

This impression of a man of purely literary interests is reinforced by the scanty knowledge available about his private life. He had two sons and a daughter. One son composed a treatise on geography—a rather ironical choice of topic in view of his father's inadequacies—and one showed interest in rhetoric. Livy's daughter married a rhetorician called Lucius Magius, whose recitations, the elder Seneca acidly suggests, drew an audience because of his father-in-law's fame. This was clearly a household with pronounced academic preoccupations.[3]

---

[1] Pliny, *Ep.* III, 5, 16.

[2] The full title of the work would be *Historiarum ab urbe condita libri* (Roman historians usually specified their point of commencement in their titles). For the admission of weariness see Pliny, *N.H. praef.* 16.

[3] For Livy's family see Quint. x, 1, 39; Sen. *Contr.* x, *prooem.* 2. The tomb-inscription (see below, 19, n. 2) mentions two sons.

What of Livy's relations with Augustus? There is no doubt that the *Ab Urbe Condita* was commenced in an atmosphere of renewed hope. After two decades of the horrors of fratricidal war, the years 29–27 saw the introduction of peace both at home and abroad, which was marked by the solemn closure of the temple of Janus. There was general enthusiasm and willingness to work for the restoration of Rome's greatness, and a strong belief, nourished by Augustus' studied moderation, that not merely the symbols but also the spirit of Republican government could be reintroduced. It is inconceivable that Livy did not react to this new spirit of optimism, nor respond to the leadership of the Princeps with enthusiasm; he must have welcomed Augustus as the second founder who was needed to put a halt to the progressive degeneration, political and moral, to which Sallust and others had drawn attention. This notion of Octavian as a second Romulus was strongly current at Rome after the final defeat of Antony.[1]

In this sense Livy can be termed an 'Augustan' historian. It is significant that the greatest writers of this great literary age were all born in Republican days. Like Vergil and Horace, Livy looked back in shame and anger at the anarchy and savagery of the twenty years preceding Octavian's triumphant return in 29; those harrowing experiences on sensitive minds seem to have been a formative element in the growth of the patriotic literature of the finest creative period ever experienced by Rome. In particular there is a remarkable correspondence between the spirit animating the first decade of the *Ab Urbe Condita* and that of Vergil's *Aeneid*. The same central concept of Rome as *pulcerrima rerum* dominates both works. Both conceive the city as divinely founded and providentially guided; both emphasise her imperial

---

[1] Dio LIII, 16, 7; Suet. *Aug.* 7, 2; Florus II, 34, 66. See E. C. Wickham's edition of Horace, I (Oxford, 1896), 199f.

mission to establish the *pax Romana* throughout the inhabited world. It is abundantly clear that such patriotic sentiments were encouraged by Augustus himself; Livy's history was 'fostered by the government....The Emperor and his historian understood each other.... Livy, Virgil and Horace of all Augustan writers stand closest to the government.'[1]

But it is a very different matter to claim that Livy prostituted his historical talents to the service of the regime. The impression has been frequently conveyed that he was little more than a propagandist, and that his message was the recommendation of the principate.[2] Others go further, even claiming that in Livy's characterisation of Romulus, Hercules, and Numa there are allusions to Augustus, with the clear intimation that he is divine.[3] Elsewhere we read that in his Preface the historian sets the seal of approval on Augustus' proposed social and political reforms.[4] Another scholar alleges that the historian's characterisation of Cicero reveals the extent to which Augustus dominates his thoughts: 'In no single passage has Livy sought to bring back into public favour the memory of a man who was to the last an object of dislike to his imperial patron.'[5]

There is no evidence whatsoever for this view of Livy as a blinkered spokesman of Augustus. Perhaps Tacitus

---

[1] See R. Syme, *The Roman Revolution* (Oxford, 1939), 463, 317f. Compare E. Burck, *Die Erzählungskunst des Livius* (Berlin, 1934), 241: 'Wie Vergil mit seinem großen Epos, wie Horaz mit seinen römischen Oden, so stellt sich auch Livius mit seinem Geschichtswerk im Sinne des Augustus in den Dienst der nationalen und ethischen Erneuerung Roms.'

[2] So C. N. Cochrane, *Christianity and Classical Culture* (Oxford, 1940), esp. 103 ff.

[3] G. Stübler, *Die Religiosität des Livius* (Stuttgart–Berlin, 1941), 43: 'Augustus, Gott, Gottes Sohn, ist gekommen, die Welt selig zu machen.'

[4] H. Dessau, *Festschrift O. Hirschfeld* (Berlin, 1903), 461 ff., with reference to the contemplated social legislation of 28 B.C.

[5] J. Carcopino, *Cicero and the Secrets of his Correspondence* (English edn., London, 1951), 18. But contrast the anecdote at Plut. *Cic.* 49 for Augustus' view of Cicero. Livy's judgement (see Sen. *Suas.* VI, 17) is influenced by the remarks of Pollio (*ibid.* VI, 15), and is in fact a fair if critical assessment.

is at the root of this disordered growth when he claims that after the battle of Actium impartial history could no longer exist. But the outspokenness of historians such as Cremutius Cordus was tolerated by the emperor; there was complete liberty for Livy to write what he pleased. True, Augustus obviously made a determined effort to befriend the historian, and from Tacitus one learns that they were on intimate terms. The evidence is important: 'Titus Livy... praised Cnaeus Pompey to such heights that Augustus called him a Pompeian, but this did not detract from their friendship.' Confirmation of Livy's popularity at the imperial court is found in the fact that he was at hand to encourage the youthful Claudius to write history.[1]

Tacitus' statement, it might be thought, is a sufficient guarantee that Livy's presentation of the fall of the Republic showed his integrity unimpaired in spite of his close relationship with Augustus. Tacitus further remarks that Brutus and Cassius were depicted by Livy 'on many occasions as men of distinction'. It has been suggested, however, that Augustus wished to encourage such a pro-Pompeian view to further his own political ends; Pompey is to be praised as another Augustus championing the Free State against military despotism. So Julius Caesar is ostracised from the poetry of Vergil and Horace, except for a 'veiled rebuke' in the *Aeneid*, and in the *Odes* the mention of the *Iulium sidus*, the soul of Caesar purged of all earthly stain.[2] The implication that Vergil and Horace are here the mouthpieces of official policy seems forced. The obvious reason for such reticence about Caesar is the sense of communal guilt which haunted the collective conscience of the Augustan age, and the feeling that Julius was especially guilty in precipitating the conflict.

[1] On the dearth of historians after Actium see Tac. *Hist.* I, 1. On Cremutius Cordus' outspokenness, Quint. x, 1, 104; Suet. *Cal.* 16, 1, *Tib.* 61, 3. On Livy's friendship with Augustus, Tac. *Ann.* IV, 34. On his encouragement of the young Claudius, Suet. *Claud.* 41, 1.

[2] So Syme, R.R. 317. (Verg. *Aen.* VI, 834f.; Hor. *Od.* I, 12, 46ff.)

It may be noted also that the epic of Varius, friend of Vergil, which sought to glorify Julius was not suppressed; and more obvious still, why did the sycophantic Ovid take such pains to eulogise Julius in the *Metamorphoses* and *Fasti* if he did not consider this to be agreeable to Augustus?[1] It seems probable, then, that too much credence has been lent to the view that there has been collusion on these political topics between Augustus and the influential writers of his age.

In Livy's case we must take the praise of Pompey at its face value, and dismiss the subtle theory that this was part of a deliberate campaign sponsored by Augustus. The opposite may in fact be nearer the truth. So far from Augustus' having brought political pressure to bear on Livy, the early books of the *Ab Urbe Condita* reinforced the effects of Varro's writing in giving inspiration to Augustus' programme of religious and moral reform. True, the restoration of the temples had begun in 28 B.C., but the other manifestations of concern with religion—the *Ludi Saeculares* in 17 B.C., and the many revivals of obsolete ceremonial introduced after Augustus became Pontifex Maximus in 12 B.C.—all took place long after the publication of Livy's first decade, which laid emphasis on the picturesque and salutary religious observances of ancient days. Again, Augustus became curator of laws and morals no earlier than 19 B.C., and his social legislation to encourage marriage and child-bearing and to discourage adultery was not enacted until 9 B.C.; Livy's lessons on the important role of chastity (*pudicitia*) in the well-ordered state, in the cases of Verginia and Lucretia, had been pondered by his readers as early as 25 B.C. The conclusion must be that Livy was construc-

---

[1] For Augustan feelings of guilt see e.g. Hor. *Od.* I, 35. On Varius' poem see W. Y. Sellar, *Roman Poets of the Augustan Age, Virgil* (Oxford, 1908), 50. For Ovid see *Met.* xv, 745 ff.; *Fasti* III, 155 ff., 697 ff.; and the discussion of L. P. Wilkinson, *Ovid Recalled* (Cambridge, 1955), 253 f.

tively forming public policy in this direction rather than sedulously praising it.[1]

There is no *a priori* reason, then, for assuming that Livy adapted his history to the service of the regime. Nowhere is there flattering mention of the Emperor. A Horace could show adulation with the lines

> *Lucem redde tuae, dux bone, patriae:*
> *Instar veris enim voltus ubi tuus*
> *Adfulsit populo, gratior it dies*
> *Et soles melius nitent.*

And a Vergil could write

> *Hic vir, hic est, tibi quem promitti saepius audis,*
> *Augustus Caesar, divi genus, aurea condet*
> *Saecula....*[2]

But we must distinguish between this fulsome, if sincere, flattery and the less obsequious approval of Livy, who naturally enough acclaims the end of civil strife, but seeks no personal favours from Augustus.

What references are made to Augustus in the *Ab Urbe Condita*? The first is in connection with the closing of the temple of Janus: 'The gods allowed our age to see this second closing, when Augustus Caesar after the battle of Actium won peace on land and sea.'[3] Here there is no great expression of enthusiasm for the Princeps; Livy attributes the credit to the gods. A more controversial passage is that where he describes the offering of the *spolia opima* to Jupiter by a certain Cornelius Cossus. The traditional accounts said that Cossus was a military tribune at the time, but Augustus claimed to have found the *spolia* with an inscription proving that Cossus was consul. 'When I heard', says Livy, 'that Augustus Caesar,

---

[1] For Augustus' revival of ceremonies see Suet. *Aug.* 31. For Lucretia, Livy 1, 58; Verginia, III, 44 ff.

[2] *Od.* IV, 5, 5 ff.; *Aen.* VI, 791 ff.

[3] 1, 19, 3: '...quod nostrae aetati di dederunt ut videremus, post bellum Actiacum ab imperatore Caesare Augusto pace terra marique parta'.

the founder or restorer of all the temples, had entered the shrine of Jupiter Feretrius—he restored it when it had decayed with age—and had personally read this inscription on the linen corselet, I thought it well-nigh sacrilegious to deny to Cossus as witness of his spoils the testimony of Caesar, the builder of that very temple.'[1] Some scepticism has been expressed at this discovery, especially in view of Augustus' refusal to allow the proconsul Licinius Crassus to lay the *spolia opima* in 27 B.C. on the grounds that he was not consul. Though such suspicions cannot be proved, there is a distinct possibility that Augustus has forged this evidence to discourage a possible political rival.[2] Whatever the truth of the matter, Livy's remark can hardly be construed as adulatory, though the tone is naturally respectful and his approval of the Emperor's concern for religion is manifest. But his regrettable failure personally to confirm the discovery hardly marks him as a conscious conspirator in the suppression of the truth, but is rather symptomatic of his major defect as historian—his failure to peruse the documentary evidence.[3]

Augustus is mentioned in other places factually and without flattery, as where Livy writes that Spain was subdued under his leadership, or again, where Augustus' use of Q. Metellus' speech for his social reforms is recounted.[4] In the complete absence of any obsequiousness which is explicit, imaginative denigrators have embarked upon a microscopic search for signs and symbols. Some have analysed his uses of the word *augustus*, claiming that these have allusive reference to the Princeps, or at least that

---

[1] IV, 20, 7: 'hoc ego cum Augustum Caesarem, templorum omnium conditorem aut restitutorem, ingressum aedem Feretri Iovis quam vetustate dilapsam refecit, se ipsum in thorace linteo scriptum legisse audissem, prope sacrilegium ratus sum Cosso spoliorum suorum Caesarem, ipsius templi auctorem, subtrahere testem'.

[2] See H. Dessau, *Hermes* (1906), 142 ff. G. De Sanctis, *Problemi di storia antica* (Bari, 1932), 237 f., regards this as hypercritical.

[3] Below, 112 ff.   [4] XXVIII, 12, 12; *Perioch.* LIX.

Livy was seeking to make clear the true significance of the title Augustus,[1] his object being to point the way to the deification of the Emperor. Recently the inconclusiveness of these claims has been demonstrated in detail, and the more tenable theory put forward that the conferring of the title in 27 B.C. gave a wider currency to the adjective. And, by a *reductio ad absurdum*, one can point to thirty-six usages of the word *divinus* where *augustus* could have been used if there had been an ulterior motive in the employment of the word.[2]

Still more popular is the view that Livy depicts the great figures of the past in such a way that the reader sees in them the image of Augustus. So Romulus, Numa, Camillus, Decius, and Scipio Africanus are all to be regarded as portraying facets of Augustus' greatness. Livy, it is claimed, uses Romulus' story to stress Augustus' divinity, for phrases like *deum deo natum, regem parentemque urbis Romanae*[3] awaken the reader to their contemporary significance. (The difficulty afforded by *regem*—how Livy's almost pathological abhorrence of kingship at Rome can be reconciled with such an alleged allusion to Augustus— is glossed over.) Numa's role is still more relevant: 'He prepared to found the city afresh by justice, laws, and customs.'[4] Yet Vergil expresses a similar idea, a fact which suggests that it may be reproduced from Ennius.[5]

But it is Camillus above all who rouses the enthusiasm of the symbolists—Camillus, who not only saved Rome from the invader, but prevented the citizens from abandoning Rome in favour of a new capital. So he is hailed as a Romulus, a second founder and saviour of Rome (*Romulus ac parens patriae, conditorque alter urbis*).[6]

---

[1] Stübler, 10ff.; K. Scott, *TAPA* (1925), 99; L. R. Taylor, *CR* (1918), 158ff.

[2] H. Erkell, *Augustus, Felicitas, Fortuna* (Göteborg, 1952), 19ff.   [3] 1, 16, 3.

[4] 1, 19, 1: '...iure eam legibusque ac moribus de integro condere parat'. For identification with the Princeps see Stübler, *loc. cit.*

[5] *Aen.* VI, 810; see E. Norden, *Aen.* VI³ (Leipzig, 1957), *ad loc.*

[6] V, 49, 7; see Syme, R.R. 305 f.

This is a more convincing thesis, in the sense that the echoes of titles accorded to Augustus are very strong; elsewhere, Camillus is called *diligentissimus religionum cultor* when he proposes the restoration of the shrines.[1] But the comparison should not be carried too far. It is very doubtful whether Camillus' opposition to the proposed transference of the capital to Veii can be construed as an echo of Octavian's propaganda against Antony, who was said to be planning to move the seat of empire to Alexandria (though it is clear that Cleopatra's part in this plan inspired Vergil's depiction of the Dido episode, the attempt to detain Aeneas at Carthage). Livy was composing this episode of Camillus at least four years after Actium and Antony's death; such propaganda had lost its immediate purpose. It is much more likely that this whole episode in the career of Camillus was invented by an earlier annalist, perhaps shortly after Carthage was being mooted as the site for a new capital.[2] Another powerful argument against identifying Augustus too closely with Camillus is Livy's criticism of the ancient hero for a triumph in which 'he exceeded the proper limit'; his action in riding conspicuously into the city, drawn by white horses, seemed to show conduct 'unbecoming to him not only as a citizen, but also as a man'.[3] Is this then a warning to Augustus not to consider himself more than a man? Such critics cannot be so selective as to have it both ways.

The truth is surely that Livy, like all historians, can never completely dissociate the past from the present. In depicting historical occasions which have some parallel in his own day, his ears are subconsciously attuned to the echoes of the present, and he employs anachronistic

---

[1] v, 50, 1.

[2] Plut. *Cam.* 31 f. adverts to this agitation for the transference of the capital to Veii; the story must therefore have been in the Sullan annalists. See now E. Fraenkel, *Horace* (Oxford, 1957), 268, n. 1. Also F. Klingner, *Römische Geisteswelt* (Leipzig, 1943), 436.

[3] v, 23, 5: '...parumque id non civile modo sed humanum etiam visum'.

phrases evocative of the features of his own day. But to go beyond this, and to allege that Livy is a subtle salesman for the regime by cryptic identification with Augustus of the heroes of legend and history, is neither provable nor plausible. A weapon of propaganda which preaches its message by such symbolism is hardly likely to be efficient; if Livy had been concerned to stress the benignity and greatness of Augustus, he could surely have found the opportunity to link one complimentary adjective with his name.

The claim that the Preface indicates explicit approval of Augustus' projected social and religious reforms of 28 B.C. can hardly be substantiated. Livy's introductory message goes no further than does Sallust's in the *Catiline*, where the pattern of Roman history is similarly seen as a gradual decline from greatness because of increasing moral decadence. Livy seeks to depict the desperate condition to which the Romans have come, and to demonstrate by reference to the past his ideas of how their pre-eminence must be retained, but nowhere is there any hope expressed that such an achievement is immediately possible. He speaks of his own times 'in which we can endure neither our vices nor the remedies for them', and elsewhere his pessimism is equally explicit. No one can read the *Ab Urbe Condita* without the realisation that Livy has burning moral convictions about the state of contemporary Rome, and the need for a spiritual and moral awakening; but there is also clearly discernible a scepticism about the feasibility of immediate reform.[1]

Livy, then, lived for forty years in friendship with Augustus, directing great influence on him and retaining a sturdy independence in his interpretation of the past. He probably resided in Rome for most of his adult life.[2]

---

[1] This scepticism is expressed at *Praef.* 9; VII, 2, 13; 25, 9; compare VIII, 11, 1; IV, 6, 12.

[2] This is the commonly held view. V. Lundström, *Eranos* (1929), 1 ff., and R. Syme, *Tacitus*, 137, suggest that he spent most of his life in Patavium. The

Towards the end of his life he must have retired to Patavium, where he died, according to Jerome, in A.D. 17. But more probably the date was A.D. 12, two years before the Princeps' death.[1] This retirement to his native city is confirmed by the existence of a tomb-inscription found at Padua, which commemorates a Titus Livius, and which has been ascribed to the Augustan age.[2]

question cannot be definitely decided, but note that the Spaniard from Cadiz visited Rome to see Livy (Pliny, *Ep.* II, 3, 8); presumably he knew that he resided there. Livy's friendship with Augustus and his encouragement of the young Claudius' historical studies (12, n. 1.) are further indications. The argument from silence—that Livy does not appear in literary anecdotes in connection with his famous contemporaries—may be suggestive of character and habit rather than place of residence.

[1] Hieron. (*ad. Euseb. Chron. ad ann. Abr. 2033*) may have made the same mistake with Livy as with Corvinus. The length of life is accurate, but both birth and death are postdated by five years. For a dissenting view which defends Jerome's dating of Corvinus' death, see R. Hanslik, *RE* 8 A 1, 131 ff.

[2] *CIL*, v, 2975 (Dessau, 2919).

II

THE TRADITION OF ANCIENT
HISTORIOGRAPHY

BEFORE the Augustan age, history-writing at Rome
had never been regarded as the exclusive task of the
scholar. Whereas in our own day almost all historians
live their lives in a library, and comparatively few have
experience as political or military leaders, in Republican
Rome such a dichotomy between the student and the
man of action was impossible. Her small number of
highly literate men was needed to guide state policy, to
carry out diplomatic missions, to give leadership on the
battle-field, and to administer the laws.[1] And when,
in the middle of the first century B.C., intellectuals
like Cicero began to emphasise the need for academic
historians at Rome, the unsettled political scene did not
allow of it; Livy's most important immediate predecessors, Sallust and Asinius Pollio, both served the state in an
active capacity before they wrote history. Polybius' thesis
is unanswerable—that such experience was essential for the
ancient historian, who had so often, in the absence of works
of reference, to rely on his own knowledge and judgement
when evaluating his sources. But the Romans, forgivably
preoccupied with the paucity of their historiographical
tradition, were concerned to match Greek achievements
rather in literary elegance than in scientific accuracy.[2]

[1] See the remarks of Sallust at *Cat.* 8, 5.
[2] It is worth recalling that, for the ancients, philosophy and history were the
main types of literature composed in artistic prose; they had not the genres which
we associate with creative writing, though a form of romantic fiction eventually
emerged. History was therefore the primary medium for literary prose writing.

With Livy Roman historiography becomes a more academic pursuit. He came to history-writing without any of the practical experience demanded by Polybius, and, though he is conscientious according to his lights in the recording of the facts, his talent is largely literary. Fortunately, however, he was able to benefit from the extensive discussions on the theory of historiography which had preoccupied Roman intellectuals for some years. As has been frequently observed, his work incorporates many of the virtues which Cicero in his treatises (especially the *De Oratore*) demanded of the ideal historian: 'Was Cicero ersehnte, hat Livius erfüllt.'[1] Cicero's opinions, however, are not always consistent, for they vacillate under the stimulus of the particular historians before his eyes on the various occasions when he pronounced on the question. For the Ciceronian dogmas are in no way original, but represent an attempted synthesis of earlier historiographical theory, especially that of the Hellenistic period. In brief, Livy is indirectly the heir to the views of numerous Greek historians, moulded by Cicero into a doctrine not wholly consistent, about what the form and content of history should be. A brief study of these earlier influences is desirable to obtain a fuller understanding of Livy's approach to history.

Greek historiography reached its peak in the fifth century with Herodotus and more especially with Thucydides, whose narrative is perhaps the nearest approach to the ideal history of contemporary events the West has yet known. In particular, his survey of causes and effects, his impartiality in securing evidence from both sides, and his rigorous accuracy of detail established scientific standards which one might confidently have expected to be maintained and revered by his successors.

---

[1] R. Heinze, *Die augusteische Kultur* (Leipzig, 1930), 96. Compare J. Bayet, Budé Livy I (Paris, 1940), xxxvii, xli; H. Bornecque, *Tite-Live*, 33 ff.; M. Rambaud, *Cicéron et l'histoire romaine* (Paris, 1953), 121 ff.

In fact, the tenuous surviving material of the historians of the fourth and third centuries suggests that these standards were largely abandoned. Admittedly amongst lost historical writings were some outshining those which have survived. The unidentified author of the *Hellenica Oxyrhynchia*, for example, appears to have been far superior to Xenophon who wrote on the same period:[1] Ephorus, a pupil of Isocrates, is praised by Polybius for the wide scope of his history, and he emphasised the supreme importance of truth, and is said to have avoided pathetic and sensational effects;[2] and, at a more prosaic level, the chronicle of the Cretan Nearchus' voyage down the Indus and along the Asian coast to the Tigris, made after the Indian expedition of Alexander, and, again, the history of Alexander by Ptolemy I, which was based on the official *Journal* and other documents, both appear (in the extracts reproduced by Arrian) to be thoroughly trustworthy. Mention must be made also of Hieronymus of Cardia, whose reliable history of the half-century following the death of Alexander was used by Diodorus, Arrian (for his *Diadochi*) and Plutarch in his *Eumenes* and *Demetrius*.[3]

But the majority of histories written in this period were not so laudable. This is not the place to discuss detailed reasons for such a retrogression, but they are undoubtedly connected with the growth of the schools of rhetoric which followed upon the activities of the sophists. From these developed theories of 'rhetorical' history aiming at effects not always compatible with the truth. It is not until the second century that a worthy extant successor to Thucydides appears in the person of Polybius, to

[1] Text in F. Jacoby, *Die Fragmente der griechischen Historiker*, IIA, 17–35. See G. T. Griffith in *Fifty Years of Classical Scholarship* (Oxford, 1954), 160ff.

[2] See Polybius v, 33, 2; xII, 28, 10f. Ephorus, like Thucydides, passed over the early mythology, beginning his history with the return of the Heraclidae. But his claim to have excised the fabulous is disputed by Strabo (IX, 3, 11f.), who also complains of inaccuracies (VII, 3, 9; compare Seneca, *N Q*. VII, 16, 2).

[3] For the fragments of Hieronymus see Jacoby, IIB, 829–35.

maintain that the truth must always take precedence over literary considerations, and to reassert that the historian's primary concern is the discovery of what was actually said or done on any occasion, 'however commonplace'. In this respect he goes further than Thucydides, who was content to conform with the convention of composing speeches in a manner apposite to the occasion; Polybius censures Timaeus for this very practice.[1] Cicero speaks with approval of both Thucydides and Polybius, and his theories owe much to the standards of truthfulness and serious treatment which they exemplify.

Thucydides and Polybius are at one in asserting that the study of history will be of practical benefit to the statesman, a view also propounded by Aristotle. Thucydides regarded his work as a κτῆμα ἐς αἰεί for those who wished to have a clear vision 'both of the events which have happened and of those which will at some time again occur in the same or in a similar way'. (The influence of Hippocratic medical theory—the need for prognosis—is evident here.) And Polybius believed that his history had a great practical utility, equipping the student with a method of dealing with any future contingency.[2]

Very different from this sober, factual, and didactic treatment was the influence of those who regarded history as closely akin to rhetoric. Isocrates, himself no historian, plays an important role in this development through his influence on his pupils. One of these, Ephorus, could be content with insisting that history should be clothed in a worthy literary garment, and that due regard for truth should be maintained; but indications of Isocrates' less exacting historical standards[3] are conspicuous in the work of another pupil, Theopompus, who sought to display his rhetorical powers by the choice of

[1] Thuc. I, 22; Pol. XII, 25 a, 5.
[2] Thuc. I, 22; Pol. IX, 2, 5; XII, 25 g. Compare Aristotle, *Rhet.* I, 9, 40.
[3] Isocrates developed the encomium, with its tendency towards exaggeration: see e.g. *Busiris* 4 ff.

topics most congenial to such presentation. So in his work fables abounded, embodying 'everything strange and wonderful found on every land and in every sea'.[1] This emphasis on exotic topics was continued and accentuated by the chroniclers of Alexander's achievements, and in particular Callisthenes' and Clitarchus' accounts of the Asian expedition succumbed to the worst features of rhetorical history—exaggeration, sensationalism, and love of the marvellous.[2] Similar criticisms can be made of one of the most outstanding historians of the Hellenistic period, Timaeus, whose history of the Western Greeks was vitiated by over-emphasis on 'dreams, prodigies, and...womanish love of strange events'.[3] For such writers the purpose of history was not to offer practical instruction in statesmanship, as it was for Polybius, but to charm and entertain the reader.

A more detailed scrutiny of an historian of this type will illustrate this. Duris of Samos, who covered the period from the battle of Leuctra to 280 B.C., recalls in some respects Herodotus at his most delightful and his most irrelevant. There is the same *cherchez la femme* attitude in his narration of the Sacred War, when he claims that it was provoked by a Phocian's rape of Theano. There is the same love of anecdote, as in his story of the dolphin who fell in love with the child of Iasos and carried him off for a ride, or of the dog who threw him-

---

[1] Compare Cic. *De Leg.* 1, 1, 5: 'apud Theopompum sunt innumerabiles fabulae'. Also Dionysius, *Ad Pomp.* 6; Strabo 1, 2, 35.

[2] For general criticism of Callisthenes' incapacity in military matters, see Pol. XII, 17 ff. For typical examples of his rhetorical approach, Strabo XVII, 1, 43 (the flattering account of Alexander's godhead proclaimed by oracular agencies); Cic. *De Div.* 1, 74 (where is described, 'ut ait Callisthenes', the supernatural opening of the doors of Hercules' temple at Thebes before the battle of Leuctra). On Clitarchus' inaccuracy see Quint. x, 1, 75; Cic. *Brut.* 42 ('concessum est rhetoribus ementiri in historiis, ut aliquid dicere possint argutius...sic Clitarchus...'). There were other equally sensational chronicles of Alexander's expedition. Onesicritus, who did geographical exploration for Alexander, is condemned by Strabo (XV, 1, 28) for painting imaginary pictures; Hegesias is included by Gellius amongst the writers 'miraculorum fabularumque pleni' (IX, 4, 3). [3] Pol. XII, 24, 5.

self on his master's funeral pyre. There are the scandals about the private lives of prominent men like Demetrius of Phalerum. There is the same unremitting search for portents and marvels, and equally inevitably emphasis on the erotic element, with weird and wonderful stories of the intercourse some Indians have with beasts.[1]

It is Duris, too, who is prominent in another tendency found in some Hellenistic historians—the imitation of tragedy in its aims and methods. The distinction between this and 'rhetorical' history is not always clear-cut, because some 'rhetorical' historians had recourse also to 'tragic' methods; it is therefore misleading to speak of 'tragic' history as a separate genre used exclusively by a specific school. One cannot say precisely when it originated; Aristotle's clear distinction between the historian and the tragedian ('not that one writes prose and the other verse, but that one tells what happened, the other what might have happened') suggests that the problem was already controversial in his day. The general assumptions that the Peripatetic school or alternatively Isocrates originated it are highly improbable, and indeed it may well go back to the fifth century.[2]

Those writers addicted to 'tragic' techniques sought to thrill (ἐκπλήττειν) their readers by evoking feelings of pity and fear, by emotional persuasion (ψυχαγωγία), and by emphasis on the unexpectedness of events (τὸ παράδοξον) and the vicissitudes of fortune (τύχης μεταβολαί). Certain types of description are particularly amenable to this type of treatment, such as the fate of conquered cities, or the deaths of famous men; but dramatic effects were

---

[1] The causes of the Sacred War, Athen. XIII, 10; the dolphin, *ibid.* XIII, 85; the dog, Pliny, *N.H.* VIII, 143; Demetrius, Athen. XII, 60; the Indians' strange sex life, Pliny, *N.H.* VII, 30. The schol. on Apollonius Rhodius records another erotic touch from Duris—the allegation that Prometheus was punished, not for the theft of fire, but because of a love-affair with Athene. For a collection of these texts see Jacoby, IIA, 138, 140–50.

[2] On the origins of 'tragic' history see now F. W. Walbank, *Bulletin of London Institute of Classical Studies* 2 (1955), 4ff.

also sought in the more common scenes like battle-accounts, meetings of assemblies, and the like. Further, the composition of these writers sought to incorporate the structural principles of tragedy, so that the depiction of episodes had a clear pattern of beginning, middle, and end.

Equally as notorious as Duris for seeking such 'tragic' effects is Phylarchus, who is strongly criticised by Polybius for acting the tragic poet by recording harrowing details of the scene in Mantinea in 222 B.C.—dishevelled women with breasts bare, and children and aged parents lamenting as they are led away to slavery.[1] Similarly Duris' description of the Athenians' atrocities (reproduced by Plutarch with the significant preface Δοῦρις δ' ὁ Σάμιος τούτοις ἐπιτραγῳδεῖ...) when his birthplace Samos capitulated to Pericles contains details of brutal treatment to Samian trierarchs and marines which are quite fictitious. He also has a pathetic description of how a sole survivor from an Athenian force sent to plunder Aegina was surrounded by Athenian womenfolk who 'stood around him, some asking what had happened to their husbands, others to their sons, others to their brothers'—a description echoed by Livy's portrayals of Roman matrons after signal defeats.[2]

Another dominant feature in Hellenistic historiography, which can be traced back to Isocrates,[3] is the moralistic function given to history; the depiction of the lives of great men should fire the reader to emulation of their deeds and thus ensure the moral betterment of mankind. Amongst many writers of the Hellenistic age, the purpose of history is thus to enshrine the virtues and to deter men from the paths of vice. It inculcates the lesson that the man who seeks to live in harmony with gods and men by espousing virtue will achieve prosperity, but that

---

[1] Pol. II, 56, 7; also Plut. *Them.* 32, *Cleom.* 30. Phylarchus continued the history of Duris to Cleomenes' death in 219.

[2] Samos, Plut. *Per.* 28; the episode at Athens, Schol. M Eur. *Hec.* 934.

[3] Isoc. *Antidosis* 76; *Evagoras* 76 f.

if he neglects his duty disaster inevitably follows. So Timaeus, as an illustration of the poetic justice guiding men's affairs, claims that the Athenian disaster in Sicily was attributable to the mutilation of the statues of Hermes, perpetrated just before the expedition sailed![1] This sense of ethical purpose in historiography, this attempt to depict history with an invariable moral, takes immediate root in Roman history-writing, being congenial to the national temperament, and especially to a man like Cato, the first to essay the writing of history in Latin. Nor must one forget the role which the Stoics play in allotting this purpose to history. Panaetius, the illustrious second-century Stoic, had profound influence on first-century political philosophy (for example, in Cicero's *De Officiis*) with its inevitable impact on historical interpretation. Other Stoics, conspicuously Posidonius, themselves wrote history and thus strengthened the Stoic grip on this genre. The following chapter will show how powerful an influence this exerts on the approach of Livy.

It is clear then that, with a few honourable exceptions such as Hieronymus and Polybius, Hellenistic historiography had strikingly declined from the standards of Thucydides. Its purpose was now not to give practical instruction, but to charm, divert, and edify. The overwhelming preoccupation is literary. Though some writers pay lip-service to truth, few are willing to make the physical effort to acquaint themselves with the terrain they depict, or to come to grips with original documents. If they deal with events already narrated by others, their overriding aim is not to outdo their predecessors in accuracy or balanced judgement, but to outshine them in splendid and dramatic description. Often the theme is chosen on artistic criteria, being a self-contained whole like a plot for tragedy. The narrative is made more attractive by concentration on topics most conducive to

[1] 'Longinus', *De Subl.* 4, 3.

dramatic treatment; Thucydides' resolute exclusion of τὸ μυθῶδες, the fabulous element, is rarely emulated. The impact of the professional rhetorician is felt not merely in the dramatic scenes but also in the regular insertion of composed speeches, which may or may not have been inspired by genuinely historical circumstances, and in digressions (ἐκφράσεις) which discuss the character and history of peoples or cities, the deaths of great men, and other such topics to alleviate the tedium of continuous narrative.[1]

The distinguishable threads in the historiography of the Hellenistic period—the concern of the minority (as represented by Polybius) for truth and serious political treatment, the emphasis laid by the majority on rhetorical presentation ultimately affecting not only the form but also the content of history, the attempts made by some to produce effects similar to those of tragedy, and the popular view that history should have a didactic function closely addressed to the sphere of morals—all exercise a considerable effect on the Roman tradition of history-writing. Unfortunately the extent of such influence on the early Roman historians cannot be closely measured, as only fragments of those anterior to Caesar and Sallust have survived. Clearly the period of some two hundred years was one of trial and experiment, for the only indigenous historical records prior to the Punic Wars were the *tabulae pontificum*, the rude community chronicles originally compiled for each year by the *pontifex maximus*. Even so, the surviving fragments of Q. Fabius Pictor and L. Cincius Alimentus, the first prose historians, exhibit a degree of fluency and sophistication which is surprising to those who take Cicero's strictures[2] too much to heart, and which is explicable only by regarding them as close

---

[1] Posidonius is an outstanding example, πολλὰ παρὰ πολλοῖς ἔθιμα καὶ νόμιμα ἀναγράφων (Athen. IV, 36). See his comments on the Celts, Jacoby II A, 229–31.

[2] See *De Or.* II, 51, *De Leg.* I, 5 for the comment that Fabius wrote in the bald style of the *annales maximi*; for his alleged *brevitas*, *De Or.* II, 53. But these passages may refer to the *Latin* annals of Fabius.

students of Hellenistic methods. The same is true of A. Postumius Albinus, whom Cicero describes as *et litteratus et disertus*, and of C. Acilius, who acted as interpreter when a distinguished group of philosophers from Athens visited Rome in 155 B.C.[1] All these early Senatorial historians wrote in Greek, not because Latin was inadequate for the task (witness the vigour of the Latin of Plautine comedy, though admittedly prose developed more slowly than poetry), but in order to reach a wider audience, and thus to impress the whole of the Greek-speaking world with the growth of Roman power and influence.

In these early Roman writers there are few indications of their conception of the historian's task. But the second-century historians who, beginning with Cato, wrote in Latin offer abundant evidence that they are influenced by Hellenistic theories in analysing the purpose of their writing. Sempronius Asellio, who composed a history covering the period from the Punic Wars to the Gracchi, claims that for an historian to recount the bare facts is not enough; plans and methods must also be outlined. The debt to Polybius is notable here.[2] Asellio is also influenced by the ethical aim given to historiography by Isocrates and other Hellenistic writers, for he criticises earlier Roman chronicles because they do not make men readier to defend the state, or slower to commit wrong; such works, he claims, are not history.[3] Perhaps Cato was making the same point when he refused to reproduce the contents of the *tabulae pontificum*;[4] he too wished to write *res gestae* rather than *annales*, interpreting the events of the past rather than merely relating them.

The Romans responded also to the stylistic enticements

---

[1] Albinus, Cic. *Brut.* 81; Acilius, below, 120.

[2] Asellio *ap.* Gell. v, 18: 'non modo...quod factum esset...id pronuntiare, sed etiam quo consilio quaque ratione gesta essent demonstrare'. On Polybius' influence, see M. Gelzer, *Hermes* (1934), 48.

[3] *ap.* Gell. v, 18, 9.   [4] Cato, HRR 77 (Peter).

of the Hellenistic historians. The taste for the sensational and the marvellous, with its opportunities for rhetorical treatment, so characteristic of Theopompus, Timaeus, and others, is soon acquired by such writers as Coelius Antipater, and 'tragic' effects are discernible in Livy's account where they are obviously inherited from Valerius Antias.[1] Sisenna, too, whom Cicero regards as far superior to any previous Roman historian, is explicitly said to have modelled his writing on that of Clitarchus.[2] Thus in spite of Cicero's lament that earlier history-writing at Rome was from a stylistic viewpoint negligible, it is clear that an attempt has been made to introduce colour and dramatic interest by the adoption of Hellenistic techniques, and that this experimentation has paved the way for the more mature achievements of Sallust and Livy.

But Hellenistic influences were by no means the sole factors affecting early Roman historiography. Equally important is the consideration that history-writing in Latin was in origin official and religious, and that this character remains impressed upon it even in its maturity. For the first historical records, the *tabulae pontificum*, were venerated by Roman historians in a spirit markedly in contrast to that of the Greeks. A Hecataeus could exult in his intention to break away from the 'laughable' accounts of earlier chroniclers,[3] but the Roman enshrined his written traditions, believing it important to perpetuate them whether true or not. So Livy prefaces his work by saying of the early legends: *ea nec adfirmare nec refellere in animo est*. But by the very act of recounting them he underlines the sentimental value set upon them.

This attitude of veneration towards Roman traditions is reflected in the importance attached to the old registers. True, Cato and Sempronius Asellio were unwilling to

---

[1] For further details of Hellenistic influences on these writers see Ch. v.
[2] Cic. *De Leg.* 1, 1, 7.
[3] Hec. *fr.* 1 a. For the contrast between Greek and Roman see G. De Sanctis, *Problemi di storia antica*, 225 ff.

reproduce them, but they were greatly outnumbered by the second- and first-century annalists who faithfully recorded from them even the most trivial detail. Livy in his turn copied many items almost verbatim from the later annalists, and the form of the original chronicles can be clearly seen in many passages.[1] In the later decades these extracts are supplemented by accounts of senatorial transactions recorded by his annalistic sources. Though there was no official documentation beyond the *senatusconsulta* and the names of the drafting committees, records from private archives[2] existed to provide the chroniclers with a factual basis for their highly imaginative versions of such debates.

For within this framework, which lent plausibility to their work, the later annalists did not scruple to insert fictitious details, to amend what they found uncongenial, and to omit embarrassing facts. These distortions were chiefly motivated by an undiscriminating patriotism, and also by a desire to glorify their own family names and to denigrate those of their rivals. This complex of patriotic and gentile partiality became the 'authorised version' of earlier Roman history; and though inconsistencies and inaccuracies in it are legion, the absence of Greek and Etruscan testimony elevates it to the status of an indispensable *pis aller*.

Why did these annalists (including Livy) incorporate these records into their accounts rather than extract the information and encase it in a more elegant framework? Clearly an attitude of reverence to these repositories of Rome's early history did not preclude the presentation of the documentary evidence in a more congenial narrative form. It may well be that this formal arrangement of elections, allotments of provinces, army-lists, prodigies, and the like was retained because it lent an air of authenticity to an historian's account. Even here, when con-

[1] E.g. II, 16, 1; 19, 1; 40, 14; III, 31, 1; IV, 30, 4; VII, 15, 9, etc.
[2] Below, 112.

fronted with Roman traditional influence on the form of Livy's history, one cannot ignore the effect of Greek theory. The three *narrandi virtutes*, according to Isocratean tenets, were *lux, brevitas, fides*—clarity, brevity, *plausibility*.[1] Such annalists as Valerius Antias could invest their narrative with more πιθανότης by reproducing the form of the old registers.

All these considerations, Hellenistic and Roman, are prominent in the discussions which Cicero records. The basic canons of history are ably propounded by Antonius in the *De Oratore*. 'For surely everyone knows', he says, 'that the first law of history is to dare to say nothing false, and again to omit nothing which is true. And in writing there should be no suspicion of either partiality or hatred.'[2] It is in this spirit that Cicero condemns the debasement of history in family records, especially in funeral laudations, and stresses the difference between history, where truth prevails, and encomium, where exaggeration is allowed.[3] Elsewhere he maintains that historians should exclude the element of the fabulous, and he seeks to make a clear distinction between legend and sober history.[4] He is at pains to distinguish clearly between the functions of history and oratory, showing that history is different both in its material and in its treatment, for chronological order and geographical clarification are essential. Again, the historian should analyse motives or intentions, and survey results, so that there is a sequence of *consilia, acta, eventus*; and causes of events must be explained. Finally, in the case of illustrious persons a description of their actions is insufficient, for there should also be an account of their careers and characters.[5] History is thus to have an ethical function, and be the *magistra vitae* as Isocrates had demanded.

---

[1] See Quint. ii, 5, 7. For the influence of Isocratean theory see M. Gelzer, *Hermes* (1935), 269 ff.

[2] Cic. *De Or.* ii, 62.   [3] *Brut.* 61 f.; *Ad Att.* i, 19, 10.

[4] *De Inv.* i, 27; *De Rep.* ii, 10, 18–19.   [5] *De Or.* ii, 63.

Such prerequisites of the historian Polybius would have heartily approved, and his influence on Cicero is here indisputable. But Cicero was not content with such sober aims. We see the influence of the Hellenistic rhetorical tradition when he compares the form (not the content) of history with that of sophistic rhetoric and epideictic oratory.[1] On this point, however, he is somewhat inconsistent. At one moment he praises the simplicity of Caesar, or upbraids the over-rhetorical nature of Callisthenes' writing; at another he says that 'in history everything should be spoken after the manner of Isocrates and Theopompus', and he praises Duris, the most unabashed exponent of 'tragic' history, as a diligent historian.[2] But in general he espouses Isocratean theory. He is emphatic on the place to be accorded by the historian to speeches and digressions,[3] the fairest fields for the rhetorician. Above all, it is in his comments on earlier Roman historiography that Cicero shows his concern for *eloquentia* as an essential attribute of the good historian. It is not necessarily true that he wished to restrict history-writing to orators,[4] but he judges the earlier Roman annalists to be inferior to the Greeks not on any historical criteria, but because they were mere *narratores* and not *exornatores rerum*.[5] To this extent his concern for truthful history seems to be overshadowed by his emphasis on literary standards.

Yet it might be fairly claimed for Cicero that he sought to encourage a view of history-writing which would embrace the best of both worlds. Scientific and truthful

[1] *Or.* 37.
[2] *Brut.* 262; *De Or.* II, 58; *Or.* 207; *Ad Att.* VI, 1, 18 (though this praise of Duris is within the context of condemnation of the Eupolis–Alcibiades story).
[3] *Or.* 66.
[4] Bornecque justifies this thesis by citation of *De Leg.* I, 5–7 and *De Or.* II, 62. But in the one case Atticus, and in the other Antonius, need not be expressing Cicero's personal view. So P. Defourny, *Et. Class.* (1953), 156 ff.
[5] *De Or.* II, 54.

history demands a worthy literary setting; then indeed it will become the *testis temporum, lux veritatis, vita memoriae, magistra vitae*.[1] These are the Ciceronian standards which Livy consciously sought to attain, and these are the standards by which he is to be judged.

The modern student, accustomed to the more sophisticated fare of modern historians, may find such aims and standards unsatisfactory. He will search in vain in Livy for any analysis of economic and social factors. The central feature of ancient history-writing always to be borne in mind is the prominence attached to the individual—his thoughts, his emotions, his words, his acts, his character; these are the stuff of history, the motivators of events. So Thucydides, in his analysis of the Peloponnesian War, and Polybius, in his discussion of the origins of the Hannibalic War, both assume that the causes lay in human decisions, thoughts, and emotions.[2] And Cicero recommends the historian to recount the causes of events, 'whether they are attributable to chance, wisdom, or rashness'.[3] Human qualities, then, and beyond them chance (and divine intervention) are regarded as the only considerations necessary to explain the past. Inevitably it is the leaders of communities, the men who make decisions, who alone are important in such a view of history, a fact which explains why Cicero demands from the historian an account of the careers and characters of illustrious persons.[4]

One can therefore readily appreciate why the history

---

[1] *De Or.* ii, 36. For useful surveys of Cicero's historiographical theories see J. F. D'Alton, *Roman Literary Theory and Criticism* (London, 1931), 508 ff.; M. Rambaud, *Cicéron et l'histoire romaine.*

[2] So F. M. Cornford, *Thucydides Mythistoricus* (London, 1907), 67 ff. Other scholars (e.g. Gomme) claim that Thucydides was aware of economic issues, but rejected them as an explanation of the Athenian conflict with Sparta.

[3] *De Or.* ii, 63.

[4] The attempt to get behind the leading figures of a period, and to examine the significance of minor personages in the formation of policies, is an innovation comparatively recent in history-writing.

of Livy is in modern eyes so narrow in scope. Another important limiting feature is the extent of the period which he chose to depict. The first six hundred years of Roman history are largely concerned with the wars of a state which had first to be aggressive to establish itself, and which then embarked upon a long series of overseas campaigns. Livy's theme embraces not only this saga of conquest but also the momentous one hundred and fifty years following, in which the Republic collapsed following a surfeit of civil strife. Even in one hundred and forty-two books his treatment of so vast a period could be no more than panoramic. The result is that the *Ab Urbe Condita* is by and large a history of Roman armies, with occasional glimpses of the activities of politicians and legislators at Rome, as the battle is joined first for the hegemony of Italy and later to establish Roman dominion on three continents.

In Livy's treatment of this predominantly military theme, three different types or categories of historical material can be distinguished. First, there is the narrative of the campaigns themselves. Secondly, much of his writing is devoted to the spoken word—assemblies at Rome and elsewhere, conferences between great leaders, speeches made to the troops before battle. Thirdly, he usually gathers together (at first in a chapter or two, and more extensively in the later, more historical books) the official appointments to magistracies and priesthoods, the celebration of state festivals, the reports of dreams and prodigies, and so on; he thus preserves the annalistic framework which goes back to the *tabulae pontificum*. We must be prepared to find little beyond this, except in the early books where Livy devotes considerable attention to internal politics. This general framework of words and deeds—the λόγοι and ἔργα of Thucydides—is above all well suited to the indirect delineation of character, for a man's basic attitudes and attributes can best be judged by his deeds and words, and by the remarks made by others.

Within this framework Livy seeks to embody the principles of the ideal rhetorical, or Isocratean, historian which Cicero had so ardently desired. So far as truth and impartiality are concerned, he does not feel the necessity, as Sallust did, to state that he would write with mind 'uncommitted by hope, fear, or political allegiance', *quam verissume*; or again to promise, as Tacitus did, that his account would be *sine ira et studio quorum causas procul habeo*.[1] Such avowals are necessary only for those with axes to grind, and Livy succeeds in being less biased than either, though the absence of his version of first-century history makes such comparison unfair. But Livy never approximates to the impartiality of a Thucydides. His main fault is a too uncritical patriotism, a traditional Roman bias which began when Fabius Pictor, the 'father' of Roman history, was writing his propaganda history for the benefit of the Greek world.[2] This is the greatest stumbling-block to Livy's attempt to attain objectivity. In reviewing the savage barbarity of Roman arms in Sicily, for example, in the Second Punic War, one is tempted to doubt the sincerity of a man who is not sickened by the massacres at Henna and Leontini and by the sacking of Syracuse, and who makes Marcellus a symbol of the qualities to which later ages should aspire. In general, however, Livy's sincerity of belief in Roman greatness is so blatant that we should attribute such bias rather to a defect of vision. It is precisely the attitude of a Charles Kingsley when he depicts the Elizabethan pirates as paragons of virtue, unquestionably superior to the Dutch, French and (of course) Spaniards, worshipping the God of the Church of England and contemptuous of 'foreign cults', and dutifully slaughtering the inferior

---

[1] Sall. *Cat.* 4, 1; Tac. *Ann.* 1, 1 (compare *Hist.* 1, 1).
[2] Below, 117 ff.

races in the most blood-curdling manner. Livy is hardly so blind as this.[1]

The second cause of partiality in Roman history-writing was the political acrimony which marked the last hundred years of the Republic. The traditions of earlier days were distorted by an unscrupulous, often clumsy manipulation in the interests of the anti-Senatorial campaign; and on the other side, those who wrote from a Senatorial viewpoint were not loth to use this weapon to attack the hostile opposition of the Populares. The position is further complicated by the use made by many historians of family archives which not unnaturally glorified the achievements of individual families at the expense of the truth. In his handling of such biased source-material, Livy steers a reasonably impartial course. Politically speaking, he clearly favoured an aristocratic type of government, with statesmen motivated by Roman *virtus* rather than Platonic philosophy, and he is fully aware of the dangers of mob rule. In addition, the Patavian environment of his early life implanted in him much pro-Senatorial sympathy. But in the extant books the only indication of anti-plebeian bias can be seen in his discussion of agrarian legislation in the first decade. Here his hostility towards the plebeian tribunes is undoubtedly provoked by first-century events, and especially by Caesar's Agrarian Law of 59, which was put directly to the popular assembly when the Senate rejected it. For Livy was markedly pro-Pompeian, and correspondingly sceptical of Julius' claim to greatness; in his own words, 'it is uncertain whether Caesar's birth was of more benefit to the state than if he had never lived'.[2]

---

[1] Compare R. Heinze's apposite comment on the effect of Stoic thought on the advocates of Roman imperialism (*Die augusteische Kultur*, 53): 'Eine überaus lehrreiche Parallele zu diesem Glauben bietet die theologische Färbung des heutigen Imperialismus der Engländer, die ja auch meinen das auserwählte Volk zu sein und Gottes Willen zu erfüllen, wenn sie sich die Welt unterwerfen.'

[2] Sen. *N.Q.* v, 18, 4. For condemnation of plebeians see below, 69.

The question of Livy's veracity will be discussed later at greater length; one traditional feature may be noted here. As has been mentioned, Thucydides often adopted the practice of composition of speeches not according to the letter of what was said, but with words which would have been apposite to the occasion. In spite of Polybius' castigation of this practice, the technique became a salient feature of Roman historiography, and writers regarded it as a legitimate expression of their function to invent speeches allegedly uttered on historical occasions. Sallust and even Caesar pay due deference to this convention. The central importance of rhetoric in Roman education and public life made such composition one of the most desirable attributes of the equipped historian, and Livy's talent in this direction is one of the chief reasons for the enthusiastic recognition accorded to him by such prominent writers as Tacitus, Seneca, and Quintilian. He is not unfaithful to the material which he found in his sources, but he transforms the expression of it in such a way that he attains the double effect of increased elegance and more subtle characterisation.[1]

The other rules laid down for the historian by Cicero Livy faithfully observes. He avoids the element of the fabulous except in the early books, where such material alone is available; and he implicitly warns us in the Preface not to regard this as historical fact. Though his geography is weak, he is most conscientious in his attempts to clarify points of topography.[2] His analysis of motives and intentions can be exemplified especially in the fourth and fifth decades, where under Polybius' influence he invariably prefaces any account of decisive action with a psychological observation on the motives of the participants. As Cicero demands, he investigates the causes of important events,[3] but his deeply religious interpretation

---

[1] See Ch. IX. [2] Below, 153 ff.

[3] E.g. his analyses of the causes of the Samnite Wars (VII, 29, 3 ff.), the Hannibalic War (XXI, 1, 3 ff.), the Second Macedonian War (XXXI, 1, 9 ff.), the war with Perseus (XXXIX, 23, 5 ff.). And he goes beyond his allotted scope in recounting the Greek events of 192, since they were *causae cum Antiocho belli* (XXXV, 40, 1).

is not content with the alternatives of 'chance, wisdom, or rashness'; he draws repeated attention to the part allegedly played by the gods in human affairs. It need hardly be added that he follows Cicero's injunction to characterise illustrious men, for this is the central feature of his work.[1] In his formal arrangement he follows the annalistic method recommended by Cicero, even though this detracts from his artistic aims when he has to break off the description of events in one field of operations to bring us up to date in another. In short, he is faithful to the Ciceronian dogmas on the historian's task— theories which preach the essential connection between history and oratory as branches of *eloquentia*, but which also emphasise the separate discipline of the historian.

Livy's writing is also conspicuously affected by the view that history is a medium for moral instruction, which took root in Hellenistic historiography. Today most historians in theory attempt to eschew moral judgements, however difficult they find the practice. But the Romans continued in the Hellenistic tradition. Tacitus expressly states that the purpose of his work is a moral one—to record good and evil deeds to inspire or deter posterity.[2] When Cicero calls history *magistra vitae*, he is presumably making the same point. Livy in his Preface is still more explicit, exhorting his readers to examine the way of life of those who raised Rome to her pinnacle, and to mark the subsequent decline, in order that they may arrange their lives accordingly. The great heroes of his history symbol- ise the qualities which he believes made Rome great, the *bonae artes* of religious, political, and private life. 'Let men jibe nowadays at admirers of former times; I believe that if there existed a community of philosophers fashioned by the imagination and not the experience of thinkers, there would never be leaders of greater sobriety and lesser ambi- tion for power, nor a common folk of better morality.'[3]

[1] See Ch. IV.   [2] *Ann.* III, 65.   [3] XXVI, 22, 14.

Livy combines with this moral function for history a conviction of its practical utility for the statesman. So in the Preface there is an exhortation to scrutinise the past as a guide for future political organisation. Here Livy's debt to Thucydides and Polybius is clearly marked.[1] Many would quarrel with this attempt to build the future on the basis of the idealised past, for the setting for human actions can never be the same; we have to reckon with different personalities in different environments. The fallacy, in Livy as in Thucydides, is in reducing human beings to types which react identically in all circumstances.

Finally, there is the literary problem of Livy's debt to the theories of 'rhetorical' and 'tragic' history, so widespread in the Hellenistic world. Though one cannot say with certainty that he was a practising rhetorician, there is evidence that he had a keen interest in the subject.[2] Not only in the speeches, but also on the rare occasions when he takes the liberty of extended personal comment—as in the Preface or in the digression which compares the Rome of Papirius Cursor's day with Alexander's Macedon[3]— he shows complete mastery of the orator's equipment.

But it should be carefully noted here that Livy specifically rejects the aims of pleasing and charming the reader so common to rhetorical historians of the Hellenistic period. 'From the beginning of this work', he says, 'it can be seen that I have no intention of straying from the order of events more than is justifiable, nor of seeking pleasant digressions (*deverticula amoena*) for my readers, and relaxation for my mind, by adorning my work with variation of topics.'[4] Such a procedure would distract

---

[1] Livy occasionally gives such advice as this: 'Roman commanders will always have to be careful...not to put trust in foreign troops to such a degree as to fail to have superior numbers of their own picked, exclusively Roman troops in their camp' (xxv, 33, 6).
[2] Sen. *Contr.* ix, 2, 26.   [3] ix, 17 ff.
[4] ix, 17, 1.

his audience from the didactic purpose of his work. Occasionally, however, he relaxes this close discipline to digress on topics which were often the theme for an ἔκφρασις in Hellenistic historiography. So in relating how the Spartan Cleonymus ventured to lead a Greek fleet up the Adriatic, and to land on Paduan territory, he patriotically includes gratuitous details of geography and local custom.[1] Again, the epitome of Book CIV suggests that there was a long excursus there on the Germans; now the character and customs of peoples and cities were popular topics amongst rhetorical historians as a respite from factual narration.[2] Another favourite theme was the manner of death of famous men, as in Ephorus' account of the death of Alcibiades at the hands of Pharnabazus;[3] in the same way, Livy records the circumstances of Philopoemen's death, presumably because of the fame of the man and the strangeness of the event, for its connection with Roman affairs is tenuous.[4] Noteworthy, too, is the occasional excursus in the early books on topics of antiquarian interest, as in his description of the fetial ceremonies.[5] And there are other 'set pieces' beloved of the 'rhetorical' and 'tragic' historians observable in Livy's account—notably the siege and capture of cities, dramatic dialogues, and human situations, in which horrific, pathetic, or romantic effects are sought.[6] It is in these scenes that Livy gives his rhetorical training full play.

There is also abundant evidence for the impact of 'tragic' history on his writing. In a later chapter[7] one

---

[1] x, 2, 4–15.

[2] E.g. Phylarchus on the Egyptians (Jacoby IIA, 168–9); Posidonius on the Celts (above, 28, n. 1); Sallust on the Africans (*Jug.* 17); Tacitus on the Germans and Britons (*Ann.* IV, 32–3; *Agric.* 10); Livy on the Gauls (v, 33–5).

[3] Diod. XIV, 11, 1–4.

[4] XXXIX, 49–50. See also Hannibal's dramatic death, XXXIX, 51.

[5] I, 24, 4ff.; 32, 5ff. (But this, as Mr R. M. Ogilvie points out to me, may have been firmly embedded in the source-tradition.)

[6] See Ch. VIII.   [7] See Ch. VII.

may note how he has often applied the principle of the composed episode according to the Aristotelian theory of tragedy, with a distinct beginning, middle, and end. In these episodes many of the effects sought after by Hellenistic writers, such as lively presentation and dramatic thrill, are clearly attempted. The influence, then, of such writers as Duris, Clitarchus, and Phylarchus is incontrovertible. But it is one thing to admit such influence but quite another to claim a direct debt to one or other of these historians, as some have sought to do.[1] There is no convincing evidence for such assumptions. More probably, the techniques which these writers employed were assimilated by Livy in his training in the school of rhetoric, where historical episodes had often to be discussed with an eye to pathetic effects. Relevant, too, is the fact that such methods were already being habitually exploited by some of Livy's sources, notably Coelius Antipater and Valerius Antias; even the sober Polybius cannot always exclude such treatment from his account.[2] Above all, one can detect in the writing of Sallust the close familiarity with Hellenistic techniques enjoyed by Roman first-century historians.[3] It is clear that Livy has made no startling innovations in Roman historiography by these methods, but he has used them more moderately and with a greater degree of control than have his predecessors, so that in his account we do not meet with the excesses of which both Hellenistic and earlier Roman writers were guilty.

The most important of Cicero's discussions of the duties of the historian, on which Livy bases his approach, is to be found in the *De Oratore*, which appeared in 55 B.C.

---

[1] E. Burck, for example, suggests that Livy is an historian of the Peripatetic school, i.e. in the tradition of Duris and Callisthenes. It should be noted that there is no necessary connection between these historians and the Peripatetics.

[2] F. W. Walbank, *JHS* (1938), 65–8.

[3] V. Paladini, *Sallustio* (Milan, 1948), 103–84.

Accordingly the remarks made there on the Roman historiographical tradition could not take into account the writings of Caesar, Sallust, and Asinius Pollio.

There is little doubt that Livy paid close attention to the writings of all these historians as source-material for the last fifty years of the Republic; but there is such a gulf between his conception of history and theirs that they appear to inhabit a different world. Livy's immediate predecessors, all men of political and military experience, viewed their collapsing world from close quarters with experienced eyes, and wrote realistically of what they knew. Their successor first sought to turn away from such harsh realities, and idealised earlier times; tragically enough, the books in which he depicted contemporary events, through which he might partially have vindicated his reputation as historian, are lost.[1]

The sole possible link with his predecessors lies in considerations of style. Of these predecessors, Caesar exercises the most direct influence. Livy learned a great deal from the narrative of the Gallic and Civil Wars; the influence of the *Commentarii* may be noted in Livy's method of describing troop dispositions and certain other techniques of military narration. Caesar, however, did not write *historia* proper. The account of his campaigns represents an intermediate stage between the ὑπόμνημα, the bare skeleton of facts, and the more elaborate composition of Livy.[2]

Sallust on the other hand holds an important place in the development of *historia* at Rome. As a former Senator and governor of Africa, he had an intimate knowledge of contemporary politics, not excluding the more unsavoury facets; during his career he was expelled from the Senate, and after his office in Africa he was

---

[1] The point is well developed by R. Syme, *Tacitus*, 139.
[2] See F. E. Adcock, *Caesar as Man of Letters* (Cambridge, 1955), 7ff. For Caesar's influence on Livy see below, 203.

impeached for extortion. He availed himself of this experience by his choice of a contemporary theme, like Thucydides avoiding the legends of the past. In his *Catiline*, he studied the complex forces of his own day— the ideas, the passions, the dominating personalities, the corrupting influences. Though later he chose an older theme in the Jugurthine War, he was still discussing movements and passions which were relevant to and understood in his own times. And when he graduated from these monographs to the *Historiae*, he began where Sisenna had ended so as to narrate the congenial theme of the downfall of Senatorial oligarchy from 78 B.C. onwards.

Sallust seeks to expound these themes by the scientific Thucydidean method which had for too long been ignored;[1] but the mental climate pervading his work is utterly different. Thucydides, reflecting the positivist teaching of the sophists, is sceptical about oracles and alleged manifestations of divine power; in his work the gods are absent and indeed irrelevant. Sallust on the other hand embraces the ethical preoccupations of earlier Roman chroniclers, so that he views all history in terms of man's duty to gods and fellow-men. It is the adaptation of Thucydidean historical analysis to the traditionally Roman ethical approach which lends Sallust such significance as a precursor to Livy. He himself is not always successful in emulating Thucydides' accuracy and impartiality, but his recognition of these as necessary virtues is of great importance for his successors. And his analysis of the moral causes of Rome's decline, the work of a man who had helped to precipitate the disintegration he describes, has undoubted influence upon Livy's preliminary philosophising in the Preface. Perhaps such moralising was a cloak to enable Sallust to wallow in the

---

[1] G. B. Grundy, *Thucydides and the History of his Age* II (Oxford, 1948), 16; P. Perrochat, *Les Modèles grecs de Salluste* (Paris, 1949), 3–39.

scenes of vice and violence which he denounces;[1] but more probably it is a deliberate evocation of *prisca antiquitas*, in keeping with the affected archaisms of style.

These stylistic effects—paratactic sentence structure, verbal archaism, abrupt brevity of expression—are the studied antithesis of Ciceronian *latinitas*, and as such are rigorously condemned by Livy, who was a strong admirer of Cicero and Demosthenes.[2] There is thus no conscious imitation by Livy of Sallustian language. Yet there are elements in the Sallustian style, notably a striving for variety in expression, which contribute to the formation of Augustan prose and thus exercise an indirect influence on the *Ab Urbe Condita*.

Asinius Pollio, Senator, Caesarean officer, and ex-governor of Cisalpine Gaul, was well-versed in both political and military facets of his historical theme, the Great Civil War. His analysis started at 60, and extended to a point beyond the battle of Philippi. Like Livy, he was aware of the pitfalls of contemporary history. He eschewed the period of the Principate, and this passivity has been over-praised, as if discretion were solely a concession to honesty.[3] His governorship exacted severe requisitions from Patavium, which thus suffered for its opposition to revolution;[4] hence Livy may have reciprocated the antipathy which the taunt of *patavinitas* reveals. But Pollio's influence on Livy's surviving books is negligible, for his presentation, jejune and unadorned, was the antithesis of the stylistic requirements which Livy envisaged for *historia*.[5]

[1] As suggested by R. Syme, *Tacitus*, 135, and others.
[2] Sen. *Contr.* IX, 1, 13; 2, 26.
[3] See R. Syme, R.R. 5 ff.
[4] Macrobius, I, 11, 22.
[5] See below, 270.

III

RELIGIOUS, PHILOSOPHICAL AND MORAL PRECONCEPTIONS

THE biographical background—the home influences and the friendship with the imperial court—and the tradition of historiography within which Livy wrote are both obviously important for a fuller understanding of his work. Equally vital is the need to appreciate the preconceptions, religious, philosophical, and moral, with which he approaches the events of the past. There is little external evidence to assist us in this, but fortunately the history itself offers abundant indications. Yet it is surprising to find how differently this evidence has been interpreted. One scholar lays emphasis on the *rationalisme sceptique* of Livy, and explains his interest in religious ceremonial as a purely academic study; the historian is credited with an appreciation of the importance of religious phenomena in ancient history. More recently an interesting analysis of Livy's religious thought comes to exactly the opposite conclusion: 'It stands beyond doubt that Livy had unshakeable belief in the old gods.'[1] Such disparate views indicate the complexity of the problem, but may also point to a solution, for both contain important elements of truth.

The dilemma, simply stated, is clear. If one studies the beliefs of the official Roman religion, and the attitude

---

[1] For Livy as sceptic see J. Bayet, Budé edition of Book I, xxxix; as orthodox believer, G. Stübler, *Die Religiosität des Livius*, 205: 'Daß Livius von echtem, unerschütterlichem Glauben an die alten Götter beseelt ist, steht außer Zweifel'—a view supported by M. A. Levi, *Il tempo di Augusto* (Florence, 1951), 214ff.

towards them of first-century intellectuals like Varro, Caesar, or Cicero, one is soon convinced that no intelligent man after their time could ever have given unreserved assent to such beliefs. The Roman religious calendar was based on the activities of an agricultural society; the religious formulae and rites, recited solely by the religious officials of the state, were of interest only to antiquaries. Many religious offices were filled by unbelievers like Caesar, who saw in them opportunities for political prestige and nothing more. The philosophers of the Epicurean and Academic schools had directed withering criticisms against the illogicalities inherent in such beliefs, and against the crude superstition on which they were based.[1] Yet Livy, who must have read these damaging attacks, writes as if the fall-away from religion had been a national disaster, and stresses the desirability of a revival.

Does Livy then give unqualified assent to Roman traditional beliefs? One has only to read the early books with a little care to answer this question decisively. Here indeed is abundant evidence for Livy's *rationalisme sceptique*. After pointedly emphasising that he does not intend either to defend or reject the early legendary material (a sure sign of scepticism in conflict with Roman veneration for tradition), he repeatedly qualifies the traditional version of divine intervention in Roman affairs with an alternative, more rational explanation. Thus he throws doubt on the claim that Mars was the father of Romulus and Remus, and again on the alleged apotheosis of Romulus.[2] Frequently, too, he prefaces his account with such expressions as *dicitur*, *ferunt*, *traditum memoriae*, *visi sunt*, so that without specifically rejecting allegedly miraculous accounts he can politely dissociate

[1] For the decline of religion towards the end of the Republic see C. Bailey, *Phases in the Religion of Ancient Rome* (Oxford, 1932), 149 ff.

[2] I, 4, 2; 16, 4. He is also non-committal on whether the twins were suckled by a she-wolf (I, 4, 7). Other examples: I, 31, 4; III, 8, 1; V, 13, 4.

himself from belief in them.[1] Especially notable is his scepticism about the activity of gods in anthropomorphic guise. There is indeed no sign of a credulous, pietistic approach here; Livy has not deliberately closed his eyes to the absurdities inherent in the state religion.

More persuasive as a possible explanation for Livy's advocating a religious revival is that like Polybius and Cicero[2] he understood the *social* value of religion as the securest basis for a healthy public morality. One cannot ignore the comment made on Numa's institution of religious rites: 'Lest the citizens' minds should grow degenerate in leisure ("ne luxuriarent otio animi"), he believed that the fear of the gods should be instilled into them—a most effective weapon for a populace inexperienced and at that time unsophisticated.' Naturally (and justifiably) this motive advanced for Numa's religious innovation has been interpreted as a mark of Livy's rationalism,[3] especially as his next comment is that Numa *pretended* (*simulat*) to receive his divine instructions in nightly concourse with the goddess Egeria.[4] But it would be wrong to assume that such scepticism has extinguished all genuine religious feeling. The distinction made by Varro is a useful one between superstition and the higher form of religious feeling, *pietas*: the superstitious man fears the gods, but the truly religious person reveres them as parents.[5] So Livy's comment on the expediency of instilling fear of the gods is not the Ovidian cynicism of *expedit esse deos*; his rationalism is confined to the superstition of the lower orders, and it is this element alone in

---

[1] See I, 45, 4; 55, 5; II, 7, 2; 36, 8; VI, 33, 5; VIII, 6, 1, etc. Such qualifications are reminiscent of Herodotus' attitude: 'My business is to record what people say, but I am by no means bound to believe it' (VII, 152). So in Book VIII he prefaces the story of the pursuit of the Persians by two superhuman figures, and again the claim that the Acropolis was guarded by a great snake, with such phrases.

[2] Pol. VI, 56, 6–14; Cic. *De Rep.* II, 26f.

[3] So K. Glaser, *RE* XVII, 1245.   [4] I, 19, 4–5.

[5] Aug. *Civ. Dei* VI, 9: 'ut a superstitioso dicat (*sc.* Varro) timeri deos, a religioso autem tantum vereri ut parentes'. See Stübler, 40.

religion which has for him no more than a social value. So again, at the commencement of the sixth book, he stresses that the *vulgus indoctum* alone is bound mentally by religious awe.[1] So much stress is laid throughout the *Ab Urbe Condita* on the necessity for a right relationship between men and gods, and the importance of *religio* is so frequently emphasised, that it is impossible to believe that Livy is an utter sceptic.

We must therefore reject the views that Livy seeks a religious revival because of a blind adherence to the state religion, absurdities and all, and, at the other extreme, that he pays mere lip-service to theological concepts which he regards as absurd in order to achieve a morally healthy society. The true explanation must surely be that he sees in these beliefs a symbolic truth. He attempts to sift from the mass of superstitious myth a central doctrine of the relationship between men and gods which will lend order and significance to human life. This is the fundamental force of Livian *pietas*—a reverence for the godhead which ensures the right ordering of men's lives. It is this conviction of a symbolic truth at the heart of Roman religion which alone can explain the pattern of belief consistently and even passionately expounded in Livy's interpretation of the past.

Mention has already been made of Livy's interest in philosophy; the younger Seneca tells us that 'he wrote dialogues which one can assign to history as much as to philosophy, and books of philosophy specifically'.[2] To which school did he belong? There is evidence to suggest that he came to history under the influence of Stoic ideas —not the rigid determinism of the early dogma of the Porch, but the neo-Stoicism as preached by Posidonius, which finds little difficulty in coming to terms with much

[1] VI, I, 10.
[2] 'scripsit enim et dialogos quos non magis philosophiae adnumerare possis quam historiae, et ex professo philosophiam continentis libros...' (*Ep.* 100, 9).

of Roman religious thought. This distinction between the old and the new Stoicism is chiefly important for the increase of emphasis on ethics at the expense of physics. It has been suggested[1] that Livy cannot be a Stoic, because little emphasis is laid on the omnipotence of impersonal Fate, and because human qualities are continually prominent in shaping the course of history. But the Romans' philosophic view of Stoic determinism is coloured by their traditional regard for ethical considerations. The man who respects the rights of gods and men, who bases his religious, political, and private life on the virtues which the Stoics uphold, is regarded as living in harmony with Fate. The central doctrine of Stoic physics —that there is an essential harmony in matter, directed by a material god immanent in it—is thus surveyed from the viewpoint of ethics; and the man who follows reason and virtue, being in harmony with the universe, inevitably succeeds, whereas he who espouses rashness and vice inevitably fails. This is the determinism which Livy habitually expounds, and its close connection with Roman Stoicism can be seen, for example, in Cicero's *De Natura Deorum*, where the Stoic Balbus lists a number of reverses sustained by generals through neglect of the gods.[2]

Now Livy was pre-eminently a traditionalist and not an original thinker, and much of the outlook inherent in his history, and the language expressive of this outlook, are common to Roman history-writing from Cato to Tacitus, all of which is greatly coloured by Stoicism. But it is in Livy that the full implications of this Stoic outlook can best be measured, for he alone of the greater Roman historians presents a coherent pattern of history resting consistently on Stoic premises. Tacitus, for example, on one occasion throws off the cloak of conventional Stoic colouring to state that he is not committed to any

---

[1] Bayet, Budé Livy I, xl.　　　[2] II, 7 ff.

philosophical position;[1] and while the monographs of Sallust reflect Stoic ethical considerations, he is hardly concerned to present the process of events in any preconceived Stoic pattern.

Clearly Livy's ethical teaching does not of itself demonstrate any definite adherence to Stoic beliefs. True, the Preface stresses that the reader should look to the moral qualities of the early Romans, and that the causes of decline are the vices which the Stoics condemned—greed and soft living, lust and base ambition; and throughout his work Livy draws from the events of the past moral judgements emphasising the importance of the Stoic virtues. But this kind of Stoic influence is to be found in Sallust and Tacitus as well, though neither was an adherent of the Porch; it had become an integral part of Roman historiography. Livy's allegiance must rather be demonstrated by such cosmological views as emerge from his history, and even here one must take into account conventional phraseology which may not necessarily reflect his personal views.[2]

Negative evidence of a Stoic outlook may perhaps be seen in the vigorous condemnation of Academic and Epicurean viewpoints which is embodied in historical contexts and expressed in language suggestive of the philosophical adversary.[3] But more important is the positive evidence in the early books—the depiction of the growth of Rome as inevitable and predetermined. This is expressed not merely in theological terms which stress the conviction that Rome was founded and assisted in its

---

[1] *Ann.* VI, 22. For good comments on the conventional Stoic terminology, and its non-application to Tacitus' personal views, see B. Walker, *The Annals of Tacitus* (Manchester, 1952), 245 ff.

[2] For further detail see Walsh, *AJP* (1958), 355 ff.

[3] E.g. X, 40, 10: Sp. Papirius praised as 'iuvenis ante doctrinam deos spernentem natus', and X, 40, 14: 'nunquam humanis rebus magis praesentes interfuisse deos'. See, too, the words of the *plebs* at III, 56, 7: 'deos tandem esse et non neglegere humana'. For elaborating comment see Weissenborn, *Einl.* 17; Stübler, 80.

early growth by the benevolence of the gods, but also in language which depicts a more impersonal process, thereby suggesting the influence of Stoic physics.

Interesting here is Livy's use of final clauses to convey the impression that an impersonal constraint was exercised to ensure that the Romans were confronted with continuous difficulties from without and within. The whole of early Roman history is thus depicted as a period of trial, in which the military and civic virtues of the Roman people are thoroughly tested so that they may become physically and morally capable of world-leadership. Pressure from external races regularly recurs: '*Behold, so that the identical round of events might yearly recur*, the Hernici reported that the Volsci and the Aequi were refitting their armies despite destructive losses.'[1] Domestic difficulties trouble the Romans when they are not hard pressed from without: '*So that peace might not be universal*, conflict developed between the patricians and the plebeians who were leaders of the community.'[2] When both dangers from without and disharmony within have subsided, they are taxed with outbreaks of disease: 'Then, when L. Genucius and Q. Servilius were consuls, and the state was untroubled by sedition and war, *so that they might never be free from fear and dangers*, a great pestilence arose.'[3] It might be argued that such clauses are merely emotive rhetoric, but curiously enough they appear exclusively in the first decade, where the historian's philosophical preconceptions are most pronounced. Even if viewed as stylistic features merely, they must reflect the working of Livy's mind.

Coupled with this series of challenges to the Roman spirit of resistance is a supernatural protection which prevents the three dangers of war, discord, and disease

---

[1] III, 10, 8: 'ecce, ut idem in singulos annos orbis volveretur...'.

[2] x, 6, 3: 'tamen, ne undique tranquillae res essent...'.

[3] VII, 1, 7: 'ne quando a metu ac periculis vacarent...'; and compare VII, 27, 1: 'ne nimis laetae res essent, pestilentia civitatem adorta...'.

from overwhelming them simultaneously. So in one passage[1] Livy states that during a time of pestilence there was no external danger or internal dissension; these difficulties return only when the disease has vanished. On another occasion, domestic anarchy is averted by a sudden attack of the Aequi, made, 'one might say, on purpose' ('velut dedita opera').[2]

This depiction of the predetermined process of Roman development is hardly apposite to an historian, but would be less surprising in a philosopher with Stoic views. Livy's use of *fatum* furnishes further evidence of this standpoint, though he rarely employs the word in the strict sense of ἡ Εἱμαρμένη, the predestined end to which Providence (Πρόνοια) guides mankind. In neo-Stoicism this notion has been contaminated with the Roman religious view of the *fata* as *Göttersprüche*, divine communications made through oracles, dreams, prodigies, divination, and augury. The later Stoics Chrysippus and Posidonius both admit that the future can be foreseen by these means, because of the essential harmony (συμπάθεια) of the universe linking the macrocosm with the microcosm; order or disorder in the smaller will divulge a similar state of affairs in the larger. Neo-Stoicism therefore gives to *fatum* not the sense of an inscrutable destiny, but of one which though predetermined can be foreseen.[3]

Most of Livy's usages of *fatum* and *fata* either reflect the sense of *Göttersprüche* which emerges from Roman religious thought,[4] or are merely conventional expressions for 'death' or other calamities. But in other passages the

---

[1] IV, 52, 8.

[2] III, 30, 2. Polybius (was he likewise preoccupied with Stoic concepts?) uses a similar phrase, ὥσπερ ἐπίτηδες (I, 86, 7; II, 4, 3, etc.). Such phrases are not conclusive of a definite belief in determinism, but they suggest that a pattern of events is recognised.

[3] *Fata* as *Göttersprüche*, W. F. Otto, *RE* VI, 2048. Admission by neo-Stoicism of prodigies, dreams, etc., Cic. *De Div.* I, 3, 6; 31, 66. For a Stoic view of foreseen fate, Sen. *N.Q.* II, 38, 2.

[4] V, 16, 10; 19, 1; VIII, 24, 2 and 11; XXI, 22, 9; XXIX, 10, 8, etc.

stricter Stoic sense is found. Servius Tullius' plan to avoid the hatred of the Tarquinii by giving his daughters to them in marriage is described with the comment: 'Yet with human designs he did not break the inevitability of fate.'[1] Livy here refers to the predestined expulsion of the kings and the introduction of *libertas*. Elsewhere, when Livy recounts the celebrated episode of the young man who disobeyed his father and general Manlius Torquatus, and was executed by him,[2] the reasons given for such disobedience are 'anger, or a sense of shame at declining battle, or the unconquerable might of fate' ('inexsuperabilis vis fati'). There are two other striking phrases suggestive of Stoic influence in Book xxv. One of them is in a speech delivered by a spokesman of the punished survivors of Cannae—a piece of special pleading to account for their shameful defeat; but the phrase, 'Fate, by whose law the unchangeable order of human affairs is arranged', has obvious Stoic associations.[3] Later is recounted the death of Tiberius Gracchus, who was warned of impending danger when snakes repeatedly devoured the liver of his sacrificial victim: 'Yet by no foresight could the overhanging fate be dispelled.'[4] In each of these cases the phrase is too emphatic to betray a mere conventional utterance, written without philosophical significance or intent; here we have more positive indications of a *Weltanschauung*.

It is especially interesting to note how often the major crises of Roman history are linked in Livy's account with *fatum*. The fall of Veii (Camillus is *fatalis dux*), the Gallic sack of Rome, the disaster of Cannae, the emergence of

---

[1] I, 42, 2: 'fati necessitatem'.   [2] VIII, 7, 8.

[3] xxv, 6, 6: '...fato, cuius lege immobilis rerum humanarum ordo seritur...'.

[4] xxv, 16, 4: 'nulla tamen providentia fatum imminens moveri potuit'. But note that though Gracchus is killed, he refuses to bow before his fate: 'Leaping from his horse, he bids the others do the same, so that by their courage they can make honourable the only end which fortune grants them.' Here Gracchus shows a Stoic spirit by refusing Seneca-like to surrender to fortune meekly, by meeting her *contumeliose*.

Scipio Africanus (like Camillus a *fatalis dux*), the events leading to the death of Marcellus are all depicted as pre-destined. It is impossible to disregard here the possibility that traditional presentation of these events has affected Livy's account; and the literary attraction of the *fatum* motif is not negligible. But it would be foolish to dismiss completely the philosophical implications of such consistently expressed notions of fate,[1] though under the influence of Polybius Livy's preoccupation with such Stoic determinism recedes after the third decade.[2]

This Stoic view of fate is reinforced by contexts where Livy suggests that even the divine power is circumscribed; the gods cannot affect the inflexible course of history. 'The soldiers turned to the *praetorium*, and demanded from their leaders the assistance which the immortal gods could scarcely lend', writes Livy of the Caudine disaster, which he depicts as the result of Roman *saevitia* and *superbia*; and to bring home the lesson, Lucius Lentulus is then reported as telling the consuls: 'We must therefore undergo this indignity, however great, and hearken to necessity, which not even the gods can overcome.'[3]

Livy's use of *fortuna* has also features which reflect a preoccupation with Stoic determinism. Not long after the historian's death the elder Pliny, in a revealing passage,[4] describes the importance which his contemporaries attached to this concept. She alone in all places and at all times is invoked, praised, and blamed; she is considered blind and fickle, and favours the unworthy.

---

[1] See v, 19, 1–2; 33, 1 ff.; xxii, 43, 9; 53, 6; xxvi, 29, 9. This evidence is discounted by I. Kajanto, *God and Fate in Livy* (Turku, 1957), 54ff., on the grounds that *fatum* is a mere literary motif, though he also suggests that it excuses Roman defeats.

[2] See Kajanto, 63, for Livy's use of *fatum*—twenty-eight times in the first decade, nine in the third, and only three thereafter.

[3] IX, 2, 15: '...opem, quam vix di immortales ferre poterant'; 4, 16: '...necessitati, quam ne di quidem superant'.

[4] *N.H.* II, 22.

Even allowing for some rhetorical exaggeration in this description, one must concede that *fortuna* has become at Rome precisely what Tyche is for Hellenistic Greece. The Romans in their successive stages of belief aped the Greeks as in so much else; just as in fifth-century Athens the new scientific view of the universe propounded by the Ionian physicists corroded the belief in the Olympian deities, and left a vacuum which was eventually filled by the irrational worship of blind chance or Tyche, so at Rome the increasing influence of Greek philosophical thought hastened the disintegration of the state religion, and unwittingly paved the way for the dominance of *fortuna*. In the primitive Roman theology, where each individual deity had his or her peculiar province, Fortuna supervised the incalculable element of life, and had a number of shrines dedicated to her, so that there were respectable precedents for her worship; but her identity, under the influence of the Greek Tyche, has been radically transformed.[1]

The Stoics, postulating a universe moving on a pre-destined course and guided by the Intelligence of the world to a predestined end, had no room in their dogma for *fortuna*/Tyche, whose essential characteristics are fickleness, blindness, and the favouring of the unjust. Yet the prevalence of the concept of deified *fortuna* made it essential for the schoolmen to explain it within the contexts of their own beliefs. So the Epicureans equated it with *natura*, the natural movement of the atoms comprising the universe.[2] For the Stoics the solution was equally obvious; *fortuna* is nothing more than a symbol of the world-intelligence (Πρόνοια) or, regarded impersonally,

---

[1] For detailed accounts of Fortuna see G. Wissowa, *Religion und Kultus der Römer* (München, 1912), 256 ff.; W. Warde Fowler, *The Roman Festivals of the Period of the Republic* (London, 1899), 67 ff.

[2] Note Lucretius' use of *natura* and *fortuna* in identical contexts at v, 77, 107; and the remark of Menander, friend of Epicurus, that 'fortune is no real thing, but people give the name of fortune to what happens in nature's way' (*fr.* 594).

the operation of this world-intelligence, and therefore almost identical with *fatum*.[1] In the symbolic language of the Roman religion, *fortuna* manifests the power of the gods.

Livy allots a role to *fortuna* often consonant with this view, particularly in the early books. It is true that in a number of passages she appears in the garb of Hellenistic Tyche, but these examples chiefly occur in speeches, where Livy is concerned more with characterisation than with the expression of his own viewpoint, and in conventional phraseology.[2] In more extended references in his narrative, he carefully avoids attributing to her any of the notorious qualities of Tyche, and on several occasions specifically equates her with the divine will or power. It is interesting, for example, to see how when following Polybius, whose narrative is full of conventional references to Tyche as a capricious and vindictive deity, he pointedly ignores many such references, or replaces them with an alternative explanation.[3]

It is also noteworthy that Livy's doctrine of *fortuna* contrasts markedly with the usage of his predecessors Sallust, Cicero, and Caesar. Sallust can speak of her in the Hellenistic sense of a wilful mistress who is universally powerful: Cicero can say in the same spirit that there is nothing so unreasonable and inconsistent as she: and Caesar's writings are full of references to her importance

[1] Compare Verg. *Aen.* VIII, 333 ff.: 'Me pulsum patria pelagique extrema sequentem / Fortuna omnipotens et ineluctabile fatum / His posuere locis...', and Servius' comment thereon that the Stoics allotted birth and death to *fatum*, the intervening period to *fortuna*. See C. Bailey, *Religion in Virgil* (Oxford, 1935), 234.

[2] Kajanto, 79 ff., quotes XXIII, 5, 8; 13, 4; II, 35, 1; XXVIII, 8, 1; XXX, 30, 5, and similar extracts from speeches; from the narrative, II, 5, 5; V, 42, 4; VI, 3, 9; IX, 22, 5—all casual and conventional uses of the word.

[3] For greater detail see Walsh, *AJP* (1958), 365 ff. The passages are: Pol. XX, 7, 1–2 and Livy XXXVI, 6, 2 (the parlous condition of Boeotia, with Polybius attributing it to Tyche, Livy to moral failings); Pol. XXXIII, 10, 2 ff. and Livy XL, 5, 1 (Philip's madness, the work of Tyche in Polybius, of divine wrath in Livy). Also Pol. XV, 15, 5 and Livy XXX, 36, 9 ff.; Pol. XI, 19, 5 and Livy XXVIII, 12, 1–9.

on the battle-field.[1] The Augustan writers, Vergil no less than Livy, make a conscious effort to reconcile the conflicting claims of *fortuna* and the traditional deities. Thus Livy seems deliberately to connect the word with the gods. For example, we read how Camillus was urging the Romans to destroy Antium, and how his speech was interrupted. 'In the middle of his speech—I believe that *the gods* wanted the state of Antium to remain for longer— legates came from Nepete and Sutrium begging help against the Etruscans...*fortuna* diverted Camillus' attack there from Antium.'[2] Or again, Flaminius 'did not show sufficient awe of the laws, of senatorial dignity, *or even of the gods*, and *fortuna* had nurtured this rashness innate in his mind'.[3] Though *fortuna* here wears the conventional garb of Hellenistic Tyche, she is especially charged with maintaining harmony in the world by assisting virtue and punishing vice; she symbolises the just working of Providence. So elsewhere Livy writes: 'et successisset fraudi ni pro iure gentium...stetisset fortuna'; and repeatedly she attends on courage or foresight or justice, and lays low those who show no regard for these virtues.[4]

It is easily seen, too, how the 'sectional' power of *fortuna*, manifested in such phrases as *fortuna populi Romani*, *fortuna urbis*, and the like, can be reconciled with a Stoic

---

[1] Sall. *Cat*. 8 : 'res cunctas ex libidine magis quam ex vero celebrat obscuratque'; Cic. *De Div*. II, 7, 18. Cicero's views are in general inconsistent, but his final judgement (*Acad*. I, 7, 29) is that it is nothing but a word to hide men's ignorance of events and causes. For Caesar's conception of *fortuna* see W. Warde Fowler, *CR* (1903), 153–6, rejecting the view of Rice-Holmes that Caesar believed *fortuna* to be a supernatural power, and claiming that Caesar merely 'believes in good or bad luck as we all do'. Certainly Caesar hardly visualised *fortuna* as a mystical power, but he is somewhat superstitiously preoccupied by it, as in *B.C.* III, 10, where it appears three times in a single chapter.

[2] VI, 9, 3: 'credo rem Antiatem diuturniorem manere dis cordi fuisse...eo vim Camilli ab Antio fortuna avertit'.

[3] XXIII, 3, 4: '...ne deorum quidem satis metuens; hanc insitam ingenio eius temeritatem fortuna...aluerat'.

[4] XXXVIII, 25, 8 (quoted); V, 19, 8, etc. The notion of fortune being dependent on courage ('fortes fortuna iuvat'), virtue, etc., is traditional: e.g. Cato *ap.* Gell. III, 7, 19: 'dii immortales tribuno militum fortunam ex virtute eius dedere'

outlook, for this is suggestive of the Stoic Πρόνοια working in a particular field. This notion appears earlier in Cicero and Sallust,[1] but with increasing frequency in the Augustan writers. Here again this philosophical concept can merge painlessly with the Roman traditional belief of *pax deorum*—the guarantee of divine benevolence provided that the ritual procedure is correctly observed. Note how Livy comments on the disharmony of the Aequi and the Volsci, who prepared an attack on Rome but instead attacked each other: 'There the fortune of the Roman people, in a battle no less obstinate than ruinous, destroyed two enemy armies.'[2] This then is an extension of that providential protection which Livy claims for Rome. The same idea is still more emphatically stated a little later: 'When all was abandoned, without leader and without resource, the guardian gods and the fortune of the city lent protection, for they turned the thoughts of the Volsci and the Aequi to plunder rather than to hostile attack.'[3] Such passages as this suggest the working of a divine power immanent in the body politic.

There are of course a large number of occasions on which *fortuna* means no more than 'luck' or 'chance'. This does not necessarily suggest that Livy had reservations about Stoic beliefs of determinism; in the final analysis, such luck is sent by the gods. In his characterisation of military commanders this sense is especially common; Fabius Cunctator, for example, trusts 'more in calculation than in luck'.[4]

There is, then, a considerable body of evidence which suggests that Livy's historical perspective, especially in the first and third decades, is powerfully affected by a sympathy with Stoic ideas. This goes far to explain his ambivalence towards Roman religious beliefs—his ration-

---

[1] Cic. *Cat.* I, 15; *Phil.* v, 29; Sall. *Cat.* 41, 3.
[2] II, 40, 13.   [3] III, 7, 1; compare I, 46, 5.
[4] XXIII, 18, 8; see Erkell, *Augustus, Felicitas, Fortuna*, 167 ff.

alising tendencies in the early books contrasting with his desire for a religious revival. For the neo-Stoics encouraged such ambivalence. Their defensive attitude when confronted with the scepticism of the rival schools is explicit in Cicero's *De Natura Deorum*, where they seek to expound the symbolic value of religious beliefs by 'rationalising' the myths—'commenticiarum fabularum reddere rationem'.[1] At the same time they maintained that the popular notions about the gods were by no means to be despised, for the *consensus gentium* was a most powerful argument for the existence of the divine; and these beliefs contained an important allegorical truth, for the gods of the Roman pantheon symbolised the existence of the godhead resident in matter. Balbus in the *De Natura Deorum* is insistent on this point.[2] The marked similarities between the old Roman and the Stoic theologies are closely relevant here. The Roman pantheistic notion of *numina*, each charged with the special sphere of woods, streams, crops, and the rest, is easily reconcilable with the Pronoia of Stoic physics, the material godhead immanent in matter. The similarity contains the important consideration that in both systems the gods are not anthropomorphic as they were for the Greeks; they do not wander freely on the earth, interfering directly with human affairs. They wield their sway impersonally. There are rules of conduct on the observance of which prosperity depends. As Manlius Capitolinus puts it: 'The gods will prevent my death, but they will never come down from heaven for my sake; they must give you the spirit to prevent it, as they have granted me the power to defend you in war from the barbarian foe, and in peace from haughty citizens.'[3] The same point is made in another speech: 'The gods never personally lay hands on the guilty; it is enough for them to arm the injured with opportunity for revenge.'[4]

[1] *N.D.* III, 63.   [2] II, 12; III, 63.
[3] VI, 18, 9.   [4] V, II, 16.

Livy's Stoic attitude, harmonising so closely with traditional Roman beliefs, is partly conditioned by the spirit of the age; in no other respect has Augustan idealism so clear an impact on his writing. The attempted religious revival, reflected not merely in Vergil's and Livy's fondness for recounting ancient rites and customs but also in Ovid's *Fasti* and in the poetry of Propertius, presented its intellectual problems to intelligent minds other than Livy's. It is not surprising, then, to find his contemporaries writing poetry which reflects a similar preoccupation with Stoic doctrines. There is a sense in which the *Aeneid* can be called a Stoic poem, as its central theme demonstrates how the destiny of Rome was guided by Providence.[1] It has also been suggested that there are Stoic elements in the *Odes* of Horace—not merely the ethical commonplaces that 'nature demands little' or that 'the wise man is a king', nor the equally conventional praise of Regulus and Cato, but more notably the frequent use of the singular *deus*, much as the neo-Stoic Seneca employs it in his letters.[2] Hence when Livy views history from this philosophical standpoint, he is not an isolated witness to the doctrine; one feels that it was in harmony with the official religious revival.[3]

This is the religious view of life which Livy regards as sane and objective, in contrast with the subjective superstition of foreign religions, which he repeatedly condemns for the mental illness or the bodily corruption which they cause. He is especially outspoken about the *Bacchanalia* scandal of 186 B.C.—'this ruinous scourge', he says, 'spread to Rome from Etruria like a contagious disease'. And a similar condemnation is made of a less serious outbreak in the Hannibalic War.[4]

It is within the context of neo-Stoicism reconciled with

[1] As at *Aen.* I, 205, 257, 382; II, 294, 777; III, 395; IV, 224, etc.
[2] *Od.* I, 3, 21; 12, 14; III, 4, 45; 29, 29.
[3] So J. F. D'Alton, *Horace and his Age* (London, 1917), 101.
[4] XXXIX, 9; XXV, 1; compare IV, 30, 9–11.

Roman religious thought that Livy's attitude towards prodigies and dreams—a favourite target for the nineteenth-century critics writing in the 'age of reason'—can best be apprehended. Beginning from the first year of the Second Punic War, he regularly lists the events of a miraculous nature which had originally appeared in the *tabulae pontificum*.[1] There are eight such lists in the third decade, and there is a catalogue for each year between 201 and 167 B.C., with a few exceptions. Livy himself tells us the reason for his inclusion of these lists: 'I am well aware that, because of the religious indifference (*neglegentia*) today inspiring the general belief that the gods foretell nothing, no prodigies are publicly reported or listed in historical works. But as I write of ancient days my mind somehow becomes old-fashioned (*antiquus*), and a kind of religious awe prevents me from regarding as unworthy of my history the events which those famous and far-sighted men decreed should be dealt with by the state.'[2]

This is a defensive statement, an appeal to the wisdom of the past to counter the criticisms which his contemporaries were making of his work; for the word *antiquus* in the Roman mind evoked not the derogatory sense attached to our 'old-fashioned', but a notion of simple purity and excellence. When Livy contrasts his own *religio* with the general *neglegentia*, he is defending what he believes to be the older and better values. The very fact that he reports the prodigies so conscientiously—in the face of contemporary convention—suggests that he accepts the *possibility* that they express the divine will—a view accepted by the neo-Stoic Posidonius.[3]

On this issue, however, the neo-Stoics had been

---

[1] On the *tabulae pontificum* see below, 110f.

[2] XLIII, 13, 1.

[3] Above, 53, n. 3. This view is proposed by M. L. W. Laistner, *The Greater Roman Historians* (Berkeley, 1947), 68ff.; but rejected by Kajanto, 52. One must not of course neglect the sentimental and literary motives for recounting the prodigies. See below, 175ff.

divided. Though Livy may accept such a possibility in principle, he is frequently caustic about the great numbers of prodigies claimed. He is aware of the dangers of religious psychosis in time of terror and defeat, and he knows that the announcement of one miracle can provoke a rash of them. So in one place he states: 'In that year many prodigies were reported, and their numbers increased in proportion to the credulity of the ingenuous and superstitious.'[1] And again: 'Many prodigies occurred that winter, or, as usually happens when once men's minds are turned to religious dread, many were reported and rashly believed.'[2] He is even more scathing when he recounts that at Cumae some mice were reported as having gnawed the gold in the temple of Jupiter: 'To such an extent does base superstition involve the gods in the most trifling matters.'[3]

There are, however, prodigy lists where no such comment is made. For example, before his account of the great defeats at Trasimene and Cannae, Livy has placed a list in close juxtaposition in a very significant way, as if to emphasise the divine displeasure.[4] Later in this decade, after remarking on how the sacrifices offered by the consuls M. Claudius Marcellus and T. Quinctius Crispinus were unfavourable immediately after the announcement of prodigies, he writes: 'The deadly outcome of the prodigies turned upon the consuls' persons whilst the state remained unharmed.'[5] Here and elsewhere Livy has opened his mind to the possibility that a prodigy may be the medium for a divine warning. But it need not be assumed that by giving credence to the importance of such occurrences as ship-shapes shining in the sky, lakes running with blood, and unborn children

[1] XXIV, 10, 6. [2] XXI, 62, 1.
[3] XXVII, 23, 2; also XXVIII, 11, 1; XXIX, 14, 2.
[4] XXII, 1, 8. See E. Burck, *Einführung in die dritte Dekade des Livius* (Heidelberg, 1950), 80, n. 16.
[5] XXVII, 23, 4.

crying from the womb *Io triumphe*, Livy is reverting to the unthinking fear and superstition of a primitive society. These incidents do not appear to him as the direct acts of some malevolent god, but in the complex and sophisticated cosmology of the Stoics he sees the prodigies as possibly symptomatic of a disordered universe, portending future disaster. It is instructive in this connection to read Plutarch's account of the Patavian augur Cornelius, who divined from a flight of birds the time and the result of the battle of Pharsalus. Livy, Plutarch insists, attests to the truth of this claim.[1]

Such philosophical and religious views, reflecting so closely Stoic dogmas, can be seen to have encouraged Livy in the view that the Romans were a master race. His account of the foundation of Rome begins with the uncompromising statement that it was divinely chosen: 'sed debebatur, ut opinor, fatis tantae origo urbis maximique secundum deorum opes imperii principium'.[2] And the alleged providential protection lent to the city in the early years has already been noted. His patriotism is thus accorded philosophical justification, and he has no hesitation in proclaiming that the Romans were superior to all other peoples in the moral qualities on which greatness depends. 'Either my love for the task I have undertaken deceives me, or no state was ever greater, purer, or more abounding in good examples; in no state did greed and extravagance enter so late, nor was honour accorded so long to frugality and moderate living.'[3] The indomitable spirit shown by the Romans after Cannae leads him to the view that 'certainly no other race would have avoided destruction under such grievous calamity'.[4] The discipline of the Roman *plebs* is superior to that prevailing in other towns.[5] If a foreigner like Timasitheus is honourable and just, he

---

[1] Plut. *Caes.* 47.
[2] I, 4, 1.
[3] *Praef.* 11.
[4] XXII, 54, 10.
[5] IV, 9, 8.

is 'more like the Romans than his own people', and if a Roman like Tarquinius Superbus achieves his ends by guile and deceit, this is a non-Roman trait.[1] Most incredible of all are Livy's words after condemning the execution of the Alban leader Mettius, who was tied to waggons which were then driven in opposite directions: 'This was the first and last punishment exacted by the Romans which showed insufficient regard for human laws; in other cases we can boast that no other race has been more gentle in its punishments.'[2] In every book such undisguised chauvinism can be exemplified.

It must however not be assumed that this bias was extended to the praise of first-century Rome. There is one patriotic outburst in which he claims that Rome's soldiers can drive off 'a thousand armies more imposing than the Macedonians and Alexander',[3] but this is exceptional, and his more consistently expressed view is one of pessimism. The Romans of his day, he alleges, cannot match their ancestors, and the reward which he seeks from the study of the past is an anodyne to relieve the despondency induced by the contemplation of the present. Such frank admissions in the Preface are reinforced by similar comment in the body of his work. Typical are his remarks on the election into office by the plebeians of three patricians, though the *plebs*' own representatives were by now eligible: 'The people appointed as military tribunes all patricians, content that some account had been held of the plebeians. Where nowadays could you find in a single person the moderation, the fairness, the magnanimity which then possessed the whole community?'[4]

Livy's patriotic sentiments, then, are qualified by his explicit awareness of the moral defects of his own society, in contrast to his idealising of the remote past. Our estimate of his impartiality is thus lower than it might

[1] V, 28, 3; I, 53, 4.   [2] I, 28, 11.
[3] IX, 19, 17.   [4] IV, 6, 12.

have been had we possessed his analysis of the fall of the Republic; if the Preface is any guide, we should have found there much emphasis on the moral degeneration which overtook the state.

In the extant books, Livy's history is dominated by ethical preconceptions. He looks at the past as at a battle-field of manners, and seeks to illustrate the moral qualities needed for a state to thrive, and for individual prosperity. His idealisation of the past depicts such qualities in sharp outline, so that our vision of them is not blurred by trivial human inconsistencies. His patriotism leads him to depict the Roman people as a whole as uniquely possessed of these virtues, and successive Roman leaders as typical examples of her uniqueness. Hence moral and patriotic considerations are united for didactic purposes, to demonstrate to posterity that national greatness cannot be achieved without the possession, especially by the leading men of the state, of the attributes which promote a healthy morality and wisdom in external and domestic policies.

These attributes are the principles of religious, political, and private activity. Due observance of the gods (*pietas*), and readiness to uphold treaties and promises solemnly made (*fides*); harmonious collaboration in the body politic (*concordia*), with due deference to authority both military and civic (*disciplina*); the application of foresight (*prudentia*) and reason (*ratio*) in politics and in war, and the exercise of mercy (*clementia*) when appropriate; at an individual level, the maintenance of chastity (*pudicitia*) and of courage (*virtus*), the need to comport oneself in accordance with one's status (*dignitas*) with the requisite seriousness (*gravitas*), and yet to espouse a simple way of life without luxury (*frugalitas*). These abstract qualities, clothed in the accidental garb of the leaders of each generation, are the true and enduring heroes of the *Ab Urbe Condita*.

Livy draws attention to the religious observance of the

ancients on every possible occasion. The shrines are thronged at every crisis; commanders vow and dedicate temples and offerings to individual deities for success in battle. The historian feels it his duty to record even unimportant events if they have a religious connection. 'I should pass over an affair trifling to relate', he begins when recounting details of a musicians' strike, 'if it did not appear to have reference to religion.'[1] If possible, he prefers the topic to be edifying, and is prepared to omit it if it is not. So in describing how C. Flaccus, a man of loose and degenerate habits, amended his ways after being appointed *flamen dialis*, he writes: 'I should gladly have omitted to mention the reason why the priest of Jupiter was compelled to be consecrated, had the story not passed from notoriety to edification.'[2] The implication is that he would have suppressed details of the appointment had he not been able to draw attention to the new-found *sanctitas vitae* of Flaccus, caused by his revived devotion to the ancestral religion.

Pietas towards the gods and *fides* towards men are in Livy's philosophy of history closely interconnected. His account of the Roman defeat at the hands of the Gauls in 390 B.C. attributes the disaster to the lack of these virtues. It is true that military deficiencies are taken into account. The military tribunes are blamed for conducting an inadequate levy and for lack of a battle-plan, but these occur subsequently to the grievous neglect of a divine warning; more important still is the emphasis laid on the contravention of the *ius gentium*, when the Roman ambassadors abused their privileged status by fighting on behalf of Clusium against the Gauls, and when the Senate and people not only failed to surrender them at the Gauls' request, but also made them their supreme commanders. The immediate military defects are thus to be viewed as the outcome of a lack of *fides*, the failure to observe inter-

---

[1] IX, 30, 5.   [2] XXVII, 8, 5.

national law, with which is associated the divine displeasure which the Romans ignored.[1]

Similarly the defeat at the hands of the Samnites near Caudium is the result of the Romans' rejection in a haughty manner of the just restitution offered by the enemy. This pride (*superbia*), which causes the Romans to disregard the claims of justice, is the fundamental cause of the humiliation which ensues. As the Samnite C. Pontius says: 'I shall have recourse to the gods who take vengeance on unsupportable pride, and I shall beg them to turn their anger against the Romans.'[2]

A specific example of disaster following upon non-observance of the gods is afforded by the description of the *débâcle* of Flaminius at Lake Trasimene. His *impietas*, which Livy regards as the cause of the defeat, is stressed by this comment: 'He showed insufficient fear of laws and Senatorial dignity, and even of the gods...so it was quite clear that he would act fiercely and hastily without consulting gods or men.'[3] This sums up his neglecting to pay the customary visit to the temple of Jupiter, and to perform the other necessary religious ceremonies when he assumed office, and also his disregard of the evil portent when the bull-calf which he was sacrificing leapt from his hands.[4] In all these disasters, such lack of *pietas* and *fides* is at root the dread sin of ὕβρις, which meets its inevitable ἄτη. Here Livy succumbs to the 'tragic' concept of history, which is also discernible in Thucydides' characterisation of Cleon, and affects even Polybius in his portrait of Philip V of Macedon.[5] Such a presentation of Roman calamities was of course not Livy's invention; and it is

---

[1] Neglect of the warning, v, 32, 6f.; contravention of the *ius gentium*, v, 36, 6 and 8–11.

[2] IX, 1, 6–8; and compare IX, 1, 10: 'iustum est bellum, Samnites, quibus necessarium, et pia arma...'.

[3] XXII, 3, 4–5.   [4] XXI, 63, 13.

[5] Cleon's tragic career, Cornford, *Thucydides Mythistoricus*, 110ff.; Philip's, F. W. Walbank, *JHS* (1938), 65ff.

interesting to note how the neo-Stoics had espoused the message to stress the inevitable result of neglect of the gods.[1]

Livy's emphasis on the civic virtue of *concordia* can be seen especially in his portrayal of the struggle of the orders in the early books. Every possible opportunity is seized of praising the measures which advanced such concord, and of condemning the selfishness of sectional interests. Beginning with the very first chapter of the second book, where he lauds the appointment to the Senate of the outstanding men of equestrian rank ('This had a remarkable effect in achieving concord in the state by reconciling the spirits of the plebeians to the patricians'), he singles out the measures which helped to achieve political harmony. Bulk buying of corn, nationalisation of salt, the exemption of the poor from taxes, the establishment of sovereign laws in the Twelve Tables, the concessions made to the *plebs* by the Valerian and Horatian laws and by the *lex Canuleia*—all these measures have his approval. He condemns the patricians on occasion for their enslaving free citizens, their attention to private interests ('which have always impeded and will always impede the common good'), the thuggery and licence of their younger members, their refusal to give the plebeians even untenanted land, and in general their failure to serve the *plebs*; and the plebeians are castigated for their repeated agitation for agrarian legislation ('the poison of the *plebs*') as well as for fomenting unjustified hatred against the patricians.[2] These are the roots of discord. It may be noted that Livy lays emphasis especially on economic and social differences; though he does

[1] Above, 50. For emphasis on the *positive* concept of *fides Romana* see v, 27, 11; vi, 33, 8; vii, 31, 1, etc. This is one of the prominent attributes of Augustan patriotic literature.

[2] For measures achieving *concordia* see ii, 9, 6 ff.; iii, 34; iii, 55; iv, 1 ff. Condemnation of patricians, ii, 23; ii, 30, 1–2 ('sed factione respectuque rerum privatarum, quae semper offecere officientque publicis consiliis...'); iii, 11, 9 ff.; iii, 37, 7–8; of plebeians, ii, 41, 3 ff.; ii, 52, 2 ('suo veneno, agraria lege'); iv, 48.

not ignore the political concessions made within the body politic, he has not fully appreciated that these are the foundation of concord. For example, he does not sufficiently advert to the importance of the extension of the citizenship in the peaceful evolution of the Roman state.[1] His interest is primarily in personalities, not in policies; and when he comments on domestic discord, his remarks are usually psychological. 'A moderate attitude in defence of freedom is difficult when the individual makes pretence of a desire for equality, yet exalts himself in such a way as to bring down his neighbour. Men gratuitously convert themselves into objects of terror by taking precautions against terrorisation; the injuries which we have warded from ourselves we inflict upon others, as though we must either be aggressive or suffer.'[2]

Concordia cannot be achieved without *disciplina*, a lesson which Livy brings home with the anecdote of Brutus, the deliverer of Rome from kingship, who was forced to execute his own son for treason.[3] The virtues of harmonious co-operation and unquestioning obedience are equally as vital in warfare as at home. So Livy emphasises the guilt of such commanders as L. Sergius Fidenas and M. Papirius Mugillanus,[4] and M'. Sergius and L. Verginius,[5] whose jealous rivalry towards each other was the cause of Roman defeats; and equally vehemently he praises the conduct of those who subordinate their personal desires and judgement to the orders of their commander. So the army's gracious acceptance of a rebuke from Cincinnatus is accompanied by this remark: 'But in those days a man's spirit was so calmly amenable to superior orders that this army was more mindful of the benefits received than of their shame, and the soldiers decreed a golden crown to the dictator....'[6]

---

[1] Below, 164. [2] III, 65, 11.
[3] II, 5. [4] IV, 46.
[5] V, 8, 4 ff. [6] III, 29, 3.

Though Livy's treatment of the *disciplina* motif usually reflects the presentation of his sources, one can occasionally demonstrate his personal imprint. Compare, for example, his account of the duel of Manlius (later Torquatus) and the Gaul with the extant version of Claudius Quadrigarius; Livy has added that Manlius agreed to fight only if his commander consented.[1] In the Hannibalic War Rome's Italian allies remained faithful 'because they were not unwilling to obey their superiors —the sole bond of loyalty';[2] and again, it is the sense of the sacredness of discipline which makes the Saguntines resist until death.[3] Such discipline is maintained only by firm leadership; hence the emphasis on Camillus' severity in refusing booty to his troops.[4] Several chapters are devoted to the disobedience of Q. Fabius Rullianus, whom the dictator Papirius Cursor finally spares, but only when the lesson of discipline has been well learned.[5]

The importance of *prudentia* and *ratio* as attributes of great military leadership is underlined especially in the characterisation of Fabius Cunctator. Livy is at pains to emphasise that the good commander should leave nothing to chance, and duly tells how Fabius 'reconnoitred the routes with the utmost care, intending nowhere to trust to luck unless necessity compelled it. . . . And indeed Hannibal felt immediate apprehension of the dictator's *prudentia*.'[6] Fabius stresses that 'fortune is not important; the mind and the reason (*rationem*) are the controlling powers'.[7]

It is the lack of these qualities in a commander which so often causes disaster. Even the great Marcellus is not excluded from such criticism, for he was killed in an

---

[1] Livy VII, 10, 2 ff.; Claudius, *ap.* Gell. IX, 13. Compare XXIII, 46, 12 ff., the duel between Claudius Asellus and the Campanian Cerrinus Vibellius, in which again the Roman asks permission of his commander before fighting.

[2] XXII, 13, 11.   [3] XXI, 7, 3.

[4] V, 26, 8.   [5] VIII, 30 ff.

[6] XXII, 12, 2–6.

[7] XXII, 25, 14 f. Polybius (I, 35, 5) passes similar comments on the γνώμη of Xanthippus.

ambush laid by Hannibal when his zeal to join battle over-rode his caution: 'The death of Marcellus was sad on general grounds, but especially because he endangered himself, his colleague, and one might say the whole state with a thoughtlessness unbecoming to his age—he was over sixty—and to the *prudentia* of a veteran commander.'[1] Small wonder, then, that Livy castigates the *temeritas* and *ferocitas*—the very antonyms of *prudentia*—of Sempronius, in his account of the defeat at the Trebia. There is a long description of his outrageous conduct in insisting on battle while his colleague Scipio was on his sick-bed, in which a vivid picture of his rashness, violence, and base ambition is built up. Livy has deliberately expanded the traditional account to emphasise these moral causes of defeat.[2]

Similar emphasis is laid on the rashness of Minucius in one of the most scathing passages of the *Ab Urbe Condita*, and the account of his being ambushed and the rescue operation of his colleague Fabius Cunctator allows Livy to moralise about the dangers of trusting fortune.[3] But the most striking example of all is the denigration of Teren-tius Varro, whose *temeritas* is said to have been the cause of the disaster at Cannae. Livy here follows Valerius Antias' propaganda against the plebeian commander, in which the decision to fight is not the Senate's, as in Polybius,[4] but Varro's alone. Before the battle there are speeches by Fabius Cunctator and Aemilius Paulus which foretell the disaster; and in the preliminary operations Varro's rashness almost results in his falling into ambush. These details have no basis in fact, but Livy prefers the tradition which lays greater emphasis on the moral delinquency allegedly the cause of the disaster.[5] It is interesting to

---

[1] XXVII, 27, 11.
[2] XXI, 53, 1–7; for the more moderate version see Pol. III, 70, 2 ff.
[3] XXII, 29, 1.   [4] III, 107.
[5] The same lesson is frequently taught in the first decade. Camillus condemns the *temeritas* of his troops at VI, 24, 5; another example is the condemnation of C. and P. Manlius for *temeritas* and *inscitia* after a defeat by the Volsci (VI, 30, 6).

note how Livy's views on *prudentia* in generalship are in accord with those of Augustus, but there is no need to suspect any contemporary influence at work in a view which Thucydides and Polybius had already expounded.[1]

One of the benefits which Roman Stoicism can justly claim to have advanced in the West is the more enlightened humanitarianism which eventually mitigated the effects of Roman savagery. Julius Caesar's mercifulness had doubtless been motivated by political expediency, but in the Augustan age the notion of *clementia* was elevated to the ranks of the sacred virtues, with the result that Livy re-interprets Rome's past to stress her enlightened policy in this respect. But the Roman doctrine of *clementia* does not of course embrace the Christian idea of universal forgiveness; it implies the according of merciful treatment only to those who willingly surrender.

Camillus initiated the tradition, according to Livy, with his treatment of the Tusculans, whose policy of non-resistance had ensured that their city was not harmed. 'Tusculans,' said Camillus, 'you alone up to this day have found the true weapons, the true strength with which to defend your possessions from Roman anger.'[2] Livy's patriotic bias shows through here; he condemns, for example, the slaughter of the inhabitants of Satricum by the Volsci and Praenestini, and the murder of Roman prisoners by the Tarquinienses; but the permission given by a Roman commander to three armies to sack Anxur he regards as an act of kindness to the Roman *plebs*, and the brutal massacre at Henna is half excused by the statement 'So the Romans kept Henna by a deed either wicked or necessary'.[3] On the other hand, he does condemn the

---

[1] Suet. *Aug.* 25. For Thucydides see 68, n. 5; Polybius' account of the disasters in 218–216 also takes into account the rashness of inexperienced commanders.

[2] VI, 26, 1. But compare III, 2, 5 earlier for the *offer* of clemency by Q. Fabius to the Aequi.

[3] Satricum, VI, 22, 4: 'foedeque in captis exercuere victoriam'. Roman prisoners, VII, 15, 10: 'qua foeditate supplicii...'. Anxur, IV, 59, 10: 'ea... benignitas imperatorum'. Henna, XXIV, 39, 7.

execution at Rome of the Tarentine and Thurian hostages after they escaped and were recaptured, and shows how such harsh treatment led to the loss of Tarentum; likewise he shows indignation at Pleminius' harsh handling of Locri.[1]

But it is in his characterisation of Scipio Africanus that Livy above all personifies Roman clemency; the attention is focused on his kind treatment of hostages, his liberation of Masinissa's nephew, his mercy towards the Spaniards Indibilis and Mandonius, and his cordial reception of legates from Greek and Asian cities. The picture is certainly idealised; one must repair to Polybius' account to discover that Scipio ordered his men 'to slaughter those they met' after the capture of New Carthage, for Livy merely tells us that 'slaughter took place'.[2] In his praise of Roman *clementia* Livy inflicts the greatest damage on his claim to historical impartiality.[3]

It is interesting to note how frequently the historian draws attention to Roman clemency in the fourth and fifth decades, where the dominant theme is Rome's disinterested liberation of Greece, and where ruthlessness would have been less excusable than in the earlier struggles for survival. So the speech of the Roman legate to the Aetolian council in 200 B.C. is a spirited defence of Roman treatment of vanquished peoples, culminating in the words: 'This is the greater danger, that through over-generosity in sparing the conquered, we may encourage more races to try the chances of war against us.' Flamininus can tell the Aetolians in 197 that the Roman tradition of sparing the conquered goes back to remote antiquity, and justifiably points to the terms granted to Car-

[1] Hostages, xxv, 8 and 15. Pleminius at Locri, xxix, 8, 7 ff.
[2] Kindness to hostages, xxvi, 49; to Masinissa's nephew, xxvii, 19, 8. Indibilis and Mandonius, xxviii, 34, 3. Legates in the East, xxxvii, 34. Treatment of New Carthage, Pol. x, 15, 4 and Livy xxvi, 46, 10.
[3] Below, 151 f.

thage as 'an outstanding proof of clemency'; and Livy claims that two years later his 'restraint, justice, and moderation after victory were admired by the whole of Greece as much as his courage in war'. The Greeks indeed at a conference in 185 urge Philip to imitate the Roman people, 'who prefer to win allies by kindness rather than fear'; and in the Third Illyrian War of 168 the praetor Anicius is said to have won over many cities by his *clementia* and *iustitia*. Senatorial *clementia* is also conspicuous, as when the consul M. Popillius is ordered to restore freedom and possessions to the Statiellates because of the previously good record of that Ligurian community; this is an echo of an earlier decision by which the praetor M. Furius was ordered to restore to the Cenomani their arms, and to vacate their territory.[1]

Of the personal qualities to which Livy attributes Rome's rise to world dominance none is more vital than *virtus Romana*. Its importance is first epitomised by Romulus in his message to neighbouring races: 'satis scire origini Romanae et deos adfuisse et non defuturam virtutem'—the city, divinely founded, would be supported by Roman courage. So Camillus rejects the stratagem of demanding the surrender of Etruscan Falerii by the treacherous seizure of the children of prominent burghers: 'I shall conquer this, as I conquered Veii, by Roman qualities—courage, toil, and arms.' Such idealised manhood is again represented by Mucius Scaevola's proud deportment after his failure to assassinate Lars Porsena: 'et facere et pati fortia Romanum est'. The emphasis on *virtus Romana*, carried through from the legendary sections to the more historical books, is reiterated so frequently, when Livy compares Roman troops with those of

---

[1] Speech at the Aetolian council, XXXI, 31, 16; Flamininus, XXXIII, 12, 17; XXXIV, 22, 5; Greeks in 185 B.C., XXXIX, 25, 15; Anicius' *clementia*, XLIV, 31, 1; Senatorial *clementia*, XLII, 8, 8; XXXIX, 3, 2–3.

Carthage, Macedon, and Asia, that further exemplification is superfluous.[1]

The importance of chastity (*pudicitia*) is demonstrated especially by the famous legends of the first decade. The rape of Lucretia and her suicide, and the murder of Verginia by her father to keep her chaste from the hands of Appius Claudius, both serve to illustrate that high ideals of chastity are essential for the well-being of society. It is the lust of Sextus Tarquinius, directed against the 'tenacious chastity' of Lucretia, which leads to the expulsion of the kings, and Appius Claudius' lascivious desires similarly lead to the end of the Decemvirs' rule.[2] In the fourth decade is narrated a similar occurrence in the course of a campaign in the East. When Manlius Vulso was encamped at Ancyra, one of his centurions did violence to a captive barbarian princess, Chiomara. Eventually the centurion allowed her to be ransomed, and as she was being handed back to her tribesmen, she ordered one of them to kill the centurion, and carried back his head to her husband as a mark of her fidelity.[3] The prominence which Livy gives to this story, so unedifying from a Roman viewpoint and so trivial that it could have been omitted, shows the importance he attaches to the lesson of *pudicitia*. The beauty and chastity of the princess, and the lust and greed of the centurion, are duly stressed, and Livy appends an edifying conclusion to the anecdote: 'We are told that she preserved to the end the glory of this womanly deed by her general piety and dignity.'

The Roman ideal of behaviour towards women is illustrated by the delineation of Africanus' conduct. Livy studiously ignores Polybius' comment that Scipio was

---

[1] Romulus, I, 9, 4; Camillus, V, 27, 8; Scaevola, II, 12, 9 (compare Dionys. v, 27 ff. to observe the fresh motivation introduced by Livy here); see also IX, 31, 13; XXXVI, 41, 12, etc. For numerous other examples see H. Hoch, *Die Darstellung der politischen Sendung Roms bei Livius* (Frankfurt, 1951), 33 ff.

[2] I, 58–9; III, 44.

[3] XXXVIII, 24.

'fond of the fair sex', and tells at some length the anecdote about a girl whom Scipio restored to her future
husband with the remark that he too could appreciate the
joys of love within their proper context.[1] The more famous
account of Sophoniba contains an exhortation to Masinissa to master the unquiet impulses of the flesh: 'Believe
me, there is not so much danger to our age from the
armed enemy as from the pleasures all around us. The
man who controls and subdues them by temperance has
won a much greater distinction and a greater victory than
ours over the conquered Syphax.'[2] Behind Africanus the
authentic tones of Livy the Stoic are audible.

Another lesson which Livy is anxious to stress is the
necessity for simple living (*frugalitas*), and the avoidance
of demoralising luxury. The edifying legend of Cincinnatus' simple life in a hut across the Tiber gives the
historian his most obvious opportunity. It is a story 'well
worth hearing for those who reject all life's gifts except
riches, and who think that there is no seat for great honour
or excellence other than where wealth abounds in plenty.
The sole hope of the empire of the Roman people,
L. Quinctius, was cultivating four acres across the Tiber.
...He was either digging a ditch, his weight on the spade,
or ploughing when the legates hailed him there....' He
wipes the manly sweat from his brow, dons his toga, and
proceeds to the city to take up the dictatorship, choosing
as his master-of-horse L. Tarquinius, a patrician so poor
that all his service had been in the infantry.[3] This honourable poverty is also stressed in men like Valerius Publicola and Menenius Agrippa, neither of whom left
sufficient money for a private burial.[4]

The complementary lesson, that love of luxury is
disastrous to communities and individuals, is illustrated

---

[1] Pol. x, 19, 3: '...φιλογύνην ὄντα τὸν Πόπλιον...'. For Livy's version see
xxvi, 50 and the phrase (50, 5) 'recto et legitimo amore'.
[2] xxx, 14, 7.   [3] iii, 26–7.   [4] ii, 16 and 33.

especially by the example of Hannibal's alleged wintering in Capua in 216/5. Livy claims that this was the main cause of the Carthaginian defeat in the Second Punic War; previously the troops had been hardened and unused to luxury, but during that winter they submitted themselves to sloth, feasting, harlotry and drunkenness— an error regarded by men of experience as greater than the failure to march on Rome after Cannae. This disastrous relaxation, Livy argues, impaired the effectiveness of Hannibal's war machine.[1] Livy's anxiety to bring home a moral lesson has here resulted in a distortion of the truth; in fact, Hannibal besieged and captured Casilinum during this winter, and Polybius expressly tells us that during sixteen years of warfare in Italy Hannibal never brought in his men from under the open sky. Here again the dangers of edifying history are demonstrated.[2] Capua is once more the target for such criticism in Livy's account of the Samnite Wars, when the city is described as 'by no means healthy for military discipline', for its pleasures soften the spirits of the Roman troops and make them oblivious of their fatherland.[3]

Livy's insistence on the need for personal dignity and becoming sobriety (*dignitas* and *gravitas*) in the conduct of affairs may cause the irreverent reader some amusement. In vain does one thumb the pages of the *Ab Urbe Condita* in the hope of finding one of the great Romans laughing; there is an occasional flicker of a smile, but no more. This suppression of all jocular elements tends to mislead us about the over-sobriety and high seriousness of the Roman character. Livy dehumanises leaders like Marcellus and Flamininus when he excises their laughter and their jokes.

[1] XXIII, 18, 11–16.

[2] For Hannibal's activities in this winter see XXIII, 19 and 22, the siege of Casilinum before the consulship of Gracchus (XXIII, 24). Gracchus entered office in March, and as the calendar was at this time two months in advance of the seasons, there was little time for wild life in Capua. See H. H. Scullard, *Roman World*[2] (London, 1951), 206f.

[3] VII, 38, 5.

In his account of the conference at Nicaea between Flamininus and Philip of Macedon, he has methodically suppressed all traces of the joking recorded by his source Polybius. He considers that Philip had 'more wit than becomes a king, and insufficient control over laughter even in serious discussion'.[1] When during the siege of Syracuse Archimedes with his devices lifted from the water the Roman ships, and destroyed the assault-ladders (*sambucae*, a word which also means 'harps'), Marcellus wryly remarked: 'Archimedes is drawing water from the sea with my ships, but my harpists have been flogged and expelled from the feast in disgrace.' Polybius recorded the joke; Livy carefully left it out.[2] Like Tacitus, he is sensitive about unseemly behaviour; he is scathing about his authorities' version of the duel between Manlius Torquatus and the Gaul, because they reported that the Gaul stuck out his tongue in derision before the engagement; 'even this has been thought worthy of record'.[3]

The sort of *gravitas* and *dignitas* which Livy approves is epitomised by the pompous attitude of the three legates who went to the camp of Gracchus Cloelius, chief of the Aequi, to complain and demand restitution for plundering activities. Cloelius said that he was busy; they could give their instructions to the oak-tree which stood by. 'Then one of the legates moved away, and said: "Let this hallowed oak and such gods as be hearken to your breaking of the treaty...."'[4] Livy similarly turns into embarrassing rhetoric an incident in which M. Servilius addresses the popular assembly. To increase the effect of his words as he described the various campaigns in

[1] XXXII, 34, 3. For Livy's treatment of this conference see Walsh, *AJP* (1955), 371 ff.
[2] Pol. VIII, 6, 6; Livy XXIV, 34, 16.
[3] VII, 10, 5. Tacitus insists on this *dignitas* in history no less than Livy; see Syme, *Tacitus*, 342 f.
[4] III, 25, 8.

which he fought, he divested himself of his garments, and pointed to his numerous honourable scars. Unfortunately someone noticed a curious swelling on the groin, and there was a little ribald laughter in the front rows. When Servilius realised the reason for the amusement, he said: 'That very object of your laughter I have through sitting astride a horse day and night, and I am no more ashamed of this than of these scars of mine....'[1]

All these examples of Livy's concern to illustrate the devoutness of earlier generations, their good faith, their valour in war, the harmony which they sought to engender in politics, the foresight which they exercised, the moderation of their private lives, their concern for chaste conduct, the moral grandeur and high seriousness of their leaders, give us the clearest notion of the direction of his work. It is not exclusively patriotic, for he is willing to praise the characters of non-Romans who measure up to his ideal, and to condemn Romans when they do not. His preoccupations are overwhelmingly moral, and in the depiction of every outstanding personality he accounts for success and failure by reference to moral attributes. Much of this concentration on moral criteria is not original to Livy. The traditional Greek notion which expects proud conduct to be attended by disaster has infiltrated into Roman letters. Earlier Roman historiography employed the same moral criteria in analyses of the decline of the Roman Republic; Sallust's prefatory comments in the *Catiline* and *Jugurtha* exemplify this. What *is* notable about Livy's interpretation is that this moral view of the past is conceived as being desirable not merely for its salubrious effect on society, but also because it is part of a coherent and integrated philosophical outlook. The Roman virtues are to be espoused, and

[1] XLV, 39.

vices eschewed, because by so doing men are living in harmony with their destiny. And the Stoic philosophy, with its impact not only on the Roman historiographical tradition but also on Livy personally, lends to the *Ab Urbe Condita* that sense of an ordered and intelligible universe which justifies the title for Livy of 'philosophic historian'.

IV

ROMAN MORALITY
HISTORICALLY CHARACTERISED

As has been noted in the previous two chapters, Livy regards history as pre-eminently concerned with individuals, especially with leaders of communities; and in his analysis of their achievements and failures he draws attention to the moral attributes or defects which he considers solely responsible for such eventualities. Because of this moral function which he allots to history, the characterisation of individuals, and to a lesser extent of communities and nations, occupies a central position: 'I ask that each individual should keenly direct his glance *at the kind of lives and manners* of ancient times, and observe *through what men and by what attributes* in war and at home the empire was acquired and increased.'[1]

After reading this one might well expect to find Livy making extended personal judgements, after the manner of Polybius, on leading personalities; but such intrusion of opinion is in fact rare, and usually restricted to a few words. Instead of making personal observations on the character of individuals, the historian is content to use the 'indirect' methods which we associate with the medium of drama, so that the reader forms his impression of individuals in three ways. First, the speeches and remarks made by a person give the reader an insight into his character; here the historian, allowed by convention some freedom in the reporting of speeches, has his greatest opportunity to influence our assessment. Secondly, the attitudes

[1] *Praef.* 9.

82

of contemporaries towards the person characterised, as expressed in their speeches, are important; here too the historian can subtly introduce rearrangement and change of emphasis. Thirdly, the effect which the person characterised has on other people can be depicted by describing either their mental reactions on encountering him, or the courses they subsequently adopt.[1] In this 'objective' approach, Livy follows a tradition of annalistic writing which goes back to Xenophon and Thucydides, and which is undoubtedly influenced by the techniques of characterisation employed in Greek drama. It is also relevant to remember, in assessing Greek influences here, the methods used by the Greek logographers. When professional orators like Demosthenes composed speeches for others in the law-courts, they attempted to delineate a man's character in the words given to him to deliver.[2] This type of characterisation became a convention of Roman annalistic writing,[3] and is used by Tacitus in his portrayal of Augustus, Tiberius, and Germanicus.

The advantages of this 'indirect' method to the historian are obvious. He is saved the labour of personal assessment, and can leave the onus of judgement on the reader. This allows him to pose as an impartial narrator whilst he is enabled to praise particular persons or measures by these indirect methods; and conversely, he can avoid direct criticism by attributing appropriate condemnation to one or other of the historical personages involved. Such considerations are, however, incidental; Livy follows the traditional convention by which characterisation is carefully woven into the description of events.

In order to achieve consistency of method, Livy, when following Polybius, often attributes the personal

---

[1] I. Bruns, *Die Persönlichkeit in der Geschichtsschreibung der Alten* (Berlin, 1898), 18: 'den Urtheilen von Zeitgenossen, der Wirkung auf sie, und Aussprüchen der zu schildernden Personen'.

[2] For Lysias' development of this *ethopoeia* see W. Jaeger, *Demosthenes* (Cambridge, 1938), 35.   [3] So Bruns, 62 ff.

comments of the earlier historian to an historical character prominent in events. Polybius, for example, passes some observations about the Roman liberation of Greece in 196 B.C.; he remarks how wonderful it was that the Romans had undertaken considerable danger and expense for the freedom of Greece, that they had brought a force adequate to achieve it, and that no mischance had occurred in the operations. Livy places the gist of these comments in the mouths of the Greeks themselves, and can thus use complimentary language in his characterisation of the Roman people without being accused of personal bias: 'There was upon this earth a race which waged war at its own expense, toil, and danger for the freedom of others. ...They did not afford this help merely to neighbours, but they crossed the sea so that there might be no unjust empire throughout the world, but that everywhere right, duty, and law might be most powerful.'[1] On the other hand, the comment of Polybius to the effect that Prusias, king of Bithynia, was afraid of losing his territories to Roman invasion is converted by Livy into *a letter* sent by Antiochus to Prusias, condemning Roman imperialism; Livy thus avoids direct criticism of Roman policy. The same technique is to be observed in Livy's account of a letter sent by Perseus of Macedon to Eumenes and Antiochus.[2] One is reminded of his comments on the siege of Saguntum, where he avoids direct condemnation of Roman faithlessness, but attributes some words of blame to a Spanish ancient; and also of the words of Vibius Virrius, the sponsor of the Capuan rebellion against Rome, before the capture of the city by the Romans.[3]

[1] XXXIII, 33, 5; compare Pol. XVIII, 46, 14.

[2] The letter to Prusias, Pol. XXI, 11, 1, Livy XXXVII, 25, 4. For Sallust's influence here see Walsh, *RhM* (1954), 105f. Livy's motive here may be chiefly artistic, for this letter contrasts with the one received from the Scipios defending Roman policy. For Perseus' letter see XLIV, 24, 1ff. For other examples of conversion from 'direct' to 'indirect' exposition see *RhM* (1954), 106f.

[3] XXI, 19, 9f; XXVI, 13, 4ff. Note too the condemnation of Roman policy in the Samnites' speech at the Etruscan council (X, 16, 4–8).

Livy is not blind to Roman faults, but rarely criticises them in his own name.

Though the indirect methods of characterisation are the chief ones used, Livy does employ others. After narrating the deaths of important persons, he frequently inserts a brief comment on their careers. Thucydides had done this in the cases of Themistocles and Pericles, and Sallust imitated him in a few instances; Livy extended the practice to all great men.[1] Such comments are not the undiscriminating eulogy often associated with funeral laudations, but a statement of chronological detail—age at death, length of offices held, and the like—with one or two facts to indicate the main importance of a man's career. So Camillus and Fabius Cunctator are commemorated as saviours of the state, and Scipio Africanus as the man who won the Hannibalic War. Occasionally there is a word of criticism, as in the cases of Marcellus and Cicero. Of Cicero Livy writes: 'In his long career of success, he was none the less assailed by heavy blows—exile, the destruction of the party which he had represented, the decease of his daughter, and his death so grim and bitter. None of these adversities he endured as became a man, with the exception of his death....'[2] But more usually the *elogium* has the function merely of a factual précis. There are elsewhere character sketches of a brief nature, inserted at apposite points in the narrative, and based on traditional material. One such sketch is of Hannibal, set before the description of the outbreak of the Second Punic War; there is another of Cato when his candidature for the censorship is under discussion.[3] When introducing lesser-known persons, with whom the reader would not

---

[1] Sen. *Suas.* VI, 21: 'hoc semel aut iterum a Thucydide factum, item in paucissimis personis usurpatum a Sallustio, T. Livius benignus omnibus magnis viris praestitit....'.

[2] Camillus, VII, 1, 9f.; Fabius, XXX, 26, 7–9; Scipio, XXXVIII, 53, 9–11; Marcellus, XXVII, 27, 11; Cicero, *ap.* Sen. *Suas.* VI, 17.

[3] XXI, 4, 3ff.; XXXIX, 40, 4ff.

be familiar, Livy briefly indicates their most prominent characteristics.[1]

Another method of characterisation common in the ancient world is that of comparison and contrast between leaders. Fabius Cunctator, for example, is successively set against Minucius, Marcellus, and Scipio Africanus, so that the different facets of his character may be illuminated. Again, Scipio in the fourth decade is set against his brother Lucius and against Manlius Volso (not to mention the extended comparison with Hannibal). It is rare that the comparison is made explicit, as that between Papirius Cursor and the great Alexander;[2] more frequently the reader is left to see the implied connection by artistic arrangement. Thus Africanus is the symbol of *clementia*, in contrast to his more uncompromising brother; and Fabius' prudence is set against the rashness of Minucius, his leniency against the harshness of Marcellus, his attitude of doubt against Scipio's belief in the fortune of the Roman people.[3]

Livy is especially fond of contrasting foreigners, as in the case of Hiero and Hieronymus of Syracuse. Hiero's popularity with his townsmen and his good faith towards the Romans are the antithesis of Hieronymus' lordly behaviour, lust, and cruelty to his own people, and his arrogance to the Romans after Cannae. A comparison with the account of Polybius shows how this contrast is more sharply drawn by Livy's depicting Hieronymus as more hostile than he really was. His ironical humour to the Roman legates who visited him after Cannae is exaggerated, and the reasons for his hostility towards the Romans are omitted.

---

[1] E.g. of Menenius Agrippa, 'facundum virum et quod inde oriundus erat plebi carum' (II, 32, 8). Also XXIII, 2, 2, etc.   [2] IX, 16, 19 ff.

[3] Africanus and his brother, XXXVII, 6 ff.; Fabius and Minucius, XXII, 27–9; Fabius and Africanus, XXVIII, 40–4; Fabius and Marcellus, XXVII, 16, 8. Note also the contrast between Cato's moral idealism and the more pragmatic attitude of L. Valerius in their discussions on the *lex Oppia* at XXXIV, 2 ff.

In fact, Polybius' criticism of earlier historians one
can here apply to Livy; he has made this youth of
fifteen, who ruled for thirteen months, into a monstrous
tyrant.[1]

Again, the Numidians Syphax and Masinissa are contrasted. Syphax embodies the lack of good faith endemic
in barbarians, whereas Masinissa's *constantissima fides* towards Rome is for Livy a sufficient indication that he did
not desert the Carthaginians without due reason! Masinissa is in fact a foreigner with almost all the Roman
virtues. He is religious, for he tells Scipio that he was
awaiting any chance to desert which 'the kindness of the
immortal gods offered'. As a general he shows fore-
thought, but also boldness. At Scipio's command, he
controls his wayward passions by administering poison to
Sophoniba. Above all, his valour is conspicuous; even
at the age of ninety-two, just before the Third Punic
War, he leads his army to defeat the Carthaginians.
Masinissa is one of Livy's great heroes, and throughout
the fourth decade he is mentioned in speeches as an
example to the peoples of the East of all that a king-ally
should be. Hasdrubal is made to say: 'There is greater
talent of nature and mind in Masinissa than in any
previous member of his race.' And Livy calls him 'by
far the greatest king of his day'—a comment at which
Philip V of Macedon would doubtless have smiled
sardonically.[2]

Amongst his characterisation techniques Livy has not

---

[1] Hiero's *fides* to Rome, XXI, 50, 8; XXII, 37; XXIV, 4. His popularity, XXIV, 5.
Hieronymus' flashy clothes, bodyguard, contempt, hauteur, cruelty, and lust,
XXIV, 5 ff. Exaggeration of his irony after Cannae, XXIV, 6, 5 (compare Pol. VII,
3, 2). And Livy omits Hieronymus' question to the Roman legates—why had
the Romans sent fifty ships towards Syracuse on a false report of Hiero's death
(Pol. VII, 3, 5 ff.)?

[2] Syphax's lack of *fides*, XXVIII, 17, 6. Masinissa's good faith, XXVIII, 16, 11;
his *religio*, 35, 8; *prudentia*, XXIX, 30, 9; *audacia*, 32, 12; *rara virtus* (Hasdrubal's
judgement), 31, 3; Livy's comment, 29, 5. Masinissa's final victory, *Perioch.*
XLVIII.

disdained to employ anecdotes to epitomise a person's predominant attributes. There is the splendid story of the disciplinarian Papirius Cursor, who, when asked by a cavalryman for some remission of duty after a difficult campaign, briefly told him that he was excused from patting his horse: the edifying account of Fabius Cunctator, who, on meeting his son the consul, decided to try out his suitability for the office he held by not dismounting until he got the direct command, and then gladly obeyed: and the anecdote of the meeting between Hannibal and Scipio Africanus, at which the Carthaginian ranks Alexander, Pyrrhus, and himself as the three greatest generals the world had known, but implies that none of them is even comparable to Africanus.[1] Livy gladly uses such apocryphal anecdotes, as they have always been used, to illuminate a man's more conspicuous qualities. As Plutarch says, 'It is not always in the most distinguished achievements that a man's virtues and vices may be best discerned; very often an action of small note, a short saying, or a jest will distinguish a person's real character more than battles in which thousands fall, or the greatest armaments, or sieges of cities.'[2]

Livy's emphasis on specific moral attributes often causes his characters to lack individuality, to conform to definite types. This is especially true of the legendary period covered by the first decade; here the family name is often all one needs to establish a man's basic attitudes. The more obvious examples of this, such as the Decii, who symbolise the plebeian spirit of dedication to the community by successively vowing their lives for the communal safety, clearly spring from traditions long held; others no doubt owe a great deal to the *pietas* of later Roman historians towards their ancestry. Whenever a Valerius, for example, appears on the stage, he exhibits

---

[1] Papirius, IX, 16, 15 f.; Fabius, XXIV, 44, 9 f.; Africanus, XXXV, 14, 5 ff.
[2] Plut. *Alex.* 1.

enlightened plebeian sympathies. The first Valerius
Publicola is responsible for the law of *provocatio*, a descen-
dant is hated by the patricians for his political benevolence,
while the great Valerius Corvus is the perfect type of
democratic commander, with a brotherly regard for his
troops; his pro-plebeian sentiments are especially illustrated by the speeches made to his forces and to a rebel
contingent which was marching on Rome from Capua.
No doubt Valerius Antias, one of Livy's sources, seized
every opportunity to augment the already favourable
traditions of his family's benevolence. And it is not
fanciful to suppose that the activities of the *gens Fabia*,
whose representatives show a similar unselfishness in the
development of civic harmony, owe something to the
embellishments of Fabius Pictor.[1]

It is even more obvious that the constant denigration of
the *Claudia gens* is the result of political animosity at the
birth of the literary tradition. One and all of them show
insufferable haughtiness towards the *plebs*. The first
Appius Claudius is harsh in his judgement of debtors, and
tries to ignore the right of *provocatio*: his son, labelled
carnifex by the plebeians, resists the demand for plebeian
magistrates, and on one occasion decimates the ranks of
his army: Claudius the Decemvir symbolises not merely
tyranny but also brute lust: his son is hostile from the
cradle towards tribunes and the lower class, and his
grandson attacks the Licinian Rogations: C. Claudius urges
that the consuls should be armed against the tribunes:
Appius Claudius the censor opposes the extension of the
priesthood to the plebeians. Mommsen long ago exposed
the blatant nature of this denigration, which is probably
to be attributed in part to Fabius Pictor, for the Fabii in

---

[1] Pro-plebeian activities of the Valerii, II, 8, 2; III, 18, 11; III, 55; VII, 32, 14–16;
40, 4–15. Altruism of the *gens Fabia*, II, 47; VI, 34; X, 24, where the quarrel
between Fabius Rullianus and the plebeian Decius Mus is attributed not to personal
vindictiveness, but to the orders which Fabius had to carry out. For Fabius
Pictor and Valerius Antias see Chapter v.

his day were hostile to the Claudii.[1] In his concern to demonstrate the disastrous results of the haughtiness and intolerance imputed to the Claudii, Livy omits to ask himself whether such consistent *superbia* is not too bad to be true.

Another interesting feature of the fictional characterisation of the first decade is the obvious influence which the historical career of a later member of a *gens* had on the depiction of ancestral deeds. Thus the success of a certain Publius Cornelius obviously anticipates the attitude of Scipio Africanus in that 'he appeared not to have neglected his fortune'—a phrase used by Africanus about himself.[2] The rashness of Ti. Sempronius Longus at the battle of the Trebia is anticipated by a C. Sempronius who is defeated by the Volsci because he fights without caution and deliberation.[3] There is a Minucius who has to be rebuked by the dictator Cincinnatus, just as in the Hannibalic War the historical Minucius is upbraided by Fabius Maximus.[4] The legendary role of the Valerii as promoters of harmony in the state is an echo of the occasion when M. Valerius Laevinus urges the Senate to give a lead to the people in contributing gold and silver to pay the oarsmen of the fleet.[5] Even more curious is the number of occasions on which successive Servilius Ahalas are depicted in the office of *magister equitum*, unambitious figures always willing to serve in a subordinate capacity, and reminding us of M. Servilius, the supporter of Aemilius Paulus and a holder of the same office, and

---

[1] The anti-plebeian Claudii, II, 27, 29–30, 56–61; III, 44–54; IV, 6 and 36; VI, 40; X, 7. For the falsification of the Claudian record see Th. Mommsen, *History of Rome* I (trans. Dickson), App. I. For attribution of such denigration to Fabius Pictor, H. H. Scullard, *Roman World*, 99, n. I. W. Soltau, *Livius' Geschichtswerk* (Leipzig, 1897), 111, attributes it to Licinius Macer, who doubtless intensified allegations of ill-treatment to the *plebs*. (For Macer as spokesman of the Populares see Ch. v.) Cicero's reticence in the *Pro Caelio* lends support to a first-century attribution.

[2] IV, 57, 8: 'non defuisse fortunae...'; XXVIII, 44, 8: 'id est viri et ducis, non deesse fortunae...'.

[3] IV, 37.   [4] III, 29; XXII, 29.   [5] XXVI, 36, 1–9.

of C. Servilius, who served in 208 under Manlius Torquatus.[1]

Other characters in this decade faithfully portray the Roman virtues, or repel the reader by their vices. Amongst women, Lucretia is the ideal spouse, faithfully labouring at her domestic chores until dusk, offering hospitality, defending her chastity to the last, and committing suicide after she has been violated. Veturia, mother of Coriolanus, is the idealised Roman matron. Fortunately Livy's treatment in this portrayal can be compared with that of Dionysius, who followed the same source. In narrating the famous episode in which Veturia was constrained to prevent Coriolanus from leading the Volsci into Rome, Livy writes that when he sought her embrace, 'she turned from entreaty to anger, and said: "Stay; let me know before I accept your embrace whether I have come as captive to your camp or as mother, and whether to an enemy or a son."' Significantly, Dionysius' version has no mention of the rejection of the proffered embrace, and states that Veturia wept before she spoke. Livy depicts a nobler, more controlled character, whose patriotism transcends even her maternal feelings. On the other hand, Tullia, daughter of Servius Tullius, is a 'Lady Macbeth' character who in her desire for power instigates Tarquinius Superbus to kill her own father, over whose body she drives. She leaves the city 'with men and women cursing her, and calling down the furies of her parents against her'.[2]

As the political struggle is the dominant feature of the early books, many of the men involved are judged solely

---

[1] M. Servilius as *magister equitum*, XLV, 36; C. Servilius, XXVII, 33. For the tenure of this office by Servilii in the first decade see IV, 14 and 57; VI, 2. For a general exposition of family traditions in Roman historiography see F. Münzer, *Römische Adelsparteien und Adelsfamilien* (Stuttgart, 1920), 4 ff.

[2] Lucretia, I, 57, 9–58, 10; Veturia, II, 40, 2 ff. (Dionys. VIII, 45, following the same source: see Klotz, *Livius und seine Vorgänger* (Leipzig–Berlin, 1940–1), 240 f.). On this episode see E. Burck, *Die Erzählungskunst des T. Livius* (Berlin, 1934), 75 f. Tullia, I, 47, 6 ff.; her departure, I, 59, 13.

by whether they advanced *concordia* or not. Patrician moderates like Valerius Corvus and Quinctius Capitolinus (who is addressed as *parens* by the plebeians, just as Quinctius Flamininus is so called by the Greeks) are contrasted with the intransigent Claudii and with Coriolanus, and also with men like Manlius Capitolinus and Spurius Maelius, who are excessively friendly with the *plebs* out of base motives of personal ambition for kingship. On the plebeian side, agitators like the Icilii, for whom political disturbance 'is, so to speak, the charge of their name and family', are not adjudged so highly as the moderates Menenius Agrippa, Duillius, Licinius Calvus, and Marcius Rutulus.[1]

Other family names are often an indication of other virtues or vices. As was seen in the previous chapter, the outstanding example of Roman *frugalitas* is L. Quinctius Cincinnatus, with his espousal of the simple life of the farmer; a similar picture is drawn of a later Titus Quinctius, who after being lamed in battle 'decided to dwell in the country, far from the ambition of the forum'.[2] The element of *clementia* in the character of the great Camillus is equally conspicuous in his son, especially in Livy's version of a speech in the Senate, in which he pleads for gentle treatment of the Latins:

Do you wish to decree harsh treatment against the conquered who have surrendered? You can destroy the whole of Latium, and make boundless deserts of the places from where you have often, in many great wars, enjoyed a noble army of allies. Or do you wish to follow our forbears' example and increase the Roman state by receiving the conquered into the citizenship? We have the opportunity for expansion with the fairest fame. And certainly that rule is by far the strongest which men obey gladly.[3]

[1] Valerius Corvus, VII, 26ff.; Quinctius Capitolinus, II, 60ff.; Claudii, 90, n. 1; Coriolanus, II, 34ff.; Manlius, V, 31–VI, 20; Spurius Maelius, IV, 13ff. (condemned by Cincinnatus, IV, 15); the Icilii, III, 44; IV, 52, where their agitation is 'velut pensum nominis familiaeque'; IV, 54, 4, 'familia infestissima patribus'; Menenius, II, 32; Duillius, III, 52; Calvus, V, 18; Rutulus, VII, 22.
[2] VII, 39, 11.   [3] VIII, 13, 15 f.

On the other hand, other members of the Furian *gens* were notorious for rashness in battle, and the *temeritas* of Furius Fusus is re-enacted by L. Furius, the colleague of Camillus.[1]

It is clear from the conventional nature of such characterisation that Livy has not made many innovations in the traditional material, but is content to lend renewed emphasis to the moral excellences or defects for which these individuals were well known. But in some of the extended characterisation of the later books, he has been bolder in making additions to and changes in his sources, and in suppressing the less palatable evidence. Our safest procedure in analysis of such treatment is to consider the portraits for which the source-material is at least partly available. That of Scipio Africanus is the outstanding example in this respect.

Africanus, who dominates Livy's narrative in xxv–xxx (the second half of the Hannibalic War) and to a lesser extent in xxxvii–xxxviii (the war with Antiochus and the trials of the Scipios), undoubtedly approaches nearest to Livy's ideal Roman. The historian takes his side in the dramatic controversies which arose out of his policies—the conflict with Fabius Cunctator on the strategy of the closing years of the Hannibalic War, and that with the faction led by Cato which resulted in Scipio's voluntary retirement into exile. Livy's partiality is obvious from the first mention of Scipio, when he relates the divergent accounts of the rescue of his father at the skirmish of the Ticinus. After relating how Scipio was the hero, he gives the other view that the rescue was effected by a Ligurian slave. He continues: 'But *I should prefer* it to be true of the son, the version which tradition and the majority of authorities assert.'[2] But such partiality does not prevent his recounting in detail the criticisms of Scipio's opponents, without which the portrait would be incomplete.

[1] III, 4; VI, 23–4.   [2] XXI, 46, 10.

Livy's Stoic outlook sees Scipio in the same way as Vergil depicts Aeneas—as a man of fate[1] destined to lead Rome to enhanced greatness. But at the same time he regards Scipio's claims to see visions and to have divine guidance as at best superstition and at worst deceit.

Scipio was an object of admiration not merely by reason of genuine excellences, but also by the ready technique, employed from early manhood, of exhibiting them. To the people he represented many of his actions as beheld in visions at night, or implanted in his mind by the gods, whether because his spirit as well as theirs was susceptible to superstition, or because the Romans carried out unhesitatingly his orders and designs as if they had emanated from an oracular source.[2]

Such scepticism Livy reinforces by expressing strong disbelief in the stories of Scipio's miraculous birth, and condemns the popular admiration of him which 'went beyond the bounds befitting a human being'.[3] But elsewhere, in a speech which the historian has expanded greatly for the purposes of characterisation, Scipio emphasises his claim to close communion with the gods, and the Spaniard Allucius calls him *dis simillimum*.[4] Livy thus uses the indirect methods of characterisation to show that Scipio encouraged the view that he was more than human, and that he was often so regarded; but it is equally clear that Livy himself regards Scipio as something of a trickster in this connection. So in his capture of New Carthage Scipio is depicted as covering his own intelligent and careful preparation with a smoke-screen of alleged prodigies and indications of divine favour.[5]

The truth is that Livy's theological vision, formed by the interaction of Stoicism on traditional Roman religious thought, can find no place for the mysticism, the close personal union with the gods which Scipio claimed.

[1] XXII, 53, 6: *fatalis dux.* [2] XXVI, 19, 3–5.
[3] XXVI, 19, 9. [4] XXVI, 41, 19; 50, 13.
[5] XXVI, 45, 9: 'hoc cura ac ratione compertum in prodigium ac deos vertens...'.

Visions, dreams, and ecstatic utterances are possibly the occasional vehicles of a divine message, but daily meditation, and cold, rational claims to such messages are of a different order. So Livy, like Polybius, is sceptical of Scipio's claims. Yet Livy's characterisation goes beyond Polybius' in that he stresses the orthodox religious observance of the Roman leader. In depicting the departure of the expedition to Africa, he recounts the prayers made to the gods of sea and land, the archaic language of which is retained for increased effect, and again when Africa is sighted Scipio prays. Further, his duties as a Salian priest are taken so seriously that he causes delay in the movement of the Roman army into Asia.[1] In short, Livy is concerned to portray Scipio as a man with firm beliefs in the efficacy of the traditional religion, and to discount his more exotic religious activities as superstition or deceit.[2]

Polybius[3] describes how all other writers depict Scipio as favoured by fortune, whilst he himself believes that this is a view unjust to his intense prudence and diligence in preparation for operations. Livy's attitude to Scipio's fortune comes out interestingly when Fabius Maximus vehemently attacks his rashness.[4] In reply, Scipio makes it clear that this is a misrepresentation of his standpoint. He is willing to seize the chances offered by fortune, but not to abrogate his own faculties of generalship in so doing; and the fortune on which he relies is the fortune of the Roman people—a conception which has no connotation of chance, but has a close connection with the Stoic destiny.

---

[1] XXIX, 27, 1 and 9; XXXVII, 33, 7.

[2] Polybius' account (X, 2) of Scipio's religious camouflage is strongly criticised by H. H. Scullard, *Scipio Africanus in the Second Punic War* (Cambridge, 1930), 16–19, as little better than a caricature. Livy's portrait he regards as more satisfactory, for it does not assume that 'the mystical side of Scipio was a cloak and used merely as a tool', and it allows room for real piety. I cannot agree. Livy's different characterising methods result in less outspokenness, but his brief comments (see especially XXVI, 19) closely reflect the views of Polybius. See the apposite remarks of Kajanto, 44–6.

[3] X, 2.   [4] XXVIII, 40 ff.

Scipio's intrepid patriotism is first demonstrated by the dramatic account of his threat to kill the Roman nobles who were planning to flee from Italy after Cannae. Rushing into the lodging of Caecilius Metellus, he unsheathes his sword over the heads of the conspirators, and bids them swear by Jupiter never to desert Rome; they all swore, 'as frightened as if they beheld the victorious Hannibal'.[1] This fearlessness is further exemplified in his volunteering for the Spanish command at a time of such utter disaster that no one else dared accept it.[2] But the clearest picture of the patriotism attributed to Africanus can be found in his relations with Antiochus, especially in a speech for which the Polybian source is extant. Livy relates that Antiochus' ambassador offered to restore Scipio's son without ransom; then, 'ignorant of the spirit of Scipio and of Roman manners', he promised him boundless wealth and a share in the kingdom. Scipio's reply in Livy, when compared with Polybius' version, portrays the incorruptible patriot who distinguishes between the private offer to restore his son, which is accepted, and the attempt to bribe him as a public servant, which he scornfully rejects.[3]

Scipio's majestic bearing is depicted by his effect on Roman assemblies and armies, and on foreigners like Hasdrubal and Masinissa. The previous mental picture formed by Masinissa, based on Scipio's achievements, proves to be an underestimate, for the Roman's dynamic presence leaves him dazed. Whenever Scipio's activities are being narrated, Livy brings out one or other of his qualities—the self-confidence which inspired trust in the dark days of the war, his becoming modesty (illustrated by a speech to the troops in which he declares himself expend-

[1] XXII, 53, 13.
[2] XXVI, 18, 6. This allegation of general unwillingness to serve in Spain is unlikely; perhaps, as Scullard, *Roman Politics*, 66, suggests, this reflects the unpopularity of the Spanish command in the mid-second century.
[3] XXXVII, 36; Pol. XXI, 15. See E. T. Sage, Loeb Livy XI, 394, n. 1.

able), his avoidance of aggressive language when he refuses to turn his dispute with Fabius Cunctator into a slanging-match—'If my youth overcomes his age in nothing else, it will prevail in moderation and restraint of tongue.' It was noted, too, how Livy ignores the tradition of Scipio's weakness for women, and depicts him as a thoroughgoing Stoic, teaching his subordinates the vital importance of control of the passions; and also how he represents the Roman ideal of *clementia*, with Livy minimising the savagery of which he was occasionally guilty. Associated with this is a friendliness of bearing extending even to his enemies, so that Hasdrubal is charmed with such *comitas*, and exclaims that Scipio's powers of conciliation are greater even than his military exploits.[1]

Livy is implicitly critical on occasion of Scipio's political ambition. He approves his 'insatiable courage and desire for true glory' in looking to Africa after his victories in Spain, but he is not so sure of his decision to propose the measure directly to the people if the Senate rejected it, and he attributes the scandalous treatment of Locri by Pleminius to the 'ambition or indifference' of Scipio, who was intent on greater things. In his description of the trials of the Scipios, the arguments of those who supported the prosecution of Africanus—that every citizen, however eminent, should be subject to the questioning of the laws—are given full prominence. But, at the same time, Livy is concerned to show that Scipio had no thoughts of kingship, and in this connection it is instructive to compare his account of an incident in the Spanish campaigns with the version of Polybius. Whereas Polybius states that he wished to be *called* kingly by the Spaniards, in Livy Scipio bids them *not to call him king, an*

[1] Scipio's imposing presence and self-confidence, XXVI, 19–20, XXVIII, 35; modesty, XXVIII, 27–9; restraint, XXVIII, 44, 18; *verecundia* towards women, above, 76 f.; *clementia*, above, 74; *comitas*, XXVIII, 17 f.

intolerable word at Rome, but 'mentally to consider that he had a kingly mind, if they regarded this as the most outstanding feature of human capabilities'.[1]

Scipio's generalship is also praised by Livy, who even in this specialised sphere searches out moral qualities to the neglect of strategic considerations. The result is that his estimate of Scipio's skill in planning is quite inadequate. For example, Livy regards ambushes and such stratagems as unworthy of Roman arms, and more suited to Carthaginian deceit and guile. One of Scipio's most brilliant operations was the burning of the enemy camps in the winter of 204/3 in Africa, prior to which, in order to obtain exact information on the topography, he sent in spies under the guise of legates negotiating peace. When the time came for him to ratify the negotiated 'peace', he simply said that his war council would not agree; as Polybius remarks, all the negotiations had been a mere pretence. But Livy is embarrassed by such duplicity, and invents in the Carthaginian proposals some unjust terms which gave the Romans a justification for rejecting them! So Scipio can carry out his plans *libera fide*, that is, without making a breach of faith.[2] This regard for the morality of the procedure certainly distracts attention from the careful strategy of the whole operation.

Another passage in which Livy unintentionally does Scipio less than justice is when he implies that Scipio decided to attack New Carthage on the spur of the moment in spring, whereas it is clear from Polybius that he had spent the winter planning the operation.[3] As a compensating factor, the historian also ignores his faults in strategy; he does not condemn his allowing Hasdrubal and the Carthaginian army in Spain to slip away into

---

[1] Ambition approved, xxviii, 17, 2; criticised, xxix, 16, 5; judgement doubtful, xxviii, 40. Kingship, xxvii, 19, 5 (Pol. x, 40, 5).

[2] xxx, 4; Pol. xiv, 1 ff. (Livy's source here).

[3] xxvi, 42; Pol. x, 8, 9.

Italy. Military questions of this sort have not occurred to him as important.[1]

It is Scipio's moral attributes which are emphasised. His energy and hard work are demonstrated in the manœuvres held immediately after the capture of New Carthage; and the charges idly bandied about at Rome concerning his Greek habits, sloth, and slack discipline are effectively disposed of by the scene of activity, before the African invasion, which met the investigating commission's eyes at Syracuse.[2] His powers of leadership are especially to be seen in the siege of Ilorci, when after the troops' initial failure he threatens to mount the scaling-ladders himself, and thus goads his men to successful daring.[3] Hasdrubal remarks on his audacity in crossing to the hostile territory of Africa, for the conference with Syphax, with only two ships.[4] His handling of his men is especially marked by the praise and consideration shown for subordinate officers and for his troops; he ungrudgingly lauds Silanus and his own brother Lucius for successful operations in Spain, and on taking command there he thanks the soldiers for their loyalty to successive Scipios as their commanders.[5] Most interesting of all is Livy's portrait of his dealing with the Spanish mutiny. His troops are terrified by his stern expression, 'the like of which they said they could not recall even in the battle-line'; and the speech which Livy attributes to him on this occasion is very different from Polybius' more factual version. Whereas Polybius shows that Scipio dealt with the prosaic question of the troops' pay grievance, Livy completely ignores this topic, and makes Scipio's theme the soldiers' dereliction of duty; he cannot decide whether to call them citizens, soldiers, or foes. But after this condemnation, and after the execution of the ringleaders, he

---

[1] XXVII, 20. [2] XXVI, 51; XXIX, 22.
[3] XXVIII, 19, 16. [4] XXVIII, 18, 10
[5] XXVIII, 2, 14; 4, 2; XXVI, 19f.

wins over his troops by kindly looks and words, and says that the execution of the thirty leading mutineers was like 'cleaving his own entrails'.[1] This picture of Scipio the general has such an uncanny likeness to Caesar's self-portrait in the *Commentarii* that one is tempted to believe that Livy's own contributions, chiefly in the speeches, are powerfully affected by Julius' writings.[2]

Livy has no illusions, nor does he seek to delude us, about Scipio's stature as a politician; 'he is more to be remembered for his achievements in war than for his deeds in peace'.[3] It is fair to say that Livy loses some interest in him once the Hannibalic War is over, and the task allotted to him by Providence is fulfilled; his portrait does not come to life again until the possibility of conflict with Hannibal is renewed. The Romans 'wanted to ascertain whether king Antiochus would find more powerful assistance in the defeated Hannibal, or the Roman consul and legions in the victorious Africanus'.[4] It is typical of Livy's characterising methods that the final assessment of Scipio's position in Roman history is to be found not so much in the historian's *elogium* as in the eloquent speech of Ti. Sempronius Gracchus, an avowed enemy of the Scipios, which immediately precedes it.[5] Throughout the characterisation of Scipio the indirect methods have the more important role.

In Scipio's case, then, Livy has concentrated our attention especially on his moral qualities, and he has not hesitated to suppress or modify his less desirable traits in

[1] Scipio had been ill before the mutiny, and in Polybius it is the surprise of the soldiers on seeing him recovered which stupefies them (XI, 27). Livy's version expands this to depict the shattering effect which his sternness could cause (XXVIII, 26). For the speech see Pol. XI, 28 f., and the longer, more rhetorical version of Livy at XXVIII, 27 ff. The later conciliation scene, XXVIII, 32.

[2] This likeness may be partly attributable to Caesar's adoption of Scipio's techniques of *clementia*, *comitas* towards troops, praise for subordinates. But it is difficult not to conclude that Livy's version of Scipio's speech to his disaffected troops is influenced by Caesar's words to the mutineers at Placentia.

[3] XXXVIII, 53, 9.

[4] XXXVII, 1, 10.

[5] XXXVIII, 53, 1 ff.; *elogium*, 9 ff.

order to present an edifying portrait. His depiction of
Flamininus illustrates this unscrupulousness even more
sharply. Flamininus represents the spirit of Roman
altruism at its noblest when he liberates the Greeks from
the clutches of Philip; he is called their father, and he even
calls himself their wet-nurse.[1] But Livy omits to mention
the details of the intrigue in which Flamininus was involved when the Boeotarch Brachyllas was killed in
197 B.C., nor is there a hint of the antipathy which
Flamininus continually felt towards his Greek allies. One
notes also that Livy has omitted the rather discreditable
support of Demetrius by Flamininus, when the Roman
general held secret meetings with the prince and even
wrote to his father Philip urging him to send Demetrius
back to Rome at once—advice which turned Demetrius'
head and annoyed Philip. Further, a distorted picture of
the atmosphere of the conference at Nicaea in 197 is given
by the omission of Flamininus' cordial joking with Philip.
Livy's portrait of Flamininus as a man of honour and *fides*
towards his Greek allies, and one who upheld the dignity
of his race and position by a becoming *gravitas*, has been
achieved only by closing his eyes to the unpleasant truths
in the narrative of Polybius.[2]

This same selective approach has also been at work in
the characterisation of Marcellus. True, his merciless
attitude towards the Campanian garrison of Casilinum is
contrasted with Fabius Cunctator's more clement treatment,[3] and the Sicilians are quoted as saying that they
would prefer an eruption of Aetna or a tidal wave rather
than another period of government under him.[4] But Livy
constantly seeks to mitigate his savagery in Sicily. Thus

---

[1] XXXIV, 50, 1; XXXVI, 35, 4.
[2] Brachyllas, Pol. XVIII, 43, 7ff., Livy XXXIII, 27, 5ff.; letter to Philip, Pol.
XXIII, 3, 7–9, omitted in Livy XXXIX, 46–7; the Nicaea conference, Pol. XVIII,
1ff., Livy XXXII, 32ff. For an unfavourable view of Polybius' portrait of
Flamininus see Wood, *TAPA* (1939), 93ff.
[3] XXIV, 19, 9f.   [4] XXVI, 29, 4.

his *clementia* is emphasised when he orders that no free person should be harmed in the looting of Syracuse; in another speech he says that he would have preferred to save rather than to capture the city, and expresses grief at the murder of Archimedes.[1] Above all, there is the anecdote of his weeping upon entering the walls of Syracuse, and how his reflections on the ancient glory of the city led him to send legates to the enemy, asking them to surrender to avoid the destruction of the city.[2] In speeches in the Senate, when the Sicilians accuse him of the cruel sack of Leontini and the slaughter of allies, it is notable that Livy allots a longer speech to his defence than to the indictments, and that, whilst the Sicilians' speech is unobtrusively in *oratio obliqua*, Marcellus' is written in the more arresting medium of *oratio recta*. His magnanimity is stressed when he prevails in this debate, for he is indulgent to the legates' entreaties.[3]

This biased portrait of Marcellus is best explained by the realisation that he was traditionally remembered as the avenger of Cannae, and Livy often associates his name with this role. His repulse of Hannibal from Nola is 'perhaps the greatest victory of the war, for it was more difficult to avoid defeat then at Hannibal's hands than it was to conquer him later'.[4] His offensive operations in Samnium are so effective that the Samnite legates to Hannibal claim that 'Marcellus, not Hannibal, seems to have conquered at Cannae',[5] and later he fails to conquer the Carthaginian only because Claudius Nero fails in his allotted task; Marcellus claims that otherwise he 'could have won a victory similar to Cannae'.[6] Thus, after Scipio, Marcellus is the most heroic figure of the war, the man who first fought Hannibal successfully in the open field; in Vergil's words,

[1] xxv, 31, 7 and 10; 25, 7.　　[2] xxv, 24, 11–15.
[3] xxvi, 32, 8.　　[4] xxiii, 16, 16.
[5] xxiii, 42, 5.　　[6] xxiv, 17, 7.

> hic rem Romanam, magno turbante tumultu,
> sistet eques, sternet Poenos....[1]

Hence Livy, in common with the general tradition, seeks to idealise him, and does violence to the truth in the attempt.

Perhaps the most fascinating characterisation in the extant books is that of Hannibal. Like Scipio, he is a mere shadow in the fourth decade, since he has ceased to symbolise the implacable opposition of the Carthaginians. But, in the third decade, the portrait is an artistic whole, with his career depicted as a classic example of the man who trusts initially in fortune, has his confidence increased by temporary success, and finally learns in the shadow of defeat that his expectations were wrongly based. An examination of the account of Polybius will show that this is no traditional view, and that in the creation of this framework Livy has utilised especially the speeches. So before the engagement at the Ticinus, whilst Scipio, father of Africanus, in his harangue to the troops stresses that Hannibal has incurred the displeasure of the gods by his breaking the treaty, and that gods and men will take vengeance on him, Hannibal's speech is dominated by reference to fortune. It is fortune which has surrounded his men with chains and necessities: fortune puts rewards before them, fortune has in Italy brought an end to their labours.[2] But towards the end of the war, at the meeting of the two commanders before Zama, Hannibal says that he has learnt by experience to trust to reason rather than to fortune, and, comparing Africanus' present position to his own at the time of Trasimene and Cannae, he urges him in Stoic fashion to take to heart the maxim: 'Trust least of all the greatest fortune.'[3]

---

[1] *Aen.* VI, 857 f.   [2] XXI, 43, 3, 5, 10.

[3] XXX, 30: Stübler, *Die Religiosität des Livius*, 97. Erkell, in his discussion of the speech in XXI, concludes that there is no certain or probable equation of *fortuna* with Tyche. The later evidence of the speech in XXX suggests that Erkell is mistaken. In general, Livy does not exclude *fortuna*/Tyche from speeches, for these offer a medium for characterisation rather than reflect the historian's own cosmological views.

Within this general framework of Hannibal's career, with its nuance of 'tragic' influence, a certain inconsistency of detail is observable. The traditional portrait of Hannibal, which Livy has retailed in Book xxi in a manner strongly reminiscent of Sallust's pen-portrait of Catiline, is not wholly reconcilable with Livy's indirect characterisation. The list of Hannibal's vices includes 'nullus deum metus, nullum iusiurandum, nulla religio', which is at odds with his later description of Hannibal's praying to Jove and the other gods, and of the vows paid to Hercules before the march into Italy begins.[1] Another traditional attribute listed is his 'perfidia plus quam Punica', yet we later find the historian emphasising that he sent back the defenders of Casilinum 'summa cum fide' after agreeing to ransom them if they surrendered. Again, the description of Hannibal's death does not suggest a man in character with such alleged perfidy: '...calling on the gods of hospitality to witness Prusias' breach of faith, he drained the cup of poison'.[2]

Here Livy depicts a character more human and worthy of respect than that which is painted by the earlier tradition. In other contexts, an element of tragic pity is introduced in anecdotes, as when the aged Hannibal tells Antiochus of the oath taken in his youth,[3] or again, when he concedes that defeat at Rome's hands is inevitable.[4] His humanity is further shown by his sense of humour, as in his alleged remark at Cannae when he heard of Aemilius' stupid instruction to his cavalry to dismount and fight on foot: 'He should have tied them up and delivered them to me.'[5]

On the other hand, there is consistent emphasis on the Carthaginian's cruelty—a feature generally attested—and also on his guile. Beginning with the *imperium crudele*

---

[1] XXI, 4, 9; 45, 8; 21, 9.
[2] XXIII, 19, 16; XXXIX, 51, 12.
[3] XXXV, 19, 3 ff.
[4] XXVII, 51, 12.
[5] XXII, 49, 3.

which signalled the slaughter of the young men of Saguntum, Livy condemns his 'lust, savagery, and inhuman pride' with which he did violence to the inhabitants of Victumulae, his cruelty in burning alive the wife and children of Dasius Altinius of Arpi, who seceded to the Romans, and the barbarity and greed with which he ravaged Campanian territory.[1] Even more stress is laid on his guile and deceit, so that ambushes and similar stratagems are labelled Hannibalic methods.[2]

Livy's assessment of Hannibal as general suffers from precisely the same limitations as does that of Scipio. Due emphasis is laid on his moral qualities, especially on his powers of endurance, his bravery and boldness, and the consummate leadership of his polyglot army—these are mentioned especially in the brief direct assessments.[3] But insufficient credit is given to him for the competence of his strategy and the versatility which Polybius so greatly admired.[4] One example is particularly apposite. Hannibal tried to raise the Roman blockade of Capua by marching on Rome, and, when he failed in this, he attacked Rhegium at lightning speed—thus showing a resilience for which Polybius is full of praise. But Livy sees this attack in the south not as a strategic move but as a sign of moral weakness: 'Hannibal did not show so much pertinacity in defending Capua as the Romans showed in blockading it.'[5]

In the characterisation of Fabius Cunctator one can perhaps discern the indirect influence of Thucydides. The role of Fabius in the Hannibalic War is reminiscent of Nicias in the Peloponnesian conflict. Both face the clamour of demagogic elements demanding precipitate action—Minucius in this respect being the Roman Cleon. Fabius is a Nicias-like figure not only in class conflicts, but

[1] XXI, 57, 14; XXIV, 45, 13; XXVI, 38, 3.
[2] XXI, 34, 1; XXVII, 26, 2.
[3] XXI, 4; XXVIII, 12.   [4] Pol. III, 89; 78.
[5] XXVI, 12, 1; 38, 1. Compare Pol. IX, 9.

also in his general view of life. He will put his trust in human counsels alone, emphasising the dangers of dependence on fortune.[1] Apart from this distinguishing element in his characterisation, Fabius embodies the Roman virtues. His clemency is contrasted with Marcellus' savagery at Casilinum:[2] when he persuades the people to elect him consul, Livy emphasises (by the indirect method of the praise of his contemporaries) that this is no base *cupido imperii*, but a sense of civic responsibility:[3] he is steadfast in the face of unpopularity at Rome, and thus gains Hannibal's respect:[4] after the capture of Tarentum he abstains from the demoralising booty of statues and pictures, 'with greater spirit than did Marcellus': his concern for religion is stressed by his condemnation of Flaminius' impiety.[5] As general, Fabius is depicted as Hannibal's equal in the more subtle arts of war; the Carthaginian exclaims, after Rome's recapture of Tarentum by an artifice, 'et Romani suum Hannibalem habent!'[6]

It is alleged by Plutarch that Fabius, in his jealousy of Scipio, urged Crassus, colleague of Scipio, to go to Carthage himself if necessary, and that he prevented Scipio from raising money for the expedition. Livy has excised these unwholesome allegations from his portrait, and depicts Fabius' bitter opposition as based on innate caution rather than personal jealousy. This caution, he admits in his *elogium* of Fabius, went too far: 'cautior tamen quam promptior hic habitus'.[7]

The portrayal of Philip V of Macedon reveals Livy's respect for a worthy possessor of non-Roman kingship. For long passages of the fourth decade one can observe

---

[1] Nicias' conflict with demagogic elements, Thuc. III, 82–3; Fabius and Minucius, XXII, 12 ff.; Fabius' attitude to fortune, XXII, 18, 9; 23, 2; 25, 14; 29, 1, etc.

[2] XXIV, 19.   [3] XXIV, 9, 10 f.

[4] XXII, 25 ff.; Hannibal's respect, 30, 8 ff.

[5] XXVII, 16, 8; XXII, 9, 7.   [6] XXVII, 16, 10.

[7] XXX, 26, 9. Plutarch's criticism, *Fab.* 25.

the historian's elaboration of his source-material. He lays repeated stress on Philip's regal spirit, which he favourably compares with that of Attalus of Pergamum, and which serves Philip in good stead in his encounters with Roman leaders such as Flamininus and Marcus Aemilius Lepidus.[1] But he is very critical of his occasional unkingly behaviour, as when, during the Roman surprise attack on his camp near Apollonia, he fled to his ships 'half-naked, in dress scarcely befitting a soldier, let alone a king'; or when he unleashed a crushing witticism on Phaeneas the Aetolian.[2] The emphasis on Philip's kingly spirit and on the occasional lapses from *dignitas* is the chief new characterising element introduced by Livy. Though he does not hesitate to attribute to the king clear responsibility for the war, and though he exposes his cruelty, the general effect is to reflect Polybius' sympathetic assessment—his energy and resource in war, his attractive and infectious gaiety in negotiation, his helpful attitude towards Rome in the struggle against Antiochus. There is a distinct element of tragic pity in his picture of the final stages of Philip's life, when he plays arbiter at the internecine dispute of his sons and orders the death of Demetrius, only to repent of his judgement, and to die condemning his own folly.[3]

From these examples of characterisation of individuals it is clear that Livy seeks to bring out their predominantly moral qualities, and in the case of leading Romans to omit what is unedifying. He achieves this aim chiefly by the methods of indirect portrayal already enumerated.

---

[1] Kingly spirit, XXXI, 16, 1: 'magis regio animo est usus...'; XXXI, 18, 3–4; XXXII, 32, 14: 'superbo et regio animo...'.

[2] XXIV, 40, 13: 'prope seminudus fugiens, militi quoque nedum regi vix decoro habitu...'; XXXII, 34, 3: 'dicacior natura quam regem decet...'; XXXVI, 14, 4.

[3] Responsibility for the war, XXXI, 1, 9–10; cruelty, XXXIX, 34, 3; energy in warfare, XXXI, 43, 4; helpfulness to Rome, XXXVI, 14: 'miserrimus pater, iudex', XL, 8 (below, 234f.); Livy's sympathy for his lonely and bitter death, XL, 54ff. In general, see H. Hoch, *Die Darstellung der politischen Sendung Roms bei Livius*, 46ff.

On the other hand, he often gives a direct estimate of the qualities of races and nations, though not at any length except in the case of the Germans.[1] These judgements are not distinguished by subtlety or insight; some reflect Roman insularity at its most biased, and others achieve a unique level of banality. 'Tito Livio non vede che Roma';[2] in vain does one seek in his history a clear portrait of Samnites or Etruscans, Carthaginians or Greeks. Whenever the Numidians are discussed, Livy is tempted to tell us of their mating propensities; they fall headlong into love at the least provocation. The Carthaginians are of course savage and cruel, and above all unfaithful to their word, so that the third decade is full of references to *Punica fraus* and *Punica fides*. In his comments on the Gauls, the same two points are made *ad nauseam*; they are a *gens efferata*, with habits more becoming to animals than men, and their bodies, though huge, lack staying power, and so succumb to heat, malaria, hard work, and Roman pertinacity. The Greeks can use their tongues better than their weapons, and their lack of moderation and general degeneracy are frequently portrayed; especially vivid is Livy's description of their behaviour when Attalus visited Athens, and the whole city, 'wives and children as well, poured out to meet him; the priests were there in their insignia, and the very gods nearly jumped out of their niches'. The Aetolians (here Polybius' influence is manifest) are undisciplined in war, unfaithful to their promises, unreliable allies, 'an uncontrolled, anti-social people'. (Livy gives insufficient credit to their fighting qualities, and their stubborn, even heroic, resistance.)[3]

---

[1] On the Germans see *Perioch.* CIV.

[2] G. De Sanctis, *Problemi di storia antica*, 230.

[3] Numidians, XXIX, 23, 4; XXX, 12, 18. Livy also praises their horsemanship, XXIX, 34, 5. Carthaginians, XXVI, 17, 6; XXI, 4, 9; XXII, 6, 12, etc. Gauls, 'gens efferata', VIII, 14, 9; X, 10, 12; like animals, V, 44, 6; VII, 24, 5; lack of staying power, V, 48, 1–3; X, 28, 3; XXII, 2, 4; XXVII, 48, 16. A speech by the consul

The portraits of Italian peoples are equally conventional. The Campanians are always marked by their degenerate living or their hauteur or both—'populus luxuria superbiaque clarus'. The Samnites, hardy highlanders, not degenerate plainsmen, are fierce in battle but without military genius; the Etruscans and the Ligurians are equally difficult to defeat. The Sabines are noted for their incorruptibility, the Volsci for their fickleness and their readiness to engineer secret revolt.[1]

Livy, then, has not introduced any novel or penetrating views in his portraits of non-Roman races, and in his characterisation of individuals he has often reproduced the traditional judgement. But in his portrayal of a few great men like Camillus, Africanus, and Hannibal, signs of a more original interpretation emerge, owing something to Stoic influences in that there is emphasis on their predestined role in history. Secondly, Livy's moral and patriotic preoccupations lead him to depict a series of leaders as the embodiment of the Stoic virtues of prudence, justice, courage, and moderation, and of the other virtues which Roman tradition extolled. In these characterisations, Livy has allowed his pursuit of edifying examples to take precedence over a truthful account, not merely by distortion of emphasis, but even by the suppression of unpalatable facts. Contrariwise, he has sought out the signal examples of vice in all its forms in order to demonstrate its destructive effect on the individual and the community. It is this conception of history, dominated by idealised heroes and denigrated villains, which is ultimately responsible for the most serious defect in Livy's work. He has falsified history not by error but by design.

Manlius Volso at xxxviii, 17 summarises all these qualities. For the Greeks, viii, 22, 8; xxvii, 16, 1 (Tarentines); xxxi, 14, 12 (passage quoted); 44, 9. Aetolians, xxxi, 41, 7 ff.; xxxiii, 10; xxix, 12, 4; xxxi, 43; xxxvii, 1, 4: 'tamquam indomitae et insociabili genti'; xxxvii, 49, 2–3.

[1] Campanians, vii, 29, 5; 31, 6 (quoted); ix, 6, 5; 40, 17; xxiii, 5, 1; 8, 6; xxv, 18, 2. Samnites, vii, 29, 1 and 5; ix, 13, 7; x, 31, 11. Etruscans, ix, 29, 2; 32, 9. Ligurians, xxvii, 48, 10. Sabines, i, 18, 4. Volsci, ii, 22, 3; 37, 4; vii, 27, 9.

V

LIVY'S HISTORICAL
AUTHORITIES

THE most serious objection to any consideration of Livy as a scientific historian is in part an indictment of Roman historiography generally. It is the failure to search out and evaluate the original documentary evidence.[1] Nowhere does Livy base his account directly on such evidence; where he quotes from ancient documents, he has read them in a literary source, as becomes increasingly clear from a study of the nature of these sources.

What documentary evidence was available?[2] First, Livy could have consulted the *annales maximi*, the bare outline of the history of Rome gathered into eighty books in the late second century (about 115 B.C.) from the *tabulae pontificum*, the white boards which had been affixed each year to the wall of the *Regia*, the official residence of the *pontifex maximus*. The *annales maximi* certainly contained such details as elections of state officials, eclipses, prodigies, and similar religious information, and probably also included results of military campaigns, visits of ambassadors, and the like.[3]

The extent to which this material was strictly historical is much controverted. Scholars are virtually unanimous on the reliability of the third-century entries; the priests must certainly have kept detailed records of all events

---

[1] But Tacitus must be exonerated from this charge; see the enlightening discussion of R. Syme, *Tacitus*, 176 ff., 271 ff.

[2] For good summaries see H. Bornecque, *Tite-Live*, 60 ff.; H. H. Scullard, *Roman Politics*, 251 ff.

[3] H. Peter, *HRR* I², iii–xxix. For a comprehensive account of the content see J. E. A. Crake, *CP* (1940), 375 ff.

relevant to their office from about 300 B.C. onwards. But the fourth-century registers are more problematic. Cicero remarks of an eclipse noted in the *annales maximi* ('about three hundred and fifty years after the foundation of the city') that all earlier eclipses were calculated from it. This would suggest that authentic priestly records of a systematic nature date from at least 400 B.C., which is by no means impossible. But the claim that the Ciceronian passage should be amended to 'about *four* hundred and fifty years *post urbem conditam*', and may refer to an eclipse of 288, has received wide support.[1] The evidence certainly suggests that detailed records were kept only from 300, but this does not totally preclude the existence of more jejune *tabulae* from the fourth century, upon which the editors of the *annales maximi* may have sought to impose a probable chronological order.[2] As it is now generally accepted that the state archives were not totally destroyed by the Gallic sack in 390, some fifth-century *tabulae* could also have been unearthed by Mucius Scaevola. But, unfortunately, Livy did not consult the *annales maximi* directly; he preferred to reproduce the content at second hand from the late annalists.[3]

Secondly, there were the *libri lintei* kept in the temple of Juno Moneta and containing magistrate lists. Their authenticity is uncertain. It is known that some entries differed from those in the *annales maximi*.[4] Livy has

[1] See the discussions of K. J. Beloch, *Römische Geschichte bis zum Beginn der punischen Kriege* (Leipzig–Berlin, 1926), 86–95; *Hermes* (1922), 119 ff. After a consideration of the Ciceronian passage (*De Rep.* 1, 25), he notes that in Livy there are no prodigy lists before 296/5, and claims that the *Fasti Triumphales* have no consistently reliable entries before 300. These factors lead him to amend the Ciceronian evidence.

[2] Below, 277 f. Mr R. M. Ogilvie points to detailed records in Livy II–v (e.g. at IV, 30, 6) in support of the view that the *annales maximi* contained full fifth- and fourth-century entries.

[3] That is, from Valerius Antias and Claudius Quadrigarius chiefly.

[4] Livy IV, 7, 10. For a sceptical view of the *libri lintei* see H. Stuart Jones, *CAH* VII, 320 f. R. M. Ogilvie, *JRS* (1958), 40 ff., in a valuable analysis of relevant sections of Books IV and V, supports this viewpoint.

not used them directly, nor indeed does he attempt to pronounce on their authority. One may regret that he did not personally collate them with the *annales maximi*. As it is, our information about them is at third hand (through Licinius Macer and Livy); but there is no valid reason for totally discounting the citations from them.

Permanent records of *senatus consulta* were available in book form in Livy's day.[1] The original documents were also deposited in the Treasury, a procedure probably dating from the third century.[2] It can be assumed that Livy did not consult these directly, for his version is different from the extant *senatus consultum de Bacchanalibus*; he must have drawn on a late annalistic source.[3] Copies of laws were not carefully tended,[4] but copies of the more important treaties were more carefully preserved; Polybius claims[5] that he has consulted the text of the treaty with Carthage struck in 509/8 B.C., as well as later documents of this type.

Finally, there were the contents of private archives, in which greater detail of the transaction of state affairs could be found. They needed discriminating scrutiny because of their frequently mendacious family bias,[6] but amongst them were such vital documents as census lists, property qualifications, and others relating to the censor's function. These records, which would have furnished a useful survey of social history if preserved together as state records, were kept piecemeal in the families of those who held the office.[7]

Livy never claims to have consulted directly any of these documents, and from this fact one can infer that this

---

[1] Cicero consults those of 146 when writing to Atticus (XIII, 33, 3).

[2] Livy (III, 55, 13) claims that copies of *senatus consulta* were stored in the temple of Ceres in 449, but this seems unlikely.

[3] For the text see *CIL* I², 581. Discussion: S. Accame, *RFIC* (1938), 225 ff.; A. H. McDonald, *JRS* (1944), 26 ff.; and most comprehensively by J. J. Tierney, *Proceedings of the Irish Academy* (1947), 89–117. Bornecque goes astray here, 76.

[4] Cic. *De Leg.* III, 46.   [5] III, 22.

[6] VIII, 40, 4.   [7] Dionys. I, 74.

deficiency is not so much attributable to laziness or negligence, but rather to an unhistorical attitude towards documentary evidence. This inference is strengthened by other indications. When Polybius reports that he has obtained figures of Hannibal's troops from a column at Lacinium inscribed by Hannibal himself,[1] one might expect Livy to have adopted the figures quoted there as authoritative. Instead, he lists from different writers three varying estimates, without mentioning that the second is the statement of Polybius, and without indicating its superior authority.[2] The same attitude is evident in his discussion of the alleged discovery of Augustus in the temple of Jupiter Feretrius; it does not seem to have occurred to the historian to investigate the evidence personally.[3] He has based his account on the literary tradition that Cossus, when he won the *spolia opima*, was a military tribune; then he admits that he is convinced by Augustus' evidence of Cossus' being consul. But, subsequently,[4] he is again referred to as tribune; Livy does not trouble to modify his account in the light of the new 'evidence'.

In the historian's defence it must be said that this willingness to accept the testimony of others, without troubling to consult the original documents, is a feature familiar in Roman historiography. The remarks of the younger Pliny, when discussing his intention of writing history, are revealing: 'If my subject is an ancient period already discussed by others, my material will be ready at hand.'[5] This unhistorical attitude was encouraged by the lack of an efficient system of filing public records, which Cicero criticises,[6] and by the fact that the more detailed documentary evidence, being held by the descendants of those intimately concerned in particular transactions, was

[1] III, 33, 18; 56, 4. [2] XXI, 38, 2–3.
[3] IV, 20, 5 ff.; above, 14f. [4] IV, 32, 4.
[5] *Ep.* V, 8: 'vetera et scripta aliis? parata inquisitio, sed onerosa collatio'.
[6] *De Leg.* III, 46.

widely dispersed. To collect and to collate such scattered documents would have been the task of an historian writing on a narrower period. Livy belonged to the class of those who sought to present the research undertaken by others in a more attractive literary setting. His subject of the entire history of the Roman state involved a life's work without the detailed scrutiny of the original documents.

One can, then, regret Livy's failure to consult the *annales maximi* and the *senatus consulta* (both readily available in book form), and also his unhistorical attitude in failing to subordinate the literary tradition to documentary evidence provided by others, when he knew of its reliability. In extenuation of these faults, one must bear in mind that the tradition which he followed tended to disregard such a scientific approach.

Any consideration of Livy's literary sources is rendered difficult by the fact that ancient historians from Herodotus onwards rarely tell us explicitly the sources followed. The normal procedure was to name an authority only in criticism of his account, or when indicating alternative versions of an event described; hence it is not always possible to establish the writers followed in any particular passage. In Livy's case, after more than a hundred years' systematic research (chiefly by German scholars), the boundaries between reasonable certainty and ingenious speculation are now closely defined. We have a clear idea of the sources for the fourth and fifth decades: in the third the area of obscurity is more extended, but certain general conclusions can still be reached: whilst in the first decade the information available is so vague that no more than a speculative hypothesis can be advanced.[1] The most valuable indications in this source-research are first,

---

[1] This discussion on the literary sources owes much to A. Klotz, G. De Sanctis, H. Nissen, and U. Kahrstedt (see the bibliography).

such sections of the authors used as have actually survived; secondly, the citations of his sources by the historian himself; and thirdly, the accounts of other writers—Diodorus, Dionysius, Plutarch, and Appian—which when compared with Livy's can reveal the use of an identical source, or (equally important) can indicate a different one. The citation of sources by such writers can clearly be of material help in establishing Livy's authorities.

It has for long been generally accepted that in the first decade Livy used chiefly the late annalists Valerius Antias, Claudius Quadrigarius, Licinius Macer, and Aelius Tubero.[1] Our chief guide here must be Livy's own statements, which suggest that he may have consulted older authorities as well; more probably, however, he found citations from them in the late annalists. Fabius Pictor is quoted on several occasions;[2] L. Calpurnius Piso is also named frequently, invariably as an addition or alternative to the main account.[3] The same is true of Claudius Quadrigarius, cited four times in the second pentad.[4] The tenuous evidence suggests that Claudius has been used chiefly for confirming or refuting other accounts; Fabius and Piso may not have been consulted directly.

The three others certainly employed for the first decade are Antias, Macer, and Tubero. Antias was contemporary with Sulla, or perhaps later: Macer died in 66: and Tubero survived into the Augustan period. It is possible that

---

[1] See, for example, Th. Mommsen, *Hermes* (1871), 270.

[2] At I, 44, 2, Fabius is quoted on the numbers of a census return. At I, 55, 8, he is cited first, with Piso also quoted. At II, 40, 10, he contradicts the main source on the details of Coriolanus' death; again at x, 37, 14, he is cited in opposition to the main source. Similarly when Livy refers to 'veterrimos auctores' and 'antiquissimos auctores' (both denote Fabius) at II, 18, 5 and VIII, 30, 7, they are divergences from the main source. For a complete list of Livy's references to Fabius and other sources see R. B. Steele, *AJP* (1904), 15 ff.

[3] I, 55, 8–9; II, 32, 3; 58, 1; IX, 44, 3; X, 9, 12.

[4] VI, 42, 5; VIII, 19, 13; IX, 5, 2; X, 37, 13. Considering Livy's extensive use of Claudius later, one may suspect that he is consulted frequently in VI–X. Compare, for example, Livy, VII, 10 with Claudius, *HRR* 10b (Gell. IX, 13); Soltau, *Livius' Geschichtswerk*, 130, suggests Claudius as source here.

Tubero combined in his account the writings of Antias and Macer, and that Livy has followed Tubero chiefly, with frequent direct consultation of Antias and Macer. There is certainly evidence to suggest that Tubero used both Antias and Macer;[1] further, Livy's use of Tubero is suggested by signs of mid-first century 'contamination' in the early books. If it can be proved that there are traces there of the events of the sixties and the fifties, this would certainly suggest Tubero as immediate source. (Antias is a faint possibility, but the last extant fragment of his history refers to 91; and though this does not necessarily indicate that he died soon after that date, it seems unlikely that he could have been composing the first few of his seventy-five books in the sixties or fifties.) The conspiracy of the Vitellii and the Aquilii,[2] where the plot is exposed by 'a letter given as a pledge of good faith', certainly seems to contain a reminiscence of the

---

[1] The evidence rests on various Livian passages. At IV, 23, 1, there are differing accounts of the magistrates for 434. From Macer, C. Iulius and L. Verginius (who were consuls in 435 according to the literary tradition); from Antias and Tubero, M. Manlius and Q. Sulpicius. Tubero and Macer consulted the *libri lintei*; Macer follows them, Tubero presumably rejects them. Livy's account is far from clear, but Tubero seems to have consulted both Antias and Macer. See further A. Klotz, *Livius und seine Vorgänger*, 209.

Another passage, IV, 7, 1–12, may be compared first with Diodorus, who follows an earlier annalist, and then with Dionysius, following the same source as Livy (Klotz, *RhM* (1937), 206; (1938), 47). Livy states that military tribunes were elected but resigned in the third month, L. Papirius Mugillanus and L. Sempronius Atratinus being elected consuls. The evidence for the consuls is found in the renewal of the treaty with Ardea, and in the *libri lintei*, quoted by Macer; this documentary evidence is opposed to the statements of the earliest literary authorities and the magistrate lists (i.e. the *annales maximi*). Dionysius records the same divergence: some record tribunes, some consuls, some both (XI, 62, 3). Diodorus, however, mentions only tribunes (XII, 32), a point which reinforces Livy's claim that the literary tradition has no mention of consuls. Obviously Macer has introduced the consuls from a scrutiny of the *libri lintei*; and Tubero has set down the conflict of evidence, providing Livy and Dionysius with material for their identical survey of the problem.

For further evidence suggestive of Tubero's use of Macer see X, 9, 10ff. Beginning with the words 'Macer Licinius ac Tubero tradunt...', Livy reveals Tubero's extensive use of the earlier historian. Klotz further suggests that when Livy quotes three anonymous sources (as at VII, 22, 3; X, 17, 11f.; 18, 7; 26, 5f.), they are Antias, Macer, and Tubero. But there is no reason why Piso or Claudius (or even Fabius) should be excluded here.　　[2] II, 4.

Catilinarian conspiracy; and the secret meetings of the Decemvirs[1] may similarly have been described with the conclaves of the First Triumvirate of 60–59 B.C. prominent in the writer's mind.[2] The weakness of this 'contamination' thesis is that it does not allow for Livy's personal insertion of such detail; and at best it can be demonstrated only in isolated passages.

All that can be said for certain in the first decade is that Aelius Tubero is frequently used as main source. It is also a reasonable inference that Antias and Licinius Macer are followed from time to time, as the emphasis on the *gens Valeria* on the one hand, and on the other the occasional sentiments favouring the Populares, suggest. Claudius has been consulted as a secondary source in the second pentad to check upon factual matters; the citations from Fabius and Piso do not necessarily indicate direct consultation of them. An isolated reference to Cincius[3] is not to the third-century historian, but to an antiquary of the Augustan period, consulted for specialised information about Etruscan rites. A short section on the origins of Roman comedy may be from Varro.[4] The excursus on the entry of the Gauls into Italy in Book v may be from Cornelius Nepos or (more probably) Timagenes.[5]

A brief analysis of these first-decade sources, direct and indirect, may be useful for an assessment of their reliability and of the extent of their influence on Livy. Q. Fabius Pictor, the first Roman prose historian, was an

---

[1] III, 36.

[2] Other possible examples: 1, 46, 9 (marriage of L. Tarquinius after the murder of his brother), 'cum domos vacuas novo matrimonio fecissent, iunguntur nuptiis'. Compare Sallust on Catiline, 15, 2: 'necato filio vacuam domum scelestis nuptiis fecisse'. Also Livy's remarks about Camillus: 'sed Camillo cum vitae satis tum gloriae esse' (VI, 23, 7), in comparison with Cicero's quotation of Caesar (*Marc.* 25): 'satis diu vel naturae vixi vel gloriae'. But these are possibly Livy's own rearrangement.

[3] VII, 3, 7.   [4] VII, 2, 3 ff.

[5] v, 34–35, 3. O. Hirschfeld, *Kleine Schriften* (1913), 1 ff., and Bornecque, 83, suggest Nepos; Klotz, *Livius u. s. V.* 202, inclines to Timagenes. (The Greek element is important; see Ogilvie, *JRS.* (1958), 43, n. 49.)

important figure in the Hannibalic War. He wrote his
Roman history in Greek.[1] In the section on the foundation of Rome, he is clearly affected by Hellenistic influences; his account of the cradle of Romulus and Remus,
and its use for the dramatic purposes of ἀναγνώρισις,
stem originally from Sophocles' *Tyro*, doubtless through
some intermediary.[2] He did not seriously trouble about
the accuracy and consistency of these legends; Dionysius
repeatedly censures him for petty inaccuracies, pointing
out, for example, that Tanaquil could not have buried
Arruns, as Fabius claims, unless she had lived to the age
of a hundred and fifteen![3]

On the events of his own time, the struggle with
Carthage, Fabius wrote more carefully, but the apologetic
nature of his work, the desire to impress the Greek-speaking world, led to grave distortions of fact; Polybius out-
spokenly compares his affection for the Roman cause
with that of a lover.[4] The far-reaching effects of his
patriotic falsehoods can be detected in the writings of his
successors. For example, Livy's dating of the siege of
Saguntum in 218 instead of 219 must have originated with
Fabius; the motive for such distortion was to minimise
Rome's neglect of her ally by emphasising the alleged
suddenness of the attack upon and capture of Saguntum,
and by implying that Rome had no time to send help.
Or again, Polybius' version of a speech by Aemilius
Paulus excuses Rome's defeat at the Trebia by claiming
that Sempronius' army had arrived only the day before
the battle; Polybius, who reproduces speeches accurately,
got the version from Fabius, and the allegation is untrue.[5]

It is reasonably certain that Fabius initiated for the
Romans the tradition of annalistic presentation to which

---

[1] Above, 29.

[2] Dionys. 1, 79 ff. reproduces Fabius' version. For its Greek origin see G. De Sanctis, *Storia dei Romani* 1, 214.

[3] Dionys. IV, 30. Other errors are mentioned at IV, 6 and 64.

[4] 1, 14.   [5] III, 108, 8; the true facts are at III, 69, 8.

Livy faithfully adheres. An explicit reference to the *Graeci annales* by Cicero should be sufficient to support this view. It is possible, however, that the early events were discussed by Fabius more compendiously, and that the annalistic method was used only when the historical material became sufficiently detailed.[1]

The influence of Fabius on Livy is profound. But it is largely indirect in that it helped to mould the whole tradition of history-writing to which Livy conforms. This influence is chiefly to be found, as regards content, in the partiality to the Roman cause which results in patriotic distortion; and so far as form is concerned, in the annalistic method by which events are recounted.

The second source, L. Calpurnius Piso, who was consul in 133 and censor in 120, reveals in the surviving fragments another facet of the Roman tradition; he is strongly influenced by ethical considerations, and praises the ancient virtues of simplicity and honesty through the medium of anecdotes.[2] He shows no apparent anti-plebeian bias; indeed in one passage he is strongly critical of the high-born youths who insulted a plebeian magistrate, Cn. Flavius.[3] Gellius, with his predilection for archaism, praises his style, but Cicero complains of a certain baldness,[4] a justifiable criticism on the evidence of the fragments, for there is no attempt at elegant variation. In the anecdote concerning Cn. Flavius, almost every sentence begins identically 'Cn. Flavius, Annii filius...'. It cannot be imagined that Piso had any appreciable stylistic influence on Livy.

The two annalists used most consistently by Livy

---

[1] M. Gelzer, *Hermes* (1933), 129 ff.; (1934), 48 f.; (1954), 342 ff., believes that Fabius did not arrange his history annalistically, but grouped it into wars; and that when Cicero refers to the *annales* of Pictor, he means the Latin annals. But Cicero's phrase *Graeci annales* suggests that the Greek writings also were annalistically arranged. For other arguments against Gelzer's thesis see F. W. Walbank, *CQ* (1945), 15 ff.

[2] See, for example, the story of the good farmer Cresimus (*HRR* 33).

[3] *HRR* 27; Gell. VII, 9.   [4] Gell. XI, 14; Cic. *Brut.* 106.

throughout the extant books are Claudius Quadrigarius and Valerius Antias. Claudius' approach to history is said to have been the more scientific, for, refusing to regard the early traditions of Rome as in any way historical, he commenced his work with the years following upon the sack of Rome by the Gauls. One may be allowed to entertain the uncharitable suspicion that Claudius found uncongenial the anti-Claudian nature of the early tradition, in which successive Claudii are depicted as proud oppressors, and one of them as the arch-example of uncontrolled lust.[1] Roman historians were very sensitive of ancestral honour! Claudius' history, consisting of at least twenty-three books, continued to 82 or later. One of his sources was Acilius, a Senatorial historian closely associated with the Scipionic circle and its enthusiasm for Greek culture, who acted as interpreter for the Athenian embassy visiting Rome in 155 B.C. An anecdote recounted by Livy suggests that Acilius included characterisation amongst his historical aims,[2] and as such was a more congenial source for Claudius than was Acilius' contemporary Cato, who sought a more impersonal approach.

But the basis of Claudius' annalistic arrangement is information obtained from the *annales maximi* and from Senatorial documents, probably supplemented from private archives. It is presumably owing to exaggerations in these sources that his figures of enemy losses are so wild; for example, he gives the numbers of Philip's dead at Cynoscephalae as 32,000, whereas Polybius' figure is 8000, and again he claims 40,000 enemy dead after two battles in Gallograecia, for which Antias gives the more modest figure of 10,000.[3] In his presentation, Claudius

---

[1] Above, 89f.

[2] Livy xxxv, 14, 5.

[3] Cynoscephalae, xxxiii, 10, 8 (Pol. xviii, 27, 6). Gallograecia, xxxviii, 23, 8; perhaps Claudius misread the official report of the commander L. Manlius, who in a speech (xxxviii, 47, 6) claims 40,000 killed or captured. Or the error may be Livy's.

sought to adapt his unpromising material to produce a more interesting and exciting account; he does not adhere too closely to a chronological framework. Fronto contrasts his elegance with the more turgid narrative of Antias.[1]

Valerius Antias' seventy-five or more books, which covered the entire history of Rome to 91 B.C. or later, likewise depend largely on official records. Through the later books of Livy one can see how rigidly he clung to the presentation which he found in the documents. His year by year account plods wearily through election lists, public games, the provinces and commands of consuls and praetors, the prodigies, priestly appointments, corn prices, and other such material as the *annales maximi* had contained. For Livy, Antias' work was valuable chiefly as an easily accessible compilation of priestly and Senatorial records, which saved him the labour of approaching them in the original. But this more convenient use of an intermediary brought its penalties. Antias elaborated the bare records with additional material from family archives and from a fertile brain; he is especially fanciful on the figures of enemy losses and on numbers generally, as Livy repeatedly brings to our notice,[2] and in the first decade the prominence of the *gens Valeria* indicates the extent to which Antias has introduced family material or invented it. He is also guilty of colouring his account with contemporary reminiscences, and Livy himself recognises this when he criticises the account of the arrival at Rome of two Campanian legates demanding a

[1] Claudius' chronology, Klotz, *Livius u. s. V.* 77f. His elegance, Fronto, *Ad Verr.* 1, 1: 'historiam quoque scribsere...Claudius lepide, Antias invenuste'. For longer accounts of Claudius see M. Zimmerer, *Der Annalist Q. Claudius Quadrigarius* (diss. Munich, 1937); Klotz, 268 ff.

[2] XXXIII, 10, 8: 'si Valerio quis credat omnium rerum immodice numerum augenti...'; XXVI, 49, 3: 'adeo nullus mentiendi modus est'; XXX, 19, 12: 'impudenter ficta'. Also XXXVIII, 23, 6, etc. Some responsibility for these exaggerated figures must perhaps be attached to the generals who submitted reports of their campaigns to the Senate.

Campanian consul[1]—a fictitious addition prompted by Latin demands of much later date.

In some sections of his work Valerius was greatly influenced by the dramatic presentation of Hellenistic historians, and he gives an important role to the operations of Fortune and Nemesis in human affairs. This is observable not so much through Livy, who seeks to eradicate such motivation, as through other writers. For example, Appian's account of the destruction of Carthage, taken from Antias, emphasises the retribution which Nemesis brings; and Dionysius' version of Camillus' leadership depicts the fall of Rome as a disaster brought by Fortune and Nemesis to avenge his overweening pride at the capture of Veii.[2]

In spite of these manifest faults of exaggeration, over-dramatisation and turgidity, Antias has his virtues and importance as historian because he based his account on the documentary evidence. By using him Livy has been able to transmit a far fuller picture of Senatorial activity and organisation during and subsequent to the Hannibalic War than we should otherwise possess. For this reason the stylistic defects—stereotyped presentation of monotonous appointment lists, as reproduced by Livy —should be viewed more indulgently.

Definite knowledge of the writings of C. Licinius Macer, who was tribune for 73 and a vehement supporter of the Popular party,[3] and who committed suicide in 66 after he had been accused of extortion, is meagre. Impressed by the importance of documentary evidence, he investigated the magistrate lists in the *libri lintei*, which he preferred to those in the *annales maximi*. But he seems to have succumbed to the temptation to whitewash his ancestry, for Livy[4] rebukes him for his selective account

---

[1] XXIII, 6, 8.
[2] Carthage, App. *Lib.* 85; Veii and Rome, Dionys. XII, 13.
[3] Sall. *Hist.* III, 48.   [4] VII, 9, 5.

of the consulship of C. Licinius Calvus. He is undoubtedly immediately responsible for much of the pro-plebeian element in the early books of the *Ab Urbe Condita*; conspicuous examples are the discussions on the *Lex Canuleia*, and the condemnation of the patrician thug Quinctius Caeso.[1] Macer's work is most useful to Livy for counterbalancing the patrician bias of Antias in the narration of the class struggle.

Livy may well have been acquainted with the historian who immediately preceded him, Q. Aelius Tubero. Tubero had retired to a life of scholarly research after military and legal experience (he was present at Pharsalus, and unsuccessfully impeached Q. Ligarius in 46). He wrote not only on history but also on law; and it is probable that this knowledge of constitutional law was a conspicuous reason for Livy's choosing him as a main source in recounting the struggle of the orders. Tubero was also an enthusiastic antiquary; the many formulae concerned with religious, military, and civil procedure which Livy quotes are presumably reproduced from his account. He attempted to reconcile the conflicting claims of patricians and plebeians by consulting both Antias and Macer; but though Dionysius calls him 'a careful and clever compiler', there are certain inconsistencies in Livy's account which may be attributable to him.[2] Other inaccuracies are attributable to his colouring past events with apposite detail inspired by contemporary happenings.[3] In his literary style, Tubero inclined to archaism, a trait which Livy condemns in Sallust;[4] this was perhaps a contributory reason for Livy's decision to supplant with a work more representative of Augustan letters a history which he felt did not do justice to the glory of Augustan Rome.

---

[1] IV, 1 ff.; III, 11, 6 ff.; also II, 21, 6, where the *patres* are rebuked for failing to keep at heart the best interests of the people after the death of Tarquinius Superbus.

[2] See Klotz, *Livius u. s. V.* 201 ff., though the examples seem speculative.

[3] See 116f.   [4] Sen. *Contr.* IX, 2, 26.

For the third decade, Livy consulted two writers who had not been followed in the first, Coelius Antipater and Polybius. The extent to which Polybius has been followed has been a subject of perennial controversy. Livy cites him by name on only one occasion, but his phrase of approval indicates familiarity with his work.[1] In fact, a detailed comparison of individual passages in the two writers shows that Polybius has been consulted as early as Book XXI, where Livy records an alternative version of the chronology of the siege of Saguntum coinciding with the Greek historian's account.[2] Again, the figures of Hannibal's army in Livy contain one estimate identical with that which Polybius took from an inscription at Lacinium.[3] There are other points in Livy's narrative of Italian and Spanish campaigns at which Polybius has been similarly consulted.[4]

But though the Greek historian has been *consulted* in XXI–XXII, he has not been used as a main source, in spite of the striking similarity between the two accounts. Polybius' treatment of the siege of Saguntum is much briefer than Livy's, and the chronology is different; it is also notable that Coelius Antipater is cited no less than four times in these books.[5] Now Coelius and Polybius used the same sources for the Second Punic War— Silenus for the African viewpoint, and Fabius Pictor for the Roman[6]—and the close resemblance between the accounts of Livy and Polybius is explicable by the hypothesis that Livy followed Coelius. This suggestion is borne out by a comparison of Coelius' version of the famous dream of Hannibal with that of Livy.[7] Livy's use

---

[1] xxx, 45, 5: 'haudquaquam spernendus auctor'—laconic praise, not faint approval as J. Wight Duff, *Literary History of Rome* (1910), 644, suggests.

[2] xxi, 15, 3; Pol. iii, 17.

[3] xxi, 38, 2; Pol. iii, 33. Above, 113.

[4] E.g. xxi, 19, 2 ff., Pol. iii, 29; xxii, 36, 2, Pol. iii, 107; xxvii, 7, 5, Pol. x, 7, 1.

[5] xxi, 38, 7; 46, 10; 47, 4; xxii, 31, 8.

[6] Coelius' use of Silenus, Cic. *De Div.* i, 24, 49. Polybius on Fabius, i, 14, 1.

[7] xxi, 22, 5; Coelius, *ap.* Cic. *De Div.* i, 24, 49.

of Coelius would account for the considerable differences in detail and emphasis between his narrative and that of Polybius. Another possible explanation of the general correspondence with Polybius, marked by such differences of detail, is that Livy has used a source who followed Polybius—'annalista polibiano'.[1] If such an intermediary has been employed, it could indeed be Coelius, who might have consulted his older contemporary Polybius in addition to Silenus and Fabius. Livy's account of the death of Marcellus[2] is a pointer to Coelius' possible use of Polybius; Livy's condemnation of Marcellus' foolhardiness is an echo of Polybius, yet Coelius is cited by name as the source here.[3]

Polybius, then, is only a subsidiary source in the early books of this decade, but from xxiv onwards he is frequently employed as a main authority. Livy explicitly acknowledges his authority on Roman activities in Greece,[4] and it is not surprising to find that he is followed whenever the narrative is concerned with Greece or Sicily. Two passages in xxiv, which discuss Roman operations in and off Sicily, have a close correspondence with the extant Polybian account,[5] and it is generally agreed, in view of the extensive use of Polybius for Greek affairs in later decades, that the same is true in the third. There is similar unanimity that Polybius is the source for the campaign in Africa also.[6]

---

[1] De Sanctis, *Storia dei Romani* III, 2, 180.

[2] XXVII, 27. Compare Pol. X, 32.

[3] 27, 13: 'ut omittam alios, Coelius triplicem gestae rei ordinem edit'.

[4] XXXIII, 10, 10: 'non incertum auctorem cum omnium Romanarum rerum tum praecipue in Graecia gestarum'.

[5] XXIV, 4–7, 9 (Pol. VII, 2–7); XXIV, 33, 9–34, 16 (Pol. VIII, 3, 1 ff.). For views that Polybius is here the direct source see e.g. H. Nissen, *Kritische Untersuchungen* (Berlin, 1868), 83 ff.; De Sanctis, *Storia dei Romani* III, 2, 361.

[6] Thus the following third-decade sections are from Polybius: XXIV, 4, 1–7, 9; 21, 1–39, 13; XXV, 23, 1–31, 11; 40, 1–41, 17; XXVII, 29, 5–33, 5; XXVIII, 5, 1–8, 14; XXIX, 12, 1–16; 28, 1–36, 3; XXX, 3, 1–10, 21; 16, 1–15; 24, 5–25, 10; 29, 1–35, 10; 37, 1–38, 5. De Sanctis would add XXVII, 17–19 (Spain), XXIX, 6–9 (Locri), and the Tarentum episode (see 126, n. 1).

A more puzzling problem is raised by the section of xxv embracing the fall of Tarentum—is Polybius the chief source? His extant account is so close to Livy's that several scholars believe this to be the case.[1] There are several details in Livy which do not appear in Polybius, a view which has led one scholar to argue for Coelius.[2] But most of these additions could be easily attributed to Livy's constant aim of clarification; more significant is a large number of details in chapters 9–10 which differ from Polybius,[3] suggesting the use of a different source. On the other hand, chapters 8 and 11 have a close verbal correspondence with the Greek historian. It seems probable that Livy used Polybius initially, changing over to Coelius so as to omit Polybius' strictures on his namesake Livius, commander of the garrison. (Antipater, writing from the Hannibalic viewpoint, would have little to say about affairs in Tarentum, whereas Polybius makes great play with Gaius Livius' drunkenness and unpreparedness.) He has then reverted to Polybius for the final details.

Coelius Antipater, as has been noted, was employed as main source at the beginning of the decade. He is also cited frequently in the later books,[4] but for operations on Italian soil Livy was obliged to supplement his information with more detail from the Roman viewpoint. For Coelius was exclusively concerned with the war opera-

---

[1] So H. Hesselbarth, *Untersuchungen* (Lippstadt, 1889), 489; U. Kahrstedt, *Geschichte der Karthager* III (Berlin, 1913), 257; De Sanctis, III, 2, 365 ff. The passage is at xxv, 8–11.

[2] This is the view of Klotz, *Livius u. s. V.*, ad loc.

[3] E.g. in Livy Hannibal pitches camp and calls together his men (xxv, 9, 3 f.); in Polybius he merely halts for a meal and summons the officers (VIII, 26, 6 f.). In Livy it is Nicon who gives the answering signal to Hannibal; in Polybius it is Tragiscus. In Livy, when Philemenus approaches the gate, he follows behind the boar, which is carried by two youths; in Polybius he carries the front of the stretcher. In Livy Philemenus kills the Roman guard; in Polybius all four kill him. Polybius says that Philemenus and his band had Roman bugles and players; Livy mentions only one bugle, and an incompetent player. These are trifling differences, but it seems impossible that Livy could have followed Polybius in chapters 9 and 10.

[4] XXIII, 6, 8; XXVI, 11, 10; XXVII, 27, 13; XXVIII, 46, 14; XXIX, 25, 3; 27, 14.

tions, which he described with Hannibal at the centre of his narrative. Such a procedure was not suited to Livy's patriotic approach, which lent emphasis to the virtues (and the defects) of Roman leaders. Livy also required fuller information on politics and administration in the capital. For these purposes, the late annalists Antias and Claudius were the obvious choice. Antias in particular is increasingly used as the decade progresses. The first indication of such use of the late annalists comes at the end of XXI in the dramatic account of Roman reactions to the disaster of the Trebia; there is a fanciful story of an alleged counter-offensive by Sempronius. Then an extensive prodigy list is appended.[1] There are also short sections from Antias in XXII–XXIII, but Coelius is mainly followed for the military disasters at Trasimene and Cannae, and for the campaigning before XXIII, 30. From XXIII, 31 onwards Antias is closely followed as main source. Henceforward Livy seeks to reconcile the versions of Coelius and Antias, using them alternately as main source and quoting both on differences of detail, until XXVII. Subsequently Coelius is used only for Spanish operations, with Antias increasingly followed for Italian affairs as the operations of Hannibal diminish in importance. Livy cites Antias by name on eight occasions in XXV–XXX, but not once previously in this decade.[2]

Other authorities are occasionally quoted. Fabius Pictor is named once as a subordinate source, and so is L. Cincius Alimentus, an historian contemporary with

---

[1] XXI, 57–9; 61, 5–11; 62. See De Sanctis, III, 2, 185 ff.

[2] For the use of Antias from XXIII, 31 ff. see De Sanctis, III, 2, 360. There are confidently precise figures of losses at 35, 19; 37, 6; the claim that Sempronius Longus won a victory at 37, 10; a second battle of Nola at 46 (reduplication)—all evidence of late annalistic writing. Klotz points to the prominence lent to L. Valerius Antias in a trifling sea operation at 34, 9; and also to the use of *signa militaria*, an allegedly favourite phrase of Antias. On the reason for the change to Antias Klotz well comments: 'Die Antwort ist leicht gegeben: bei Antias wurden namentlich Marcellus' Taten in viel hellerem Lichte dargestellt' (p. 158). Subsequent citation of Antias is at XXV, 39, 14; XXVᵛ, 49, 3, 5; XXVIII, 46, 14; XXIX, 35, 2; XXX, 3, 6; 19, 11; 29, 7.

Fabius.[1] Silenus is mentioned in connection with the capture of scorpions in Spain in 210, but Livy presumably obtained this through Coelius. There is one reference to a Clodius Licinus on the activities of Pleminius.[2] Calpurnius Piso is mentioned only once, in connection with enemy losses in Spain,[3] and this is also the only place in which Claudius Quadrigarius is cited by name, though he has probably been consulted in other passages.[4]

In short, for the third decade Coelius Antipater is the chief source for Spanish affairs and for the Italian campaigns whilst Hannibal's successes continue. Subsequently Livy has employed both Coelius and Antias as main sources for Italian events, but Antias is followed almost exclusively in the final books. Antias has also been used for some sections of the Spanish fighting. Polybius is Livy's authority for events in Sicily, Greece and Africa, and perhaps for part of the events at Tarentum. Claudius and Piso have been consulted as secondary sources where Livy is dissatisfied with the versions of Coelius and Antias. One cannot say with certainty whether Fabius Pictor and Cincius Alimentus were examined directly, but it appears unlikely.

Polybius and Coelius, the only sources for the Hannibalic War not employed in the first decade, both stand out in great contrast to Livy's other habitual sources. Polybius, born in Megalopolis towards the end of the third century, was brought to Rome after Pydna on a charge of resisting the regime, but was never brought to trial. After acting as tutor to the sons of Aemilius Paulus, he became the intimate confidant of one of them, P. Scipio

---

[1] Fabius, XXII, 7, 4 (Hesselbarth suggests that Livy obtained this quotation, on the number who fell at Trasimene, from Coelius). Cincius, XXI, 38, 3; this quotation too was probably obtained indirectly, for Cincius is cited in no other place.

[2] XXIX, 22, 10.   [3] XXV, 39, 15.

[4] XXV, 39, 12. Klotz well compares XXII, 61, 5–10 with a remark of Acilius preserved by Cicero, *De Off.* III, 115. As Claudius uses Acilius, he may be the source of the Livian passage.

Aemilianus. He wrote the history of the period 264–146 in forty books, but his main theme was the rise of Rome to world dominion between 220 and 168. (The final section, covering the period 168–146, was in fact an appendix.) His aim was to write a universal history, in the belief that only in this way could the reader discern the pattern of cause and effect, the demonstration of which was in his eyes the chief purpose of historiography.[1] His approach to history, then, is more scientific and rational than that of Livy's other sources, and he attempts to trace the course of events in terms of natural causes whenever possible.[2] This has a significant effect on Livy's writing. The emphasis on the role of the gods in human affairs, which so dominates the first decade and parts of the third, is largely abandoned in the fourth decade where Polybius is used extensively as sole source.

True, Polybius frequently invokes Tyche as a power which profoundly affects human destiny, and to this extent he may appear to be contradicting his own claim that he searches for natural causes. But it has often been demonstrated that Tyche is frequently a mere verbal elaboration on conventional lines—much as we talk of Dame Fortune without metaphysical implications.[3] Elsewhere, Tyche has a purposive character and seems to be identifiable with the Stoic Pronoia, the divine intelligence of the world.[4] It is very rarely that Polybius attributes any event to caprice; when he uses the word *tyche* in the sense of chance or luck, it is usually to reject it decisively as a cause of success or failure.[5] His doctrine of Tyche in fact bears a close resemblance to the use of *fortuna* in Livy;

---

[1] III, 32.   [2] XXXVI, 17.

[3] This is pointed out by many scholars, including De Sanctis. For extended discussion see P. Shorey, *CP* (1921), 280f.; F. W. Walbank, *Commentary on Polybius* I, 18–19.

[4] For the identification of Polybius' Tyche with Physis, the personification of a natural law approximating to the Stoic Heimarmene, see W. Warde Fowler, *CR* (1903), 445–9.

[5] E.g. I, 63, 9; X, 9, 2.

neither historian accords a role to the fickle, malevolent and unreasonable deity which had such a pathological hold over many of their contemporaries.

Polybius regarded personal observation and inquiry as a form of research much superior to the scrutiny of written sources. He travelled extensively in Spain, Gaul, Africa, and the East, bringing personal observation to bear on such problems as Hannibal's Alpine route, and interrogating eye-witnesses. For his account of the Punic Wars, he consulted Fabius Pictor, Philinus, and Silenus; and he used Aratus for the history of Achaea, Timaeus for Sicily, and Ephorus and Theopompus for Macedonia when he wished to record incidental information about earlier times. His evaluation of these sources, though occasionally vitiated by bias, and his use of such documentary evidence as was available, made him respected in Republican Rome as 'bonus auctor in primis',[1] and modern historians have praised him equally enthusiastically.

In his literary presentation, Polybius followed the dictum of Aristotle that history sets forth facts and has a permanent didactic function rather than the object of temporarily affecting the emotions.[2] He therefore eschewed the sensational approach of his Hellenistic predecessors, who tended to distort the facts in favour of a more colourful narrative.[3] His deliberately factual approach is not imitated by Livy, who strives to make Polybius' account more arresting by a more dramatic version of events.[4]

L. Coelius Antipater has the distinction of being the first Roman historian whose work was respected by Cicero for its literary qualities. He was the first to compose an historical monograph in Latin, choosing as his theme the Hannibalic War. For a Roman, he showed a surprising impartiality in his choice and interpretation of

---

[1] Cic. De Off. III, 113.
[2] Ar. Poet. 9, 2f.; Pol. II, 56, 11f.
[3] See Ch. II.
[4] See Chs. VII and VIII.

sources; he not only consulted the Roman writers Fabius
Pictor and Cato (as well as family archives), but also the
writings of Silenus, who reported the war from an African
viewpoint.[1] This reveals an industry unfortunately rare
in the Roman tradition of history-writing. Knowledge
of his approach can be gleaned only at second hand from
Livy's account, but it is clear that Hannibal and the
Carthaginian forces are the focal point of his work. The
Historiae, as his work was probably called,[2] was divided
into seven books, with I ending at Cannae, V embracing
the recapture of Tarentum, and VII discussing the campaign in Africa.

From the extant fragments one can observe how Coelius
was influenced by his Hellenistic predecessors in stressing
the part which observance and neglect of the gods play in
human fortunes. He relates signal examples of the
calamities which follow upon neglect of religion; for
example, the disaster at Trasimene is attributed to
Flaminius' decision to fight in spite of the unfavourable
auspices.[3] The importance of dreams as the medium for
divine warnings is especially prominent, and he tells of
Hannibal's intention to remove a golden column from
the temple of Juno, and the threat of the goddess in a
dream to take the sight of his remaining eye if he did so.
The famous dream of Hannibal, related by Livy, in which
a guide sent by Jupiter bade Hannibal follow him to Italy,
also stems from Coelius.[4] In this view of the relationship
between men and gods, Coelius is representative of the

---

[1] Coelius' use of Cato, Gell. X, 24, 6. At XXVII, 27, 13, Livy quotes from Coelius
three different versions of Marcellus' death—one the traditional literary account
(i.e. from Fabius), the second from the archives of the Claudii, the third based on
personal inquiry.

[2] See Klotz, *Livius u. s. V.* 101.

[3] HRR 20; Cic. *De Div.* I, 77.

[4] Apparition of Juno, HRR 34; Cic. *De Div.* I, 48. In the same treatise
Cicero reproduces from Coelius the story of the punishment of the slave in the
Circus before the games of 490, and Jupiter's displeasure manifested in the dream
of a rustic (HRR 49; *De Div.* I, 55). Hannibal's dream, XXI, 22, 6 ff.; see Ed.
Meyer, *Kleine Schriften* II, 368.

Roman tradition which shows its immense influence on Livy's own view of history. The narrative of cause and effect is encased in the framework of tragic historiography so dear to some Hellenistic writers.

As a literary artist, Coelius is compared favourably with his predecessors Fabius, Cato, and Piso in Cicero's *De Oratore*, and is given the title of *exornator rerum* rather than mere *narrator*; but at the same time it is suggested that his writing is rough-hewn.[1] Perhaps Cicero's criticism is directed to such forms as *poteratur*, and to such diction as *topper*, *congenuclat*, and *exfundato*,[2] which the first-century purists would find abhorrent. Coelius' general treatment, however, shows signs of the sensational approach of writers like Timaeus, as in his account of the Roman crossing to Africa; the crowd of troops was so immense that 'birds fell from the sky at the soldiers' shouts—no one seemed to be left in Italy or Sicily'. His version of the crossing is 'touched up' with imaginary hazards of sea and sky from which the troops were said barely to have escaped.[3] This introduction to Roman history-writing of ἐνάργεια, vividness of narrative, is especially important for its influence on the writings of the major Roman historians. Interesting, too, is Coelius' romantic interest in women—an echo of the Hellenistic preoccupation with erotic topics. Livy's descriptions of the famous Sophoniba episode and of the offer to Scipio Africanus of a girl whose beauty 'caught everyone's eye'[4] are adapted from Coelius' account. It is perhaps going too far, however, to express Coelius' motives as 'letteraria più che storica'.[5] Livy is greatly indebted to him not merely for his development of Hellenistic techniques of narration, but also for his careful research on sources and for his impartiality.

---

[1] *De Or.* II, 54: 'sicut potuit, dolavit'.
[2] See Peter, *HRR* 44, 46, 47. [3] XXIX, 25, 4; 27, 14.
[4] XXX, 12 ff.; XXVI, 50, 1: 'adeo eximia forma ut quacumque incedebat converteret omnium oculos'.
[5] De Sanctis, III, 2, 181.

In the fourth and fifth decades, only three sources are regularly used—Polybius and the late annalists Antias and Claudius. Most of the material in these books is concerned with operations in Greece and Asia, and for this Polybius alone is used, as is easily demonstrable from his extant account. Occasionally Livy has drawn on an annalistic source to make a short addition.[1] But his trust in Polybius is such that he rarely corrects or challenges the Greek's account by reference to other writers, contrary to his regular procedure with other sources in earlier decades.[2] Polybius is also often used for details of embassies from Eastern countries at Rome.

German scholarship has clearly established that where Polybius is not the source in these decades, Antias and Claudius are almost invariably followed. Livy found in these writers the fullest and most recent treatment of Italian and Western affairs from a Senatorial viewpoint. One persuasive theory is that for XXXI–XXXVIII Antias is the main source with Claudius used for confirmation of facts, and that subsequently these roles are reversed.[3] The reason for this change of source is presumed to be the extraordinary muddle which Antias has caused Livy to make in his narrative of the trials of the Scipios in XXXVIII.

The criticism has rightly been made that this hypothesis is more exact than the evidence allows.[4] It rests

---

[1] E.g. the anecdote of Scipio's meeting with Hannibal (XXXV, 14, 5 ff.) taken from Claudius. U. Kahrstedt, *Die Annalistik von Livius, B. 31–45* (Berlin, 1913), 97, counts ten citations of Antias and six of Claudius in the Polybian sections.

[2] For an exceptional instance see XXXVIII, 41, 12 ff. (Scipio's journey through Thrace), where Claudius is cited against Polybius. But in earlier mention of this journey (XXXVII, 7, 16 and 33) Claudius is not cited, which indicates that Livy came on his version between the writing of the two passages. This suggests that Livy keeps no regular check upon Polybius.

[3] So Klotz, *Hermes* (1915), 481–536.

[4] M. L. W. Laistner, *The Greater Roman Historians*, 84, calls this with characteristic vehemence Klotz's 'Procrustes-bed of preconceived theory'. But perhaps he could have presented the evidence more fairly. Kahrstedt's is however a more cautious and dependable survey.

mainly on Livy's own citations. Where Claudius is quoted before XXXIX, it is usually in a confirmatory comment, and when the two are named together, Antias is placed first. But in the later books Antias is cited as supporting source.[1] Less imposing evidence rests on alleged verbal idiosyncrasies. Different titles are used for governors in Spain, who were praetors with proconsular *imperium*. Antias appears to prefer *proconsul*, Claudius *praetor* or *propraetor*. Again, Claudius employs the word *barbarus* to describe the Spaniard, and Antias' apparent fondness for the phrase *signa militaria* is also an indication.[2]

These pointers are suggestive of a general thesis, but due reservation must be made. For example, in XXXVIII Claudius' name is cited first.[3] Peculiarities of vocabulary are not an infallible guide, because Livy in his transcription may have decided to change the labels in the interests of *variatio*. In short, the most sensible conclusion is that Livy has used both writers as main sources at different times throughout XXXI–XLV, but undoubtedly Antias is more prominent in the first eight books, and Claudius thereafter.

Again, the possibility has on occasion been too lightly dismissed that Cato was directly consulted in the fourth decade. It is true that his omission of names and personalities in the *Origines* made his account in general unsuited to Livy's purpose, but this is not true of Cato's own campaigns. In particular Livy's narration of his Spanish operations contains features which distinguish it from the routine battle accounts recorded from the late annalists. There is much more intelligible description, greater

---

[1] XL, 29, 8: 'adicit Antias Valerius...'; XXXIX, 43, 1: 'Valerius Antias... aliud argumentum...peragit....' Antias is cited no fewer than eleven times after XXXVIII, Claudius six times as subsidiary source in XXXI–XXXVII.

[2] On the use of *proconsul* and *praetor* see Kahrstedt, *Die Annalistik*, 55 ff.; A. H. McDonald, *JRS* (1953), 143f. *Barbarus* is found e.g. at XL, 37, 11; 39, 2; 48, 4; XLI, 3, 7; 11, 4. *Signa militaria*, XXXIII, 23, 4; XXXVI, 38, 6 (Antias cited); XXXVII, 46, 3; 59, 3, etc. For other distinguishing marks of the two annalists followed by Livy see Kahrstedt, 95.   [3] XXXVIII, 23, 8.

operational detail, and somewhat excessive emphasis on the commander's virtues. Note, too, Livy's own words: 'Cato, who certainly does not depreciate his own merits, says that many were killed, but does not give the actual numbers.' (Perhaps it was the absence of the casualty figures which caused Livy to cite Antias, with his claim of 40,000 enemy dead (!), first.) These indications prove that Cato is the ultimate source. Did Livy consult the *Origines*, or Cato's speeches *De Consulatu* (which described the operations fully), or an intermediate annalist? The answer cannot be decisive. But there is little *verbal* correspondence between Livy's narrative and the speeches' surviving fragments; the *Origines* are a more likely source. But the possibility of an annalistic intermediary, who may have reproduced Cato's account with fidelity, cannot be discounted.[1] On the other hand, Livy's narrative of the battle of Thermopylae, in which Cato was a *consularis legatus*, is from Polybius.[2]

For the fourth and fifth decades, then, Livy used Polybius for events in the East, and for details of embassies to Rome from Eastern states. Antias and Claudius are the sources for Italian and Western affairs, but Cato's own memoir may be the direct authority for the Spanish campaign in xxxiv. Since the emphasis in these fifteen books is on Eastern expansion, almost two-thirds of the narration is attributable to the information of Polybius.

In the lost books after xlv, Livy continued to use Polybius and the late annalists up to the destruction of Carthage (146 B.C.). Subsequently Posidonius was an obvious successor to Polybius, for he continued his pre-

---

[1] The passage is at xxxiv, 8–9; 11–21. H. Nissen, *Kritische Untersuchungen*, 38, believed that the speeches *De Consulatu* were the source. H. Peter, *HRR* i, cl–cliii, compares the latinity of the two, and concludes: 'res concinunt, non verba'. His arguments for the *Origines* as source are formidable. Other scholars, including Klotz and Kahrstedt, posit a late annalistic intermediary.

[2] xxxvi, 15 ff.

decessor's universal history, and his philosophical outlook was congenial. For the Sullan period, additional material was available in the highly praised writing of Sisenna,[1] as well as Sulla's own memoirs. Lucullus similarly wrote on his achievements in the East. For the period between 60 and 42 the history of Asinius Pollio was the obvious choice, reinforced by the testimony of eye-witnesses. The fragment from Livy concerning the death of Cicero has a strongly critical flavour such as we should expect from Pollio, and a comparison of their accounts of this incident makes the dependence virtually certain.[2] For Caesar's campaigns, the *Commentarii* were consulted; Book CIV contained an extended comment on the geography and customs of Germany, which presumably depended on the sixth book of the *De Bello Gallico*.

The preceding discussion has assumed that Livy used prose sources only. But the suggestion has often been made that he has also drawn directly on poetic accounts, especially in the first decade, and that sections from these sources have been incorporated almost bodily into his narrative. In particular, Ennius has been suggested as a likely authority, since the eighteen books of his *Annales*, like Livy's history, were on the broad theme of the rise of Rome from its foundation.[3] The basis of this reasoning is that Livy's narrative frequently slips into a semi-poetic mould, and can often with minor adjustments be rearranged into hexameter form. But a clear distinction must be made here between his attempt to lend the early books a poetic flavour by deliberate reminiscence of Ennian passages, which he would know by heart, and the allegation that the poetic histories are the factual basis of

---

[1] Praised by Cic. *Brut.* 228; compare Sall. *Jug.* 95, 2.

[2] Pollio's description, Sen. *Suas.* VI, 15; Livy's, *ibid.* VI, 17.

[3] For views that Livy follows Ennius see M. H. Morgan, *HSCP* (1898), 61 ff.; W. B. Anderson's (Pitt Press) edition of IX (1930), 161, 198 f.; Laistner, *The Greater Roman Historians*, 87; and (in general) W. Aly, *Livius und Ennius*.

his account. The poetic features of Livy's style—diction, word arrangement, and occasional dactylic rhythms—can be attributed partly to such deliberate reminiscence, partly to the poetic licence permitted to writers of *historia*, partly to the use of sources directly influenced by Ennius,[1] and partly to the influences of the rhetorical schools on the artistic prose of the Augustan age.[2] Nowhere can any extensive dependence on Ennius be demonstrated.

An amusing example of the dangers inherent in such speculation on poetic sources can be found in one scholar's subtle rearrangement. He takes the following passage: 'mille acies graviores quam Macedonum atque Alexandri avertit avertetque, modo sit perpetuus huius, qua vivimus, pacis amor et civilis cura concordiae'. This is transposed into hexameter form:

> mille acies avertit et avertet graviores,
> perpetuus modo sit huius, qua vivimus, ⟨urbi⟩
> pacis amor, sit civilis concordia curae.[3]

This is an impressive reconstruction; the only objection is that this subject-matter is not part of the historical narrative at all! It is part of an excursus composed by Livy himself to compare the ability of Alexander and the Macedonian forces with those of Rome. The emphasis on *pacis amor* shows it to be an Augustan sentiment. All that one can deduce here is that Livy's prose form, especially in more rhetorical outbursts, closely approximates to the rhythm of the dactylic hexameter.[4]

---

[1] Fronto, *Ad M. Caes.* IV, 3, says that Coelius emulated Ennius. For modern comments see A. H. McDonald, *OCD*, s.v. 'Coelius'; A. Klotz, *Livius u. s. V.* 185.

[2] For a longer discussion see Ch. X.

[3] The passage is at IX, 19, 17. For the reconstruction see W. B. Anderson, *op. cit.* 161, and his comment there: 'A poetical origin can hardly be doubted, as the words run naturally into verse.'

[4] For a detailed refutation of the theory of poetic sources see R. L. Dunbabin, *CR* (1911), 104 ff.

VI

LIVY'S HISTORICAL METHODS

IN the *Histories*, Polybius[1] states that the serious historian must carry out three preliminary duties before presuming to write history. He must study carefully documents and memoirs, and compare them; he should personally scrutinise cities and sites, rivers and harbours, and in general the physical features on land and sea with which his account is concerned; and he should have engaged in political activity. Later in this excursus he adds another requirement when he castigates Ephorus for his ignorance of military matters. This extract is a useful starting-point for a critical examination of Livy's quality as historian, because it indicates the standards which the best writers of the ancient world set themselves. Livy was certainly aware of these requirements laid down by Polybius.

By such standards, the *Ab Urbe Condita* is plainly deficient. If Livy had had ready access to the aids of the modern historian—manuscripts, maps, topographical charts, reference books of all kinds—his armchair existence would have brought fewer penalties. But the absence of such aids, and the inadequacy of such equipment as was available, was a severe handicap for a man with no personal experience of warfare, who apparently travelled little, and who held no political appointment. Like Theopompus, Timaeus, and Ephorus, the Hellenistic writers criticised by Polybius, Livy is compelled to rely too closely on his sources, and because of his ignorance of the areas described, and of the methods of

[1] Pol. XII, 25 e.

warfare used, he is guilty of geographical errors and factual mistakes on military matters. Sometimes these faults are inherited from his sources, but sometimes he misinterprets what he reads, or by the omission of important detail misleads the reader.

In the previous chapter, the nature of the sources was examined. He has frequently been criticised for his choice of them, but careful examination of the problems which he faced, and of his notion of the purpose of the *Ab Urbe Condita*, must force the conclusion that his selection was made with discrimination.

For the first decade, his choice of Aelius Tubero, Licinius Macer (a supporter of the Populares), and Valerius Antias allows him to present an interpretation of the domestic struggle which favours neither side unduly. Livy was well aware that problems of strict historicity of detail scarcely arise in this decade—observe the repeated use of expressions such as *ut ferunt, traditur*, and *proditum memoriae*, provisos which stress his dependence on unreliable traditions. As an accurate account was impossible, Livy is free to depict for didactic purposes the instructive struggle between the two sections of the state, to demonstrate the virtues and shortcomings of each side. Thus his choice of sources is welcome evidence of impartiality.

For the third decade, he chose Polybius where the Greek's account was fullest, but the brief treatment of such important events as the siege of Saguntum, and the paucity of comment on proceedings in Rome, made the *Histories* unsuited as a continuous source to his purpose. The frequently expressed view that Livy only gradually became aware of Polybius' outstanding merits, and so used him increasingly as the decade progressed, is quite fallacious; Polybius' virtues had been proclaimed by Cicero, whose views on history Livy closely studied, and there is positive evidence that Livy consulted the Greek historian at the beginning of the decade.[1] Livy preferred Coelius' monograph for the first years of the war because of his more lengthy account; a wise choice, because of his admirably impartial consultation of both Roman and Carthaginian sources.[2] Livy followed him for as long as was practicable, but he felt the need to depict the Roman recovery from a Roman viewpoint, with emphasis on Roman personalities; Valerius Antias is therefore increasingly used in conjunction with Coelius.

Much nonsense has been written on this consultation of Antias. 'His slothful overtrust in Valerius Antias...is rudely shaken by the tardy discovery of his exaggerations. ...Livy therefore rounds on him, chagrined to realise too late that he has incorporated and published in good faith many of Valerius' mendacities.'[3] It is naïve to assume that Livy blithely trusted Antias (whose exaggeration must have been notorious in literary circles) until disillusionment finally dawned. A remark on the very first occasion on which Antias is cited by name shows Livy's scepticism on his reliability, and the point is repeatedly made.[4] Worth remembering, too, is Livy's care in using a check source; when following Antias he always consulted at least one other authority. Above all, Antias provided indispensable detail on Senatorial administration, for which he has not always received sufficient credit.

In the fourth and fifth decades Livy rightly chose Polybius for Eastern affairs, and for Roman and Western events depended on the late annalists Antias and Claudius.

---

[1] Cic. *De Off.* III, 113. On Livy's use of Polybius see above, 124ff.

[2] Coelius, with his Hellenistic techniques, was congenial also from an artistic viewpoint.

[3] J. Wight Duff, *A Literary History of Rome* (1910), 647. Similar criticisms are made by H. H. Scullard, *Scipio Africanus in the Second Punic War* (Cambridge, 1930), 20–31.

[4] III, 5, 12: 'audet tamen Antias Valerius concipere summas': for further criticisms see Ch. v, 121, n. 2.

He had presumably no other choice; and our information is insufficient to assess whether Claudius would have been the more reliable source to follow throughout.[1]

Above all, in considering Livy's choice of sources, one should remember that he is not an original researcher; his aim was to encase reliable facts ascertained by others in a worthy literary framework. One can condemn his lack of historical sense in failing to approach directly the documentary and earliest literary evidence; but one can also applaud the astute choice of sources which were the best available for his literary and patriotic approach, and which were also easily accessible and easily read.

Livy's method of using these sources, however, cannot be acclaimed with equal enthusiasm. Generally speaking, he follows one source in the description of an event; in transcribing it he introduces his own motivation, political, religious, and moral, and reorganises the material to his own stylistic requirements. Then, at the end of this main description, he often quotes the views of other sources who voice other interpretations of the course of events, or who register a different tally of the numbers engaged or killed in an action. Such a method would be forgivable if Livy had consulted the secondary authorities *before* composing his main account, so as to amend or modify it when the subsidiary sources presented a more probable interpretation. Instead, he allows his main narrative to rest on the factual information of a single authority.

Such analysis of Livy's method has recently come under vehement attack. 'The conclusions reached by modern critics...are so often mutually contradictory or destructive that one is disposed to question the value of much that passes for scholarly investigation. Most arbitrary is the school of thought which makes it an axiom that Livy

---

[1] Claudius' figures are sometimes wilder than Antias'; see above, 120.

... always followed one main predecessor and only here and there added items taken from other writers.'[1] Such an objection is perhaps an over-simplification. Livy has indeed almost always *consulted* more than one source; but the subsidiary authorities are used merely to check upon the *facts* of the particular events described; and the main source is frequently changed within a book—sometimes indeed within a chapter—to suit Livy's requirements. The easiest way of testing this use of a single source (or Nissen's law, as it has been labelled) is to compare Livy's account with his most copious extant source Polybius, a procedure which leaves no doubt how closely he followed his main source.

In citation of sources, the historian tends to exaggerate the number consulted, speaking of *auctores* where *auctor* would be more accurate. Thus in the fourth decade, after following the narrative of Antias, he speaks of *ceteri Graeci Latinique auctores* in citation of Polybius and Claudius.[2] Another reference to *Graeci auctores*[3] has relevance only to Polybius; and mention in the first decade of *veterrimi auctores* and *antiquissimi auctores* probably embraces only Fabius Pictor.[4] Attempts to defend Livy on this charge are untenable,[5] though in some contexts the plural *auctores* may embrace the source and the authorities quoted there.

Examples of this disastrous procedure of following one main source are easily attested, and we shall presently see how this occasionally results in the narration of the same events twice over, as he passes from one source to another.[6]

---

[1] M. L. W. Laistner, *The Greater Roman Historians*, 83.

[2] XXXII, 6, 8.

[3] XXIX, 27, 13: 'permultis Graecis Latinisque auctoribus'.

[4] Livy distinguishes between the oldest (Greek-writing) annalists and the middle annalists such as Piso, whom he calls *vetustior* (X, 9, 12). There is no hint that Livy used any Greek-writing annalist other than Fabius (who may not have been consulted directly) in the first decade.

[5] As that of Laistner, *loc. cit.*

[6] See 146 ff.

Equally to be censured—the inevitable result of his method—is his tendency to summarise at the end of a description a completely opposed view, without always giving a clear indication of his own judgement. Thus, after his main narration of the siege of Saguntum, he rightly throws doubt on the chronology by quoting without acknowledgement Polybius' version. He has not troubled to evaluate the merits of the disparate views beforehand.[1] Similarly bewildering is a passage[2] describing the junction of Masinissa's forces with those of Africanus in Africa. He gives without critical comment two varying views on the size of this new cavalry contingent: 'Some say that he came with no more than 200 cavalry, several say with 2000.' Then, after describing Masinissa's earlier escapades according to the account of Polybius, he states his preference for the smaller figure in view of the Numidian's defeats.[3] It is perfectly obvious that Livy had not read this extract of Polybius when he recorded the divergences of opinion on the size of Masinissa's force.

Also to be condemned is Livy's occasional carelessness in his scrutiny of the sources. Perhaps the most culpable errors are those involving mistranslation, which can be detected by systematic comparison with the account of Polybius. In one passage Livy, confusing θυρεούς (shields) with θύρας (doors), describes men fighting in a tunnel and protecting themselves with doors instead of with shields! Elsewhere, he misinterprets a remark that the Macedonians were to *lower* their spears (καταβαλοῦσι τὰς σαρίσας) to receive the attack of the enemy, and says instead that they were ordered to *ground* spears, and fight with their swords! When describing a council of the Aetolians, he renders Polybius' remark τοῖς μὲν οὖν ὅλοις εὐδόκουν ('*on the whole*, they were satisfied') as

---

[1] XXI, 15, 3 ff. [2] XXIX, 29, 4.
[3] XXIX, 33, 10.

'ad unum omnes...accipi pacem iusserunt' ('they unanimously decreed acceptance of the peace'). In other passages, Livy has misinterpreted whole sentences.[1] It is hard to believe that he has read the account of Polybius in these places with the necessary care, even allowing for the fact that his lack of military experience closed his eyes to the absurdities perpetrated by himself. A clear and somewhat damning picture emerges of a mind rapidly and mechanically transposing the Greek, and coming to full consciousness only when grappling with the more congenial problems of literary presentation. Or, more charitably, it might be claimed that in the composition of one hundred and forty-two books fatigue has sometimes taken its toll.

Secondly, Livy unquestioningly reproduces errors and distortions from his sources which a better historian would have eliminated. Some are trivial, but none the less careless. He states that stage performances were first acted at the *Megalesia* in 194, and then makes an identical claim for 191;[2] perhaps Antias had made the same error. There are patriotic falsifications which Livy has not removed. After Trasimene, the Senate begged Hiero of Syracuse to send a force of bowmen to Rome's assistance, but in Livy's version the offer is made spontaneously by Hiero, and thus the humiliating request is omitted.[3] Such patriotic bias is also demonstrated on the many occasions when Livy allows manifestly exaggerated figures of enemy losses to go unchallenged. The supreme example is his estimate of Carthaginian losses at the Metaurus—57,000 killed and 5400 captured; Polybius' estimate of the losses is 10,000. Livy's dependence on

---

[1] See now Walsh, *GR* (1958), 83 ff. The errors occur at xxxviii, 7, 10 (Pol. xxi, 28, 11); xxxiii, 8, 13 (Pol. xviii, 24, 9); xxxviii, 9, 12 (Pol. xxi, 30, 7); xxxiii, 13, 7 (Pol. xviii, 38, 4); xxxviii, 3, 9 (Pol. xxi, 26, 2 ff.).

[2] xxxiv, 54, 3; xxxvi, 36, 5.

[3] xxii, 37, 1: for the facts, Pol. iii, 75, 7. Klotz, *Livius u. s. V.* 145, blames the distortion on Antias.

Antias necessitates a proportionate increase in the Roman losses; his figure of 8000 is four times that of Polybius.[1]

Also attributable to patriotic distortion in the sources is the confused chronology of the third decade. The siege of Saguntum is dated in 218 instead of 219 to mitigate Rome's failure to send aid to the city.[2] There is confusion, too, in the account of the recapture; it is included in the events of 214 instead of 212. The capture of New Carthage is attributed to 210, a year early. The extent of Livy's mental confusion can be measured in XXVIII, where the expulsion of the Carthaginians from Spain is dated first in the thirteenth year of the war, then in the fourteenth; and a little later he calls the *following* year the fourteenth.[3] Here again these errors may have been transmitted rather than originated by Livy.

Nor are such errors limited to problems of chronology or details of military campaigns. Livy's sources, in addition to patriotic preoccupations, were also conspicuously affected by family interests; Livy reproduces much distortion owing its origin to this fact.[4] Perhaps the classic example of his failure to disentangle fact from fable is his narration of the trial of Scipio Africanus, in which he follows Antias except in one short section from Claudius. The result is bewilderingly confused; apart from the hostility to the Cornelii for which Cato may be ultimately responsible, Antias' compendious treatment seems to have telescoped the events of several years into one; Livy would have served us better by following Claudius throughout this episode.[5]

Thirdly, many errors must be attributable to Livy's

---

[1] XXVII, 49, 6–8; Pol. XI, 3, 3. Another patriotic feature of Livy's account is his omission of the fact that after the battle the Romans found many Gauls drunk in their beds, and butchered them. This would ill accord with Augustan *clementia*.

[2] Above, 118. For the disastrous effects of this error on the chronology of XXI see H. Hesselbarth, 118 ff.

[3] XXVIII, 10, 8; 16, 14; 38, 12.   [4] Above, 88 ff.

[5] See H. H. Scullard, *Roman Politics*, 290, and the bibliography there (to which add now J. Gagé, *Rev. Phil.* (1953), 34–64).

failure to avoid confusion and repetition when passing from one source to another. The difficulties were admittedly severe; for example, the chronological problem of reconciling the Roman sources with Polybius, who dated his narrative by Olympiads beginning in the middle of the Roman year, was formidable. Again, Livy found it difficult in many cases to identify the same battle in different authorities, because of the lack of geographical precision and the wild reporting of numbers which he found in the annalists' accounts. The result is that the same battle is often recounted from two different sources as though two separate engagements had taken place.

One's sympathies are with Livy especially in the first decade, where his authorities often contradicted each other even on basic facts such as magistrate lists. 'There is such confusion of dating, with the magistrates listed in varying ways in different sources, that because of the antiquity of events and authorities one cannot say which consuls followed which, or allot the various events to specific years.'[1] In such circumstances one cannot expect more than an exposé of the differing views, and where possible an indication of the more probable version; above all, inconsistencies through a conflation of sources should have been avoided. Livy has not always succeeded in this. Did the Romans pay a thousand pounds of gold to the Gauls to obtain peace in 390? No, says Livy; Camillus arrived in time to prevent the payment.[2] Yet in later references to this event it is assumed that the ransom was paid![3] Another example of such confusion between sources lies in the report of the battle of Lake Regillus. Livy names the consuls for 499, and then suddenly changes his source;[4] the reader is confronted with a dictator, Aulus Postumius, hitherto unmentioned, who leads the

---

[1] II, 21, 4.   [2] V, 49, 1.   [3] X, 16, 6; XXII, 59, 7.
[4] This is the view of A. Klotz. R. M. Ogilvie, however (*CQ* (1959), 269 ff.), believes that II, 15–21 is wholly from Macer.

Roman forces. After dating the battle in 499 (presumably by the authority of Macer and the *libri lintei*), he hastens to return to the general tradition which allotted it to 496: 'For the following three years there was neither definite peace nor war.'[1] Some inconsistencies are the result of irreconcilable versions of the class struggle—for example, the activities of the patrician Quinctius Caeso. In Livy's account, Caeso seeks to recruit troops for an impending war with the Volsci and Aequi. But his oppressive tactics in his opposition to political concessions lead to an indictment by the tribune Aulus Verginius, and to his retirement into exile. The narration of the class struggle occupies Livy's attention to such a degree that the impending war is forgotten; he now says that there is external peace.[2] The anomalies have not been removed from the conflation of conflicting sources.

In the third decade, similar problems arise from the alternate use of Coelius and Antias. The narrative at the end of xxi is especially baffling. Hannibal's operations in the winter of 218/17 seem to be described twice; operations in Spain are partly duplicated; Hannibal's march across the Apennines, recounted in the next book, is anticipated with a fictional earlier attempt which failed. Livy has failed to recognise Antias' account of events which he also narrates on the authority of Coelius.[3] Other 'doublets' are to be observed in this decade.[4]

Also to be criticised in Livy's handling of Coelius and Antias is his failure to allot more weight to Coelius'

---

[1] II, 19–21. See Klotz, *Livius u. s. V.* 272, who also cites alleged first-decade doublets, e.g. IX, 20, 4 and 7; IX, 21 and 22.

[2] III, 10–11 (esp. 10, 8 ff.); 14, 1.

[3] XXI, 57, 5–14 and 59 (war operations); 60–61, 4 and 61, 5–11 (Spain); XXI, 58 and XXII, 2 (Apennines). Scullard, *Roman World*, 428, rejects the whole of 57–9 as reduplication, but there seems no good reason to reject 57.

[4] XXII, 57, 9–12 and XXIII, 14, 1–4 (Klotz, 152); XXIII, 50, 5–12 and XXIV, 1–3, 15 (Klotz, 158f.); XXVI, 47, 4 and 49, 7 ff.; XXV, 21 and XXVII, 1 (*CAH* VIII, 81); XXVI, 51 and XXVII, 7 (with much inconsistency of detail in two reports of Laelius' return to Rome).

account. In his list of hostages, prisoners, and equipment captured at New Carthage, two main views are given—those of Coelius and Antias. Though Livy has emphasised Antias' wild reporting of numbers, he suggests to the reader that the precise figures lie at some point between the two estimates (*media simillima veri sunt*).[1] Again, no discrimination is made between the reliable and the unreliable in two varying estimates of Roman losses in a defeat in Apulia; the question is left open (*quis pro certo adfirmet?*)[2] It has not occurred to Livy that Coelius' figures have a greater claim to reliability.

In the fourth and fifth decades, the confused use of Antias and Claudius has caused several blatant examples of *Doppelheit*, avoidable by careful revision. The dedication of the same temple to Jupiter is recounted under both 194 and 192; the erection of gilded shields on this temple is allotted to both 193 and 192. More important, the operations of C. Claudius in Etruria are narrated twice in the space of five chapters, and those of Postumius in Apulia are also duplicated.[3]

Livy also has his troubles in passing from the annalists to Polybius and *vice versa*. At the beginning of the fourth decade, he reports the departure of legates from Rome to Alexandria to solicit support in the event of a war with Philip V of Macedon; the source is Antias, the date 201.[4] Later, he turns to Polybius to describe events in Greece in 200, and reads there that only now are the legates on their way; whilst they are in Athens, king Attalus comes to confer with them. Together with the king they make their triumphal entry into the city, and,

---

[1] XXVI, 49, 6.   [2] XXVII, 1, 13.

[3] XXXIV, 53, 7 and XXXV, 41, 8 (temple dedication); XXXV, 10, 12 and 41, 10 (the shields); XLI, 12 and 16, 7–9 (Etrurian operations); XXXIX, 29, 8 and 41, 6 (Postumius' campaigning). Other examples are cited by U. Kahrstedt, *Die Annalistik von Livius*, 38 ff., and include XXXIV, 21, 8 and 42, 1; XXXII, 29, 3 and XXXIV, 45, 1; XXXVI, 21, 6–11 and 38 f.; XLII, 3, 1 and 10, 5.

[4] XXXI, 2.

when later Nicanor overruns Attica, they warn him to evacuate it. Livy excludes these details of the legates' activities for no apparent reason other than that he was aware of the chronological inconsistency they brought into his account.[1] It is extraordinary, to say the least, that he made all these changes rather than amend his dating. Again he is the victim of his faulty compositional method, by which he has framed and written his account before evaluating fully the details given in all his sources.[2]

Another signal example of Livy's confused use of his authorities in the fourth decade is his dating of Africanus' death. First, following Antias, he attributes it to 187; later he decides that the written and oral accounts of the event are so contradictory that he can accept none of them.[3] In the following book he reverts to the topic, rejecting Antias' date of 187; Africanus' speech against the tribune Naevius (whose term of office began in December 185) proves that he could not have died till the end of 185. He also notes that Africanus had been replaced as *princeps senatus* in the censorship of Cato and Flaccus; he must have died before their active duties ceased in September 183.[4] The evidence is clear; Africanus died in 184 or 183, but Livy rejects out of hand the dating of 183 given by Polybius and Rutilius. Obviously, when he first wrote on the subject, he had read Antias only; and even when he had fuller information he failed both to draw the obvious inference and to amend his earlier

---

[1] XXXI, 14, 6ff.; Pol. XVI, 25. For a recent discussion see J. P. V. D. Balsdon, *JRS* (1954), 30–42. He concludes that 'Livy did not regard either the presence of the envoys at Athens or their activities there as being of the first importance'. But from a Roman viewpoint they were of greater interest than the Athenian reception of Attalus; the chronological embarrassment is a more probable reason for the exclusion.

[2] For other chronological errors see XXIV, 21–39 (the events of Sicily 214–213), then 40, 1: 'eadem aestate...' introduces Greek affairs not for 213 but for 214. Examples in XXVII are cited by S. G. Campbell in his Pitt Press edition (1937), xxi and 102. Livy was not the only historian to experience this difficulty of reconciling Greek chronology with Roman; Diodorus is another case in point.

[3] XXXVIII, 53, 8; 56.   [4] XXXIX, 52, 1.

statement. 'One wonders how much of what he said in Book XXXVIII was in his active memory when he wrote Book XXXIX, and why the earlier narrative was allowed to stand after he was convinced that it was wrong.'[1]

From this cumulative evidence of carelessness in translation, of failure to eliminate factual errors in his sources, and of confusion in reconciling his sources, one must conclude that Livy's standards of concentration and accuracy inspire little confidence. But there is something to be said on the other side. His conscientiousness in listing the details which originally appeared in the *annales maximi* is noteworthy; one scholar has assembled the numerous passages in XXI–XLV in which are recorded such important if mundane topics as allotment of provinces, disposition of legions, and visits of embassies.[2] Again, an outstanding feature of any comparison between Livy and Polybius is the scrupulous way in which he reproduces such important matters of detail as peace terms. For example, an examination of the terms of Flamininus at the conference of Nicaea, or the details of the general settlement of Greece in 196, or the conditions enjoined by Scipio on Antiochus after the battle of Magnesia, shows how Livy has exercised care in his reproduction of them. (There are the inevitable stylistic changes in the speeches in Livy, but the accuracy of the content is not affected.)[3] Or again, note the conscientiousness with which he lists

---

[1] E. T. Sage, Loeb Livy XI (1949), 385.

[2] E. Cavaignac, *Rev. Phil.* (1915), 5–23.

[3] Nicaea, XXXII, 33, 2–4 (Pol. XVIII, 1, 12–14); settlement of Greece, XXXIII, 30 (Pol. XVIII, 44), but Livy has here made additions from an annalist (M. Holleaux, *Rev. Phil.* (1931), 5); terms imposed on Antiochus, XXXVII, 45, 11 ff. (Pol. XXI, 17). But the scrupulousness of Livy in referring also to his annalistic sources, and making additions to Polybius (e.g. for the peace terms imposed on the Carthaginians, XXX, 37, 2–6, Pol. XV, 18), raises acute historical problems. Livy's version of the treaty of Phoenice of 205 (XXIX, 12), taken from the account of Polybius now lost, has without doubt faithfully incorporated Polybius' version; but he may have added unreliable annalistic elements. See J. P. V. D. Balsdon, *JRS* (1954), 32–4, who however believes the treaty to be accurately represented in Livy.

the twelve colonies which in 210 declined to contribute further troops or taxes, and the eighteen whose conduct was more exemplary.[1] Clearly Livy cannot be convicted of continual negligence; considering the extensive scale of his work his errors are no more than occasional lapses. But they are still too frequent for him to be viewed as a model of accuracy.

More serious still, and even more damaging to his reputation, are his occasional attempts to pervert or to cloak the truth for patriotic or moral reasons. He depicts the great leaders who defended or extended the empire as men of complete integrity, occasionally ignoring evidence which indicates less noble traits, as in his edifying portraits of Scipio Africanus and Flamininus.[2] The conduct of Roman troops is on occasion similarly idealised. An amusing instance concerns the illustrious Manlius Torquatus. Claudius Quadrigarius states that after Manlius had killed the Gaul in the famous duel, he cut off his head and removed the necklace as the prize of victory. Livy's account attributes to Manlius a clemency more appropriate to the Augustan age than to the Rome of about 360 B.C.: 'He robbed the body of the necklace alone, and harmed it in no other way.'[3]

More important as concerning history rather than legend is Livy's falsification of an incident at the battle of Cynoscephalae in 197. Polybius remarks that, after the flight of Philip, Flamininus pursued the fugitives, and found the Macedonians holding their spears upright—the gesture of surrender. When he realised the significance of this, he tried to restrain his men, but the leading Romans fell upon the enemy. 'They killed the majority, but a few escaped after throwing down their arms.' Livy's version

---

[1] XXVII, 9, 7; 10, 7–8.   [2] Above, 93 ff.
[3] Claudius, *HRR* 10 b (Gell. IX, 13); Livy VII, 10, 11. See R. Heinze, *Die augusteische Kultur* (Leipzig, 1930), 97 ff.

is substantially accurate until the last sentence: 'They attacked the enemy, *the first of whom* they killed, *and the rest* were scattered in flight.' This gives a less brutal picture of the proceedings. Again, Livy has suppressed Polybius' evidence of the truculence of the troops towards their commander after the battle, when they were robbed by the Aetolians of their anticipated booty.[1]

Another noteworthy suppression of the unpleasant truth concerns the attempt to sow discord in the Attalid royal house by many senators in 167. When Attalus, brother of king Eumenes, was in Rome, they attempted to turn him against his brother by the offer of a separate kingdom. He was dissuaded from accepting the offer by Eumenes' physician, Stratius. Polybius reveals that when Attalus refrained from condemning Eumenes and asking for part of the kingdom, the Senate broke its promise to give him the two towns of Aenus and Maronea; Livy omits mention of this dishonourable gesture.[2] His portrait of the Senate is so idealised that even its panic in the early years of the Hannibalic War is played down. So, after Trasimene, though we read in Polybius that Senate and people were in confusion, Livy depicts the *terror ac tumultus* of the common folk, but says that the Senate was coolly deliberating measures to meet the emergency.[3] The conduct of leaders and people is idealised both in politics and war.

Another danger which Livy has not successfully overcome is his deference to earlier members of the *Livia gens*. Amongst his sources, Valerius Antias and Fabius Pictor both seized any opportunities to glorify their families; Livy's standards are higher than theirs, and he has cer-

---

[1] Slaughter of the Macedonians, xxxiii, 10, 5 (Pol. xviii, 26, 9 ff.); Roman truculence omitted by Livy, Pol. xviii, 27, 4.

[2] xlv, 19–20 (Pol. xxx, 1–3). See Scullard, *Roman Politics*, 215, n. 1.

[3] xxii, 7, 14 (Pol. viii, 5, 7). Elsewhere Livy suppresses details of Senatorial confusion in 183 (xxxix, 46, 6; Pol. xxiii, 1, 9); see Hoch, *Die Darstellung der politischen Sendung Roms bei Livius*, 12, n. 6.

tainly not invented material in their free fashion. But amusingly enough, in his description of the fall of Tarentum, he omits to give the name of the garrison commander, Livius Macatus. Further, he does not mention the revelry and drunkenness of both commander and garrison, which materially assisted the conspirators. Polybius[1] has regaled us with full details. Yet when Livius' role becomes a creditable one by reason of a victory for which he is responsible, his name is mentioned.[2] In the case of Livius Salinator, co-conqueror over Hasdrubal at the Metaurus, Livy is not over-extravagant in his praise; but though he recounts fully Salinator's grudge against Rome for his trial and condemnation, he does not mention the reason for this punishment, the unfair distribution of booty after a campaign against Demetrius of Pharos. Livy indeed, by his indirect method of characterisation, suggests that Salinator was innocent; the Senate, for example, ponders the fate of Camillus, likewise recalled from exile, and admits to Rome's savage treatment of Livius.[3] This reads suspiciously like Livy's own insertion; the comparison with Camillus certainly advances Livius' stature.

The use made by Livy of his sources cannot therefore be regarded as satisfactory. Given his literary purpose, his choice of them was justifiable; but his carelessness in scrutinising them, his unwillingness to amend his account in the face of superior evidence, and his moral, patriotic, and gentile distortions must enforce the conclusion that Caligula's judgement—'the inaccurate historian'[4]—was soundly based.

Polybius' second demand of the good historian—the personal scrutiny of the geographical background to the events described—strikes Livy in a particularly fragile

[1] Pol. VIII, 25, 27, 30; Livy XXV, 7–11.   [2] XXVI, 39, 1.
[3] XXVII, 34, 14.   [4] Suet. *Cal.* 34.

spot. He is vague not only about foreign lands but also about districts of Italy as well. For example, he suggests that the battle of Sentinum took place in Etruria, not in Umbria; he calls Tannetum 'a village bordering on the Po' though it is fifty miles away; and his accounts of troop movements in Italy are sometimes quite incomprehensible.[1] More forgivable are the mistakes made in foreign locations, though his confusion between Thermopylae and Thermum in Aetolia (he states that the Aetolian council met at Thermopylae) is attributable more to carelessness than ignorance. In Spain, the position of Saguntum, in the discussion of the causes of the Hannibalic War, is by no means made clear (the same criticism can be made of Polybius); and in the later campaign of Scipio Africanus, Livy calls a town Iliturgi instead of Ilorci (doubtless the error goes back to Coelius). Noteworthy too is Livy's geographical vagueness which led Mommsen to talk of a second battle of Baecula. This second engagement in Livy's account takes place near the site of the first; from Polybius it is clear that Scipio marched to meet the Carthaginians at Ilipa, over a hundred miles away.[2]

These are some of the simple errors into which Livy stumbled through lack of personal knowledge of sites and routes. But the biggest geographical problem which he has left is Hannibal's route over the Alps. In fairness to Livy it must be remembered that even geographers like Strabo and Ptolemy are vague and not free from errors; and though Polybius' version, which must represent the

[1] Sentinum, x, 26, 7; Tannetum, xxi, 25, 13; troop movements, e.g. ix, 23, a description of a march from Saticula (Samnium) to Sora (Liris valley) *via* Lautulae (near Tarracina). W. B. Anderson in his Pitt Press edition of ix calls this and other instances 'colossal ignorance of geography'. See too the comments of R. S. Conway at 39, 3–4 of his edition of II. For a defence of Livy's geography in the Samnite Wars see A. Maiuri, *Atene e Roma* (1951), no. 2.

[2] Thermum and Thermopylae, xxxiii, 35; Iliturgi, xxviii, 19 (A. Schulten, *Hermes* (1928), 298); Saguntum, xxi, 7, 2; the 'second battle of Baecula', xxviii, 13 ff.; Pol. xi, 20 (F. G. Moore, Loeb Livy viii, 56, n. 1).

fullest traditional evidence available to Livy from the Carthaginian viewpoint, is comprehensible in outline, it is remarkably bare of names of specific rivers, towns, or other landmarks.

Livy's version of the route after the crossing of the Rhône incorporates contradictory detail. Initially, his narration is generally consistent with Polybius' interpretation, which stems from Silenus.[1] The crossing of the Rhône must have been in the vicinity of Arausio (Orange) on a computation of the length of Hannibal's march from the sea. The most convincing reconstruction of the route from Arausio is that Hannibal struck off from the Rhône along the Isère to Grenoble, and finally crossed over the Little Saint Bernard or one of the Mt Cenis passes. Livy, however, rejects this final stage on the grounds that the *Cremonis iugum* (most satisfactorily regarded as the Little Saint Bernard) would not have led Hannibal to the Taurini, where his Italian operations began; he suggests by implication that Mt Genèvre was the route taken.

Inserted in this admittedly vague but interpretable version are details bewilderingly inconsistent. Livy suddenly diverges[2] from Polybius' account. Hannibal is said to strike off from Allobrogian territory (that is, from 'The Island'): 'When now heading for the Alps, he turned leftward into the territory of the Tricastini, from which he marched to that of the Tricorii, skirting the frontier of the Vocontii.' 'Leftward' (*ad laevam*) must here mean 'northward'; Hannibal is facing the Alps. The most plausible explanation is that Livy has turned to a different source, and unwittingly describes Hannibal's route not from 'The Island' but from the crossing of the Rhône. This new information is in fact a 'doublet' of the route already outlined; but the march 'per extremam oram Vocontiorum' is hardly consistent with the journey along the Isère.

---

[1] XXI, 31 ff.; Pol. III, 49 ff.　　　　[2] XXI, 31, 9 ff.

A second inconsistency arises with the statement of Livy that Hannibal crossed the Durance.[1] Such a crossing can clearly not be reconciled with the route as earlier outlined. Subsequently Livy reverts to the tradition followed by Polybius.[2]

What is the reason for this insertion of dissonant detail? It is because the traditional version is so naked of recognisable names. He accordingly seeks such information elsewhere to lend an apparent precision to his account, and to give his readers the pleasure of recognising names which more recent events had made well known at Rome. In short, the northerly route taken by Hannibal has been signposted with detail from the direct route to Spain familiar to the Romans.[3]

Though frequently Livy is in error on geographical questions, one must accord him a word of praise for his consistent attempts to clarify the topography of a battle, and to explain the location of towns, rivers, and other relevant physical features. Such clarification was an important part of the Hellenistic approach to history-writing which so influenced the Romans. Sometimes he gives protracted descriptions, such as that of the Thermopylae area or that near Caudium,[4] but more frequently the information is given in brief parenthesis. On some occasions when Polybius is followed, it is clear that Livy is not merely transcribing the source; he has taken the trouble to consult other authorities to enlighten the reader on details of topography. This explanatory technique, so

---

[1] 31, 9; 32, 6.   [2] 32, 8 ff.

[3] The voluminous literature on the problem cannot be listed here. I follow A. Bourgery, *Rev. Phil.* (1938), 120 ff. For recent discussion see A. H. McDonald, *Alpine Journal* (1956), 93 ff.; F.W.Walbank, *JRS* (1956), 37 ff., where the widely publicised views of Sir G. de Beer, *Alps and Elephants* (London, 1955), are demolished. These critics rightly emphasise that the problems are primarily literary, not geographical. In the case of Livy's confused account, I cannot subscribe to Klotz's suggestion that Livy followed Coelius' disastrous conflation of Silenus and fictitious detail from Fabius Pictor; it is doubtful if Fabius could have been familiar with the topographical data cited by Livy.

[4] XXXVI, 15; IX, 2.

frequent that there is no need to quote examples *in extenso*,[1] forces us to qualify our strictures on Livy's vagueness of geography; he has made a heroic effort to repair his deficiency. But personal investigation was above all necessary, and he had so circumscribed his leisure by the magnitude of his self-imposed task that such travel was impossible. Perhaps it would also have been uncongenial.

Livy's geographical vagueness is a weakness; still more crippling is his ignorance of military matters. The parts of his history left to us are in large measure concerned with commanders and their armies; how unfortunate therefore that he had not the mind of a Xenophon, which readily apprehended the use of weapons and mechanical devices! Equally unfortunate was his lack of military experience which made him ignorant of battle tactics.

Mistakes of translation, attributable to ignorance of military matters, have already been noted.[2] This lack of acumen and knowledge is echoed elsewhere. In a discussion of Roman weapons, Livy thinks that the *pilum* was thrust as well as thrown; and he appears to imagine that Alexander's battle forces were composed entirely of the phalanx, a situation much truer of later Macedonian armies than of Alexander's, which relied on cavalry above all.[3] Again, when recounting Hannibal's troop dispositions in the final battle of the Second Punic War, he has the temerity to contradict Polybius—or else he failed to understand him. Polybius explains that Hannibal kept in the rear 'his men from Italy' as being the most effective and steady troops, who were to remain fresh and exploit their qualities at the appropriate moment; in Livy they are *Italians*, relegated there 'incertos socii an hostes essent'. He

[1] X, 2, 5 f.; XXIX, 7, 3; XXXV, 27, 13; XXXVII, 27, 2, etc.
[2] See 143 f.
[3] IX, 19, 7–8.

is blissfully unaware that the rear would be the last place for doubtful allies or potential enemies.[1]

But it is in siege descriptions that the clearest picture emerges of a mind wholly indifferent to the techniques of war. His account of the siege of Ambracia deliberately modifies the details provided by Polybius, who tells us how the defenders divined the position of the Roman miners by thin sheets of brass which reverberated when the digging was taking place. Livy's version is that the Ambraciots simply applied their ears to the ground and heard the mining operations. Later he simplifies Polybius' version of the methods used by the townsmen to 'smoke out' the Romans. In the siege of Syracuse he avoids the description which appears in Polybius of the *sambucae*, the harp-shaped ladders attached to quinqueremes and used for storming towns from the sea. Another indication of his lack of interest in such technical apparatus is his mention of some Rhodian fire ships without the description of their mechanism which he found in his source.[2]

From all this it is clear that Livy scrutinises his sources without the insight of a military expert; he relies completely on their evidence, reproducing what he reads with stylistic elaboration. The result is that his battle accounts fall into two clearly distinguishable groups—those taken from the late annalists, and those in which he followed the more detailed and knowledgeable authorities, Polybius and Coelius. The groups are so clearly distinguishable because Livy can add little to the bald, monotonously phrased annalistic accounts, which describe almost every battle in identical terms. As one scholar puts it, 'All the battle accounts are frighteningly dull variations on an identical theme. First the Romans, through the enemy's numerical superiority or through surprise, fall into diffi-

[1] xxx, 35, 9; Pol. xv, 16, 4 and 11, 2.

[2] Ambracia, xxxviii, 7, 8 (Pol. xxi, 28, 8); *sambucae*, xxiv, 33 (not mentioned), Pol. viii, 4—see De Sanctis, iii, 2, 361. Fire ships, Appian, *Syr.* 24 (following Polybius), Livy xxxvii, 11, 13.

culties; then, through the extraordinary bravery or cleverness of their leaders, they gain the upper hand, and finally kill 40,000 or 35,000 of the enemy, or occasionally fewer....'[1] The criticism is relevant not merely to the fourth and fifth decades, about which it was written, but to earlier sections as well. Often the Romans sustain an initial defeat, later avenged by a more emphatic victory;[2] on the rare occasions when a reverse is admitted, the battle is described with greater brevity than when the Romans are victorious.[3] No definite topography, no clear picture of tactics emerges; the language is general and stereotyped. Often the foe lurks in *occulti saltus*: *pavor*, *trepidatio*, or *terror* reigns everywhere: there is an *atrox proelium* or *atrox caedes*: the enemy are *fusi et fugati* or *capti caesique*. Livy is at pains to dispel the monotony wherever possible by emphasis on such distinctive detail as the tradition offers; so a number of different motifs recur—a duel takes place, or a thick mist envelops the proceedings, or the cavalry fights on foot, or slaves fight for their freedom, or a shower separates the contestants.[4] These variations offer the historian (and the reader) some relief from the contemplation of unceasing butchery.

When following more competent narratives, Livy encounters the opposite problem; he seeks to simplify the detailed accounts of tactics employed in major battles. His indifference to the finer points of soldiering, and his awareness of a non-specialist audience, make him aim at a comprehensible and stimulating account. His methods must be studied later;[5] what effect have such aims on his historical accuracy?

It must be admitted that there is scarcely a major

[1] H. Nissen, *Kritische Untersuchungen*, 94.

[2] x, 36; xxix, 36; xxxiii, 36; xxxix, 30–1.

[3] xxxi, 2; xxxiii, 36; xxxvii, 46; xxxix, 20, etc.

[4] E.g. vii, 9, 6f. and 26 (duel); x, 32, 6 (mist as at Cynoscephalae); iv, 38 and vii, 7, 8 (cavalry fight as infantry as at Cannae); xxiv, 15, 8 (slaves); vi, 32, 6 (shower).

[5] Chs. vii and viii.

battle account which does not contain a headache for the modern historian, because of mistakes caused by inexperience, obscurity, omission of vital detail, over-dramatisation, or over-simplification. One can ignore the great conflicts of the first decade, and the improbabilities involved there,[1] and concentrate on the more historical books. His version of the battle of the Trebia is vitiated by topographical and strategic inaccuracies; he wrongly assumes that the scene of the battle was the right (eastern) bank, and accordingly confuses the tactics of both sides before the battle.[2] His limitations are also exposed by a comparison of his account of the battle of Lake Trasimene with that of Polybius; he has omitted to detail Hannibal's route before the battle, the flank occupied by his light-armed troops, and the position of the Celts—items of information necessary for a proper understanding of the outcome.[3]

There are inadequacies, too, in the account of the defeat of Mago in Northern Italy in 203, immediately before the evacuation of this area by the Carthaginians. The conflict is joined 'in agro Insubrum Gallorum'.[4] No approximate location of the site, no indication of the terrain is given; the relative positions of the opposing armies go unmentioned. 'Voilà une importante bataille', acidly remarks one critic, 'qui flotte en air, si j'ose dire, et rien ne la

---

[1] The whole of the Gallic attack is of course overlaid with legend. On the other hand, the disaster near Caudium (IX, 1 ff.) has been decked out with detail adapted from the ambush of Mancinus in Numantia in 137. (The quaestor Ti. Gracchus made a solemn *foedus* with the enemy, and 20,000 Romans were accordingly released. When Mancinus left office, Philus proposed that the treaty should be annulled by the surrender of Mancinus. Orosius (V, 5, 3) states that the Numantian ambassadors made similar demands to those attributed here to the Samnite C. Pontius.) For the dramatic element in Livy's narration see H. Nissen, *RhM* (1870), 19.

[2] XXI, 47 ff. See Scullard, *Roman World*, 427 f., and the objections to Livy's version posed by M. Dimsdale's Pitt Press edition of XXI, 185. Beloch and Grundy have tried to defend Livy's account, but unconvincingly.

[3] XXII, 4 ff. (Pol. III, 82, 9 ff.). Perhaps the inadequacies are attributable to Livy's source, probably Coelius here.

[4] XXX, 18.

rattache à un terrain quelconque.'[1] This description, typical of Livy's overriding interest in battle accounts, concentrates on the dramatic features, imaginary or real. The conversation between the two Roman leaders, Quinctilius Varus and Marcus Cornelius, when the enemy declined to engage; the sudden entry into the conflict of Carthaginian elephants, 'ad quorum stridorem odoremque et adspectum territi equi'; the Roman reserves thrown in when the line was wilting; the wound sustained by Mago, whose removal from the battle *exsanguem* (a pathetic touch) is the turning-point of the battle—these are the facets which catch Livy's eye.

More understandable is his attempt to impose on some battles an orthodox mould, describing successively the operations of right wing, left wing, and *media acies*. This procedure is a relic of Hellenistic theory; some historians, Diodorus for example, presented many battle accounts in an identical pattern.[2] Livy's account of the battle of Cynoscephalae suffers from this fault, for whereas Polybius makes it clear that there was no orthodox battle-line, Livy talks of a left wing and then of a *media acies* which stood and watched as the right wing fought.[3] Equally illustrative of the point is his account of the battle of the Metaurus—an engagement for which neither side chose the site, for the battle began as soon as the Romans caught up with the Carthaginians. Polybius shows that Hasdrubal had no time to draw up his forces properly, so he put his elephants in front, took up position behind them, and engaged Livius and the Roman left wing. There was no Carthaginian right wing and no Roman centre; the Carthaginian commander relied on a narrow front to attain defence in depth, whilst the Romans were drawn up in separate contingents under Nero and Livius. Livy's account insists on an orthodox engagement with

---

[1] R. Jumeau, *Rev. Phil.* (1939), 22.
[2] See K. Witte, *RhM* (1910), 381.　　　[3] XXXIII, 9 (Pol. XVIII, 25).

Hasdrubal on the right and the Ligurians in the enemy centre; on the Roman side Porcius Licinus is said to be in the centre. But a little later the Ligurians are depicted as fighting on the right as in Polybius, and there is no further mention of Porcius Licinus. Livy has arranged the forces of both sides without reference to the terrain or to the Carthaginian tactics.[1]

To be fair to Livy, this technique of simplification for the non-specialist reader admittedly leads to minor inaccuracies, but usually gives an approximate picture. His account of the troop dispositions at Cannae, for example, is admirably clear, though there are two minor omissions.[2] Scipio's victory at Ilipa is told in equally lucid fashion, and by comparison with Polybius it is possible to see how Livy has explained a complex Roman manœuvre in a simple, easily comprehended way.[3] In view of his audience, littérateurs rather than students of military affairs, it would be unjust to expect technical details of strategy and tactics.

The neglect of such technical factors allows free play to his psychological insight. He probes the minds of the protagonists and is concerned above all with human emotions, concentrating our attention on the fears, the anger, the joy of the participants. Indeed, he sometimes allows his imagination too much scope in this respect. He repeatedly characterises Philip V of Macedon as being paralysed with fear in battle, when he has no warrant for such an interpretation, as other authorities demonstrate. Hence on the numerous occasions when other com-

---

[1] xxvii, 48 f. (Pol. xi, 1–3). Another good example of such rearrangement is Livy's version of the battle of Magnesia (190 B.C.). Witte, 388 ff., well compares Appian, *Syr.* 33–6 (here following Polybius) to demonstrate Livy's changes at xxxvii, 39–44. For errors in Livy's account of Zama see U. Kahrstedt, *Geschichte der Karthager* iii (Berlin, 1913), 353 f.

[2] xxii, 44 ff. E. Burck, *Einführung in die dritte Dekade des Livius* (Heidelberg, 1950), 46, points out the omission of the position of the African troops, and on the Roman side of the concentration of maniples (Pol. iii, 113, 3 and 6–9).

[3] xxviii, 14, 15–18; Pol. xi, 23.

manders are similarly depicted, due reservations must be made.[1] This is one of the ways in which the excesses of some Hellenistic writers find their echo in Livy.

The last duty which Polybius impresses on the would-be historian is his need to have participated in political affairs. Unlike Sallust and Tacitus, Livy had no such personal experience. It is impossible (and it would be unfair) to judge from the extant books how vitally this impaired his insight into the manipulation of political power. Sallust and Tacitus wrote on events close to their own times; Livy's analysis of first-century history would have provided the only fair criterion to compare his achievement with theirs. The tantalisingly brief glimpses provided by the *Periochae* and by other authors do not reflect the insight of a Tacitus. The summarised account of the activities of M. Livius Drusus[2]—he is described as initially espousing the cause of the Senate in 91 B.C., and of then 'stirring up the people with the demoralising hope of largesse to gain personal power'—gives no indication that Livy has credited Drusus with the far-sightedness which saw the inevitability of the extension of the franchise and of wider recruitment to the Senate. His fervent approval of Pompey betrays his failure to appreciate how that politician had contributed to the subversion of the Republican regime by his assumption of illegal powers; Tacitus has the clearer vision.[3] Nor, in his approval of the tyrannicides Brutus and Cassius, is there any indication that he had realised the futility of the assassination of Julius Caesar in the complete absence of plans for alternative government. One suspects that

[1] For Philip see XXXIII, 7, 8 (Pol. XVIII, 21 has no mention of fear); XXXI, 34, 5, in complete contrast to Diodorus, XXVIII, 8 (also following Polybius), where Philip is depicted as fearlessly reassuring his troops. Other examples of Livy's imputation of fear to commanders, XXXI, 17, 10; XXXII, 5, 2; XXXIII, 15, 6; XXXV, 27, 16; XXXVI, 16, 6.

[2] *Perioch.* LXXf.

[3] See the apposite comment of R. Syme, *Tacitus*, 430.

Livy's preoccupation with persons as moral agents, noted in his portrayal of earlier times in the extant books, has blinded him to the fundamental causes of the civil conflict which he deprecates.

The problems of political analysis in the extant books are obviously of a different order. His efforts in the first decade are praiseworthy. There is no analysis of the nature of the Roman constitution on the lines of the sixth book of Polybius; an excursus of this type would have been foreign to his purpose, and in any case he assumed a knowledge of it in his readers. But he does attempt, without entering into the theory of the 'mixed' constitution, to discuss the evolution of the Roman state from kingship to *libertas* or the rule of law;[1] and his account of the class struggle duly embraces the landmarks by which the non-privileged gradually acquired political rights. But his primary concern is to teach the importance of *concordia* by moderation and timely concessions. Hence his narrative is more concerned with the attributes of the persons involved—moderate patricians like Quinctius Capitolinus, tyrannical ones like the Claudii, wise plebeians like Duillius—than with the significance of the changes themselves. Such emphasis on the personality of participants leads to a short-sighted view of the issues.

Such treatment can be tellingly contrasted with Dionysius' perspicacity on particular events. For example, a comparison of the two accounts of the extension of citizenship to Tusculum in 381 clearly suggests that Dionysius was far more aware of its significance in the growth of Roman dominion than was Livy.[2] Dionysius' superior treatment is again marked in his discussion of how Terentilius Harsa, tribune in 462, sought to limit consular power by means of legislation. Livy is content to plunge *in medias res*; Dionysius prefaces his narrative

---

[1] II, 1, 7f.
[2] VI, 26, 8; Dionys. XIV, 6. See A. Momigliano, *JRS* (1945), 143.

with a brief survey of previous legal and judicial procedure.[1] The dramatic framework in which Livy encases such legislative acts can also distort their import; of this same *lex Terentilia* Livy suggests that it was proposed 'not so much in the hope of carrying it through as to assail the rash behaviour of Quinctius Caeso'. Similarly the *lex Ogulnia*, by which the priestly colleges were thrown open to plebeians, is regarded by Livy as merely a piece of anti-patrician legislation.[2]

Such weaknesses may be conceded, yet there is much to praise in Livy's continual attempts to explain the evolution of Roman religious, judicial, and constitutional law. As one scholar has put it,

si l'on voulait simplement grouper dans l'ordre où elles se présentent toutes les anecdotes, parfois très étendues, par lesquelles Tite-Live met en vive lumière les progrès juridiques ou constitutionnels sur lesquels s'est construite la civilisation romaine, on serait étonné non seulement de leur intensité de vie et de leur portée, mais de l'exactitude minutieuse d'une foule de pratiques ou de détails techniques.[3]

In the third, fourth, and fifth decades, Livy's discussion of political affairs is largely confined to descriptions of meetings of the Senate and of the *Comitia* at Rome, and of councils and informal meetings elsewhere. His decision to use the writings of the Senatorial annalists has resulted in useful information about the working of the Senate and some of the family alliances within it during and after the Hannibalic War, and this has been invaluable in the reconstruction of the internal structure of Roman politics, though due allowances must be made for patriotic, party, and family bias.[4]

---

[1] III, 9 ff.; Dionys. x, 1 ff.   [2] III, 11, 10; X, 6, 4.

[3] J. Bayet, Budé Livy 1, xxxviii, exemplifying the remark with Livy's discussion of *interregnum* (1, 17); *repetitio* (1, 22, 4); *fetiales* (1, 24, 4 ff.); *deditio* (1, 38, 3); *vindicta* (11, 5, 9); *perduellio* (11, 41, 11); sacrosanctity (111, 55, 8), and numerous items of this type.

[4] Such studies as F. Münzer's *Römische Adelsparteien und Adelsfamilien* and H. H. Scullard's *Roman Politics* are based largely on Livy's information.

A clear picture emerges of Senatorial control of administration in the fields of finance, foreign affairs, military appointments, and religious matters; and Livy also indicates the various ways in which this power was circumscribed by the decision of the people, whether sitting as the supreme judicial court, or deciding in popular assembly on approval or rejection of proposed laws and on the issue of war or peace, or by vetoing Senatorial transactions or decrees through the agency of the tribunes. Unfortunately his portrayal of these political processes is heavily idealised. In particular, his picture of the Senate, already glorified by the aristocratic tradition, is further enhanced by conscious distortion, as in the careful omission of discreditable intrigue in foreign affairs, and in superfluous depiction of moral strength at critical junctures.[1]

Though Livy reveals the existence of some family rivalries within the nobility, his ignorance of power politics makes him unaware of, or at any rate reticent about, the family alliances which sought to prolong their predominance by control of elections; nor does he appreciate the manœuvres by which the 'liberal progressive' faction, headed by the Aemilii and the Cornelii, or the 'conservatives', led by the Fabii, exerted their influence on the voting; Sallust lays bare the vital elements in a single sentence.[2] Livy's failure to comprehend these hidden struggles is the cause of over-simplification in his interpretation of the strife between Senate and People at the outset of the Hannibalic War. When Minucius is appointed *magister equitum* to the dictator Fabius after the disaster of Trasimene, this may not be merely a popular choice; the Minucii were in the Aemilian–Scipionic alliance.[3] The election of Terentius Varro and Aemilius Paulus as con-

---

[1] See above, 152.
[2] *Iug.* 85, 4: 'vetus nobilitas, maiorum fortia facta, cognatorum et adfinium opes, multae clientelae'.
[3] H. H. Scullard, *Roman Politics*, 46, n. 2.

suls for 216 was a far more complex proceeding than Livy's account suggests.[1]

But the greatest injustice has been inflicted upon those consuls who were elected by popular acclaim, for the Senatorial annalists closed their ranks in denigrating them. Flaminius (who with his agrarian proposals and alleged disregard of religion might have appeared as 'the prototype of the two Gracchi') is given no credit for his honourable conduct in defeat at Trasimene.[2] Minucius' rescue by Fabius Cunctator is followed by a grovelling, highly implausible apology.[3] Terentius Varro shoulders all the blame for the disaster at Cannae; there are sneers at his lowly origin. Yet his tenure of magistracies (including the praetorship) before 216, and the important missions subsequently entrusted to him, demonstrate that this picture of an inexperienced demagogue to whom the Senate was implacably hostile is wholly false. Livy 'regarded the Senate as the hero of the Hannibalic War, and in glorifying it has done injustice to the representatives of the people'.[4]

Yet Livy, lacking experienced insight, shows intense and commendable interest in the political life of Republican Rome, and communicates his enthusiasm to the most influential circle of Augustan Rome in the hope that the lesson would not be ignored. If he is blind to the motives behind election struggles, he is certainly not unaware of their moral for Augustan Rome. Hence his lively account of the disordered scenes in the forum when Appius Claudius Pulcher canvassed his brother's candidature in 185. With similar purpose he depicts friction between consuls caused by allotment of provinces. He describes triumphal processions such as that of Livius Salinator after his victory at the Metaurus, participating so intimately that he catches and records the comments of

---

[1] *Ibid.* 51 ff. [2] *Ibid.* 45.
[3] XXII, 30. [4] Scullard, *Roman Politics*, 53.

the bystanders (!); and he is especially fond of dramatic delineation of triumphs carried through against opposition.[1]

Thus on the criteria offered by Polybius Livy as scientific historian comes out badly. He is not reliable in his scrutiny of the sources, his knowledge of geography and warfare is deficient, and he lacks insight into the techniques of the manipulation of political power. Yet in each of these fields one must acknowledge his industry and endeavour in his attempt to overcome natural defects and a fatal lack of experience.

There is a sense, too, in which Polybius' requirements are incomplete precisely because they remain on the factual level. Livy partly atones for such prosaic failures by his faculty for seeing into the minds of individuals and groups—the psychological approach so beloved of many Hellenistic historians. Collingwood's views on this facet of the historian's task form a commendation of Livy's method: 'There is nothing else except thought that can be the object of historical knowledge. Political history is the history of political thought: not "political theory" but the thought which occupies a man engaged in political work: the formation of a policy, the planning of means to execute it, the attempt to carry it into effect.... Military history, again, is not a description of weary marches in heat and cold, or the thrills and chills of battle or the long agony of wounded men. It is a description of plans and counterplans: of thinking about strategy and tactics, and in the last resort of what the men in the ranks thought about the battle.'[2]

Livy's history is full of such psychological assessments.

---

[1] Claudius Pulcher, xxxix, 32, 5 ff.; friction between consuls, x, 24 ff.; xxviii, 40; xxxiv, 43, 3 ff., etc.; Livius Salinator's triumph, xxviii, 9, 9 ff.; triumphs held against opposition, x, 37, 6 ff.; xxxiii, 22 f.; xxxix, 4 f. See W. Kroll, *Studien zum Verständnis der römischen Literatur* (Stuttgart, 1924), 361.

[2] R. G. Collingwood, *Autobiography* (Oxford, 1939), 110.

He is especially fond of analysing the motives, preoccupations, or reactions of men confronted with difficult, fearful, or exciting situations. When describing the solemn departure of the consul Licinius Crassus to the Third Macedonian War, he generalises about the anxieties of Roman citizens on such occasions: 'They then ponder the chances of war, the uncertain outcome of fortune, the risks of battle; the defeats caused by the ignorance and impetuousness of leaders, the victories won by honourable prudence and courage. What man can tell which of these mental attitudes and which outcome will attend the consul whom they are dispatching to war?'[1] The importance of Livy's skilful, unobtrusive use of *oratio obliqua* in the depiction of such attitudes should be acknowledged. Sometimes they are the reactions of peoples in assembly—as in his assessment of Athenian sentiment about the war with Philip, or the feelings of helplessness which the Achaeans experience at the Sicyon council. Frequently the opposed factions of the state are thus analysed, or the impelling motives of combatants: 'The battle became fierce on both sides, because the Romans fought with anger and hatred, and the Aequi were driven to the furthest pitch of daring and exertion through the awareness that their danger was the outcome of guilt; they had no hope that trust would again be reposed in them.'[2] In the fourth decade, under Polybian influence, a standard method of recounting operations is devised, in which there is invariably a prefatory comment on a commander's intention or an army's mental attitude before an engagement.[3]

[1] XLII, 49.
[2] Athenians, xxxi, 14; Achaeans, xxxii, 19; opposing factions in the state, v, 14, 2, etc.; Romans and Aequi, iii, 2, 11.
[3] For the fourth-decade pattern of introduction, psychological observation, action, see xxxii, 17, 4–6; 23, 4ff.; xxxiii, 17, 2ff.; xxxv, 26, etc. E. Burck, *Die Erzählungskunst des T. Livius*, 213 ff., gives good examples from i–v, effectively showing that this aspect is more important in Livy's eyes than a detailed account of the events themselves.

Also conspicuous as a feature of Livy's psychological treatment is his assessment of the influence on Roman armies of their belief in the efficacy of prayers and ritual. It is the psychological factor rather than the religious which is often stressed. When Appius Claudius Caecus vows a temple to Bellona, the gesture inspires his soldiers and himself *velut instigante dea*; compare the result in Romulus and his fellow-Romans after a temple is vowed to Jupiter: 'The Romans resisted as though bidden by a heavenly voice.'[1] The phraseology used indicates Livy's appreciation of the salutary effect such appeals to the supernatural can exercise on the morale of an army.

It can rightly be claimed, therefore, that by such insight into psychological factors Livy compensates in part for inexactitudes of fact. Further, the analysis of character (in the case of individuals like Africanus) with all its minor inaccuracies wins for the reader a readier understanding of Roman achievements. This ability to analyse personalities and motives in subtle fashion enhances Livy's claims to be considered a critical historian of some merit.[2] In this respect his insight is much superior to that of Dionysius when they recount the same event.[3]

Unfortunately, Livy has not been able to resist the allure of dramatic techniques, and so does not draw Collingwood's rigid demarcation between thoughts and emotions. The 'thrills and chills' are continually emphasised. Most notable are the lengthy descriptions of the scenes in Rome following upon the announcement of defeat or victory. His portrait of the capital after the defeat at Lake Trasimene is especially pathetic, with its evocation of the feelings of the womenfolk as they stand at the gates to witness the survivors' arrival, and its mention of the two mothers who died of happiness when

---

[1] x, 19, 18; 1, 12, 7. See I. Kajanto, *God and Fate in Livy*, 28.
[2] So R. S. Conway, *PCA* (1921), 84–6.
[3] See the comments of E. Burck, *op. cit.* 230 f.

their sons unexpectedly returned.[1] Twice as many chapters are devoted to depiction of Roman reactions after Cannae as to the battle itself, so that Livy may impress us with the native courage and determination adapting themselves to the critical situation.[2] After the disaster of the Allia, the Gauls' hesitation in entering the deserted city streets and the nervous tension of the townsfolk are brilliantly portrayed.[3] In contrast to such pictures of grief and dismay is the account of the joy and bewilderment of the Greeks when Flamininus proclaimed their liberation at the Corinthian games, or again, of the helplessness and anger felt by the Aetolian assembly when Glabrio imposed harsh terms upon them.[4]

The dangers of such emphasis on emotions are obvious, but they have also a certain justification. Livy perpetually seeks to communicate with the minds of the men of the past, to relive the mental and emotional experiences felt. Only thus, he implies, can one begin to understand that though the accidents of place and time are different, the essential experiences of humankind never change. The humane man finds no obstacle in time and space to the extension of his sympathy and compassion. So Livy invites us to travel in spirit to the scenes of desolation at Alba Longa in the first years of Rome's existence, when Tullus Hostilius decided that it must be destroyed, and the inhabitants removed to Rome:

In the meantime, the cavalry had been sent on to Alba to convey the population to Rome, and then the legions were marched there to destroy the city. When they entered the gates, there was none of the confusion and panic which one associates with captured cities when the gates have been forced open, the walls levelled with the ram, or the citadel stormed, and the shouts

---

[1] XXII, 7, 6. Note (with E. Burck, *Einführung in die dritte Dekade des Livius*, 82) the influence of Hellenistic 'tragic' methods.

[2] Burck, *Einführung*, 92: 'Er wünschst, möglichst eindringlich die nationale und ethische Wandlung und Festigung des römischen Volkes zu entwickeln....'

[3] V, 40f.   [4] XXXIII, 32f.; XXXVI, 29. See Ch. VII.

and rushing movements of the armed foe fill the whole city with slaughter and flame. Instead there was a grim silence, a speechless sorrow which so paralysed men's spirits that their minds fear-struck could frame no plan, and they repeatedly asked each other what they should abandon, and what they should take with them. Now they stood at their thresholds, now they wandered aimlessly through the dwellings which they were then to see for the last time. And now the shouts of the Roman cavalry pressingly bade them leave, the din of houses being dismantled in the furthest areas of the city was heard, and the dust rising from distant places entered the whole area like a gathering cloud. They rapidly snatched what they could, and abandoned the gods, the homes in which each had been born and bred; an unending stream of refugees filled the streets; in each one the sight of the others renewed the tears which sprang from reciprocated pity, and affecting words were heard from the women especially as they passed by venerable temples beleaguered by armed troops, and left their gods as prisoners.[1]

The anachronisms are obvious. This is what the destruction of a populous Hellenistic city would be like in the time of Ennius, who notably influences Livy's account here.[2] The city has 'distant areas', the houses are large enough to 'wander aimlessly' through, the temples are *augusta*. The scene which Livy's portrait evokes could not be more unlike an Italian settlement of the eighth or seventh century B.C. Yet this is no idle rhetoric, 'thrills and chills' manufactured by a dispassionate, unengaged craftsman. The dispossessed inhabitants, their dazed helplessness, and unavailing piety awaken in us the same compassion as we feel for Lidice. This is emphatically unscientific history. Yet there is a wider sense in which it may be called historical. Livy's imaginative insight has recaptured authentic human suffering. Such explicit awareness, when directed towards the various facets of ancestral Rome, recreates for us the spirit, the *Geisteswelt* of the Romans more revealingly than any other writer.

[1] I, 29.   [2] Below, 257.

VII

LIVY'S LITERARY METHODS

IN the eyes of the first-century Romans, the ideal historian was something more than a Polybius seeking to describe events as they happened, and accounting for them in a scientific spirit; Cicero repeatedly demands that Roman historians should pay greater attention to questions of literary presentation.[1] As Livy's achievement largely fulfils the requirements which Cicero posited, an analysis of the purely literary approach, which might well be irrelevant in the study of a modern historian, is of importance for a full appreciation of the *Ab Urbe Condita*. Livy's interests and his talent lie pre-eminently in his adaptation of the material in his sources to the elegant form of Augustan prose.

Noteworthy first is the artistic skill which lies behind the general organisation of the material; the *Ab Urbe Condita* is carefully divided into pentads.[2] The care bestowed on the construction of these units can be exemplified by analysis of the third decade; the division is not merely chronological. Book xxv ends with the defeat of the Scipios in Spain in 212—the last decisive Carthaginian success before the tide turned in Rome's favour. Each pentad has thus a compositional unity, the first being dominated by Hannibal and the Carthaginian successes, the second by Roman retaliation, beginning with the victories at Capua, Tarentum, and New Carthage in xxvi. (Note how each book in xxi–xxv begins by discussing Carthaginian activity, and in xxvi–xxx by a description from the Roman viewpoint.)

[1] Above, 32 ff.　　　[2] Above, 5 ff.

Because of Livy's decision to write annalistically, describing successively the separate theatres of activity, each book cannot invariably be a self-contained whole, embracing 'actions complete in themselves from beginning to end' as some Hellenistic historians sought to do.[1] Some early books have such an artistic unity; Book I takes in the entire Regal period, and v the capture of Veii and the Gauls' entry into Rome, events closely interconnected in Livy's narrative.[2] On the other hand the major events of the second pentad are not allotted separate books. Livy begins the First Samnite War in the middle of vii, and the Second (327–304) towards the end of viii. Again in the later decades the individual books have no self-contained unity.

Within this framework, Livy's main preoccupation in the organisation of his material is the need for *variatio*. In the early books, for example, where the two main themes are external warfare and domestic discord, it is instructive to observe how he sacrifices continuity and clarity by alternating between them in the interests of such variation. This aim should be remembered in any consideration of his annalistic arrangement, with its abrupt changes from continuous narrative of external events to the appointment lists at the termination of each year. Such lists, with their details of domestic problems and decisions, provide a respite from the narrative of campaigning in territory often unfamiliar to his readers.[3]

---

[1] Diodorus XVI, 1, 1: καθήκει τοὺς συγγραφεῖς περιλαμβάνειν ἐν ταῖς βίβλοις... πράξεις αὐτοτελεῖς ἀπ' ἀρχῆς μέχρι τοῦ τέλους.

[2] E. Burck, *Die Erzählungskunst des T. Livius*, 193, sees also a self-contained unity in iii, '...indem es in der ersten Hälfte in einer aufsteigendenden Linie die Entwicklung behandelt, die von der *lex Icilia* an zur Einrichtung des Decemvirats führt, in der zweiten aber den Sturz der Decemvirn und die Wiederherstellung der alten *res publica*'.

[3] This aim of *variatio* is observable not merely in such general organisation of material, but even in such details as magistrate lists. Note for example the incidental introduction of the names of new consuls at iii, 2, 1–2: 'Q. Servilius insequenti anno—is enim cum Sp. Postumio consul fuit—in Aequos missus.... extractum in tertium annum bellum est Q. Fabio et T. Quinctio consulibus.'

Livy's deliberate choice of annalistic presentation (emphasised by the choice of subject, *a primordio urbis* and not a unified theme) makes inevitable the commencement of each year with the inauguration of magistrates, the allotment of provinces, the disposition of troops, the enumeration of prodigies, the petitions of embassies. There follow the year's campaigning and the depiction of other noteworthy events; and finally come details of political elections and sacerdotal matters. Such political and religious detail had considerable sentimental appeal in Augustan Rome. The names and activities of petty functionaries had a local attraction for those who held the same religious and political posts, and for those alert for gentile connections, however remote. Following the example of earlier annalists, Livy heightens the sentimental and dramatic interest by lengthy depiction of religious ceremony or political controversy. The citation of archaic formulae, with their emotive overtones, in the ceremonial associated with imposing historical occasions is frequently to be observed, and accounts of political assemblies are enlivened by details of controversies involving officials or candidates.[1]

Such preoccupation with religious and political ceremonial reflects a general interest in antiquarian studies in the Augustan age; like Ovid in the *Fasti*, Livy links earlier ritual with present-day survivals.[2] Citations of archaic formulae are ubiquitous in the first decade, from the proclamation of Numa as king to Appius Claudius' solemn promise of a temple to Bellona: 'Bellona, si hodie nobis victoriam duis, ast ego tibi templum voveo.'[3] The importance attached by Livy to the evocation of the

---

Burck, *Die Erzählungskunst*, 9 f., quotes sundry other examples from this book; Kroll, *Studien zum Verständnis der römischen Literatur*, 363, exemplifies the technique from Book II. See also his general comments on Livy's *variatio*, 361 ff.

[1] Ch. VI, 168, n. I.

[2] E.g. I, 17, 9: 'hodie quoque in legibus magistratibusque rogandis usurpatur idem ius, vi adempta...'.   [3] I, 18, 9; x, 19, 17.

religious solemnity of such moments can be gauged by the lengthy quotation of Scipio's prayer before landing in Africa, and of the vow to Jupiter made by Manius Acilius after the declaration of war on Antiochus,[1] for it is only in such contexts of ceremonial that Livy quotes verbatim Latin which would grate on the Augustan ear as 'horridum atque inconditum'.

Equally significant is Livy's constant attempt to enliven the jejune lists of political and religious appointments with dramatic elaboration, though the imaginative groundwork has often been laid by his sources. Livy vividly portrays the scene when Q. Fabius' unwillingness to stand as consul provokes a demonstration:[2] 'circumstare sellam omnis nobilitas; orare ut ex caeno plebeio consulatum extraheret, maiestatemque pristinam cum honori tum patriciis gentibus redderet'. Perhaps the most notable of many such disputes described in the third decade is the lengthy contention between Fabius Cunctator and Scipio Africanus on general questions of military strategy.[3] The increasingly copious documentary evidence available on second-century political assemblies ensures that in the fourth and fifth decades almost all the appointment lists are accompanied by a commentary on differences of policy, or on problems which exercise the new officials or the Senate as a whole.[4]

Thus Livy found in his sources a framework which provided 'the means of expression by which he could evoke a response to the appeal of political and religious traditionalism'.[5] How does he build up his narrative to achieve this end? The organisation of his material can be rightly assessed only by remembering his method of composition. His choice of a main source for a particular sequence of events shapes his compositional arrange-

---

[1] XXIX, 27, 1–4; XXXVI, 2, 3–5.   [2] X, 15, 9.
[3] XXVIII, 40 ff.   [4] XXXIV, 43, 4–5; XLI, 7.
[5] A. H. McDonald, *JRS* (1957), 159.

ment; it would be wrong to assume that he first unearthed the facts, and later clothed them in a literary garb independently of the source. On the basis of his main source he constructs his historical narrative in accordance with Ciceronian canons of *exaedificatio* and *exornatio*. Cicero demands for *exaedificatio* a chronological order of events, topographical exposition, the pattern of strategy, events, result, and an analysis of the causes of this outcome; and finally an estimate of the prominent persons involved, with biographical detail.[1] Livy found much of this already in his sources. He has merely to add the necessary information, and then concentrate on enhanced literary effects.

In such expanded accounts of political controversy at Rome, and in the narrative of foreign campaigning, one can observe the indirect influence of Hellenistic techniques of 'rhetorical' and 'tragic' history. Livy parades his rhetorical accomplishments especially in speeches, which are carefully worked into an apt historical context to characterise the persons concerned, and to lend significance to the occasions on which they were uttered. In Livy's narrative there is not that perpetual preoccupation with the rhetorician's repertoire, the careful choice and arrangement of words and 'figures', which so marks the writing of a Tacitus. But rhetorical devices are prominent in those sections of the narrative which Livy seeks to portray in a dramatic way, so as to engender in the reader emotions of ἔκπληξις and συμπάθεια. The realisation that he has on occasion succumbed to these 'tragic' tendencies has its relevance to an assessment of his value as historian; he does not scruple to indulge in dramatic effects such as a scientific scrutiny of events would expose as distorted history.

Livy's purpose, then, is not merely to instruct and edify, but also to affect his readers with that 'pity and fear' at

[1] Above, 32; cf. McDonald, 160f.

which many Hellenistic historians aimed. It is worth noting how regularly the words *ira, indignatio, rabies, pavor, trepidatio, maestitia,* and the like recur. Yet because he took his duties as historian seriously, he did not seek to manufacture occasions on which such dramatic effects could be continually exploited. He follows his sources faithfully, awaiting the opportunity to create or enhance a dramatic situation only when suitable events—crises in battle, excitement in assemblies, human situations of a fearful, pathetic, or romantic kind—are being described. This temperate use of dramatic techniques has artistic value; the intervening passages, more prosaically related, enable the tension built up to be relaxed. As one notable example of such artistic restraint, observe how, at the end of the third decade, when the reader is surfeited with the drama of the closing of the war in Africa, Livy avoids the long picturesque account of the triumph of his hero Africanus which the sources contained.[1]

Livy often divides his narrative into episodes constructed according to the Aristotelian precepts governing tragedy; they have a beginning, a middle, and an end.[2] The structure of the separate episode, paralleled by Vergil's narrative technique in the *Aeneid*, embodies a main feature on which the description is centred. The events leading up to this are summarised in one or two introductory sentences (ἀρχή), and the subsequent results are briefly delineated (τέλος). For example, Polybius' account of the siege of Abydus, extending over five chapters, is compressed into an episode of a chapter's length, in which the main description (τὸ μέσον) is of the mad conduct of the Abydenes; all other aspects—the initial resistance of the townsmen, their offer of surrender, their desperate resistance to the 'unconditional surrender' call of Philip,

---

[1] xxx, 45. Compare the more dramatic versions of Appian, *Pun.* 66; Silius Italicus, XVII, 625 ff.
[2] E. Burck, *Die Erzählungskunst*, 182 ff.

and their ultimate submission—are relegated to the two-sentence introduction or to the brief conclusion. But the central section is expanded to allow Livy to depict in psychological vein the motives and emotional reactions which led to the mass suicide.[1]

The introductory sentences in such episodes are frequently constructed with the pluperfect tense, for, by thus relegating events prior to the main description to an earlier time, the historian can avoid detailed mention of them;[2] and on some occasions the insertion of a phrase like 'per eos forte dies' ('about that time *it chanced* that such-and-such happened') helps to avoid the tedious narration of minor details anterior to the central description.[3]

Another apposite example of the composed episode is the narration of the Roman capture of Gabii; Livy's technique can be observed by comparison with the account of Dionysius. In a brief summary, Livy first outlines the initial attempts of Tarquinius Superbus to seize the city by storm and blockade; Dionysius' lengthy version indicates the scope of Livy's compression. Livy's central description depicts the simulated desertion of Tarquinius' son Sextus, his energetic activity within the town of Gabii, and his appointment there as army commander. It is especially notable how the action here centres on Sextus. Dionysius recounts a long story of a messenger sent by Sextus to his father requesting instructions, which Superbus gave by the cryptic decapitation of poppies; Livy adverts to this in a single sentence, and instantly refocuses the attention on Sextus. Finally, Livy's brief conclusion records only the betrayal of the town to the Roman king, without the details of the treatment of the captured town which Dionysius outlines.[4]

[1] For Abydus see below, 194f.
[2] XXXI, 14, 6; 21, 1; XXXIII, 3, 2; 12, 1; 16, 2, etc.
[3] VI, 17, 7; XXII, 33, 1; XXXIII, 3, 6; XLII, 17, etc. See K. Witte, *RhM* (1910), 299ff.   [4] I, 53, 4ff.; Dionys. IV, 53ff. See Burck, 183.

Some events, being of a more extended nature, cannot be narrated in a single episode. This is true, for example, of the siege of Saguntum. Livy here contrives an artistic division of the whole event into scenes which develop to the climax.[1] Again, the patrician–plebeian conflict culminating in the establishment of the tribunate is organised in three such scenes. The first describes the sudden appearance in the forum of an ex-centurion, now enslaved (our pity is awakened by pathetic touches—filthy clothing, physical emaciation, and unkempt appearance in a man who had served the state with distinction), and the subsequent disagreement between Appius Claudius and the gentle Servilius on how to quell the disturbances thus provoked. Servilius promises concessions in the face of a sudden Volscian attack. After an interval of warfare, the second scene reveals how Appius prevails in his policy of renewed oppression, and in the ensuing anarchy M'. Valerius has to be proclaimed dictator to deal with further external attacks. After a second interval of fighting, the final scene details the secession of the *plebs* to the Mons Sacer, which wrings from the patricians the establishment of plebeian magistrates.[2] By such piecemeal description the dramatic tension is sustained, and the readers' emotions readily reengaged. The three acts are incontestably sections of an artistic whole, the Aristotelian ὅλη καὶ τελεία πρᾶξις.

Livy, then, plans his history largely in carefully constructed episodes; but this does not result in a series of disconnected pieces, as he skilfully links the various scenes by artistic devices; the school of rhetoric taught him a useful lesson here.[3] Often the transition is achieved by

---

[1] Below, 196.

[2] II, 23–4; 27–30, 7; 31, 7–33, 3. Dionysius' arrangement (VI, 22–90) is quite different; see Burck, *Die Erzählungskunst*, 62 ff. Another good example is the war with Veii undertaken by the *Fabia gens*. Act I, the Senate's authorisation of the request, and the moving scene as the Fabii ride out (II, 48, 7–49, 8); then, after an interval (a Veientine attack on Cremera), comes Act II, the ambush and slaughter of the Roman heroes (II, 50).

[3] Quint. IV, 1, 77.

relating the journey of a major person involved from one locality to another; in proceeding from the narrative of Antiochus' love-affair in Euboea to events in Boeotia, Livy mentions Antiochus' journey there, whereas his source Polybius had passed directly to the new topic of Boeotian affairs.[1] Again, when Livy turns from a council at Sicyon to the siege of Corinth, he avoids the bald change of topic by mentioning the decision of the council to send troops to Corinth, and by accompanying them, so to speak, to that city, describing the scene there as it met the eyes of the Achaean contingent.[2] Such integration of episodes can be achieved only within a particular theatre of operations; and Livy's decision to write annalistically, reviewing events year by year in widely dispersed areas, makes a completely unbroken narrative impossible.

Livy's dramatic power emerges chiefly in the central description of the individual episode. Here he seeks to achieve the graphic presentation (ἐνάργεια) aimed at by those who favoured a dramatic view of history; he becomes 'le peintre de la luxure, de l'avarice, de la cruauté, de l'horreur enfin',[3] and over and above this portrays the emotions of communities—their grief, their joy, their panic, their *rabies*.

One of Livy's rare scenes of horror is the sight confronting the victorious Carthaginians after Cannae:

Next day at dawn, the Carthaginian forces hastened to gather the spoils and to view the scene of slaughter grisly even for an enemy to look upon. Thousand upon thousand of Roman cavalry and infantry lay scattered in groups where they had chanced to fight and flee. Some blood-stained figures arose from the scene of carnage; their wounds had closed with the morning cold, and this had revived them. The enemy felled them. Some

---

[1] xxxvi, 6; compare Pol. xx, 7.
[2] xxxii, 23. Other examples, vii, 12, 1 f.; xxi, 49–51; xxxi, 24; 33, 5–6; xxxvi, 21, 6. See Walsh, *RhM* (1954), 112 f.
[3] L. Catin, *En lisant Tite-Live* (Paris, 1944), 148.

lay alive with sinews of thigh or knee severed, and when the
enemy came upon them they bared their necks and throats,
bidding them drain what blood they still possessed. Some
were found with heads plunged into holes in the ground, and
it was clear that they had made pits for themselves, in which
they had thrust their heads, thrown earth over them, and thus
suffocated. The chief sight which attracted universal attention
was of a Numidian who was dragged from beneath a Roman.
The Numidian was alive, but his ears and nose had been
mangled by the Roman, whose hands had been unable to grasp
a weapon, and who, failing to control his rage, had died whilst
attacking the enemy with his teeth.[1]

Grisly in a different sense is the description of the
disease which afflicted both sides in the Roman siege of
Syracuse. Here Livy has consciously adverted to Thucydides' celebrated account of the Athenian plague, but his
treatment presents the utmost contrast; Livy is concerned
not to unfold the symptoms of the sufferers but to exploit
the inherent pathos of the situation:

For it was autumn, and the region naturally unhealthy. . . . The
intolerably intense heat affected almost everyone in both camps.
First men fell ill and began to perish because of the unhealthiness
of the season and region; then the disease spread, because people
came into contact with the sick through tending them. The result
was that when men fell ill, they either died through neglect and
solitude, or they dragged to death with them their nurses, who
became equally affected by the virulence of the disease through
tending them. Every day there were burials and deaths before
men's eyes, and day and night lamentation was universally heard.
Finally they became so accustomed to and brutalised by their evil
fate that they not merely refrained from escorting the dead with
tears and customary mourning, but did not even carry them out
to burial. There the corpses lay in full view of those awaiting a
similar death; and so, through fear and disease and the deadly

---

[1] XXII, 51, 5–9. Another good example is at XXXI, 34, where the Macedonians
are confronted with the sight of their dead, mutilated by the Spanish short-
sword. One may also recall a grisly night battle between the Romans and the
Aequi and Volsci (IV, 27–9).

odour, the dead bodies brought to destruction the sick, and the sick the healthy. Some preferred to die by the sword, and rushed unaccompanied into the enemy guard-posts....[1]

But gory, lurid details such as these passages portray are rare, for they are not in harmony with the more civilised tastes of the Augustan age. Thus the description in Polybius of the manifold ghastly ways in which the Abydenes sought self-inflicted death is avoided by Livy with the phrase 'per omnes vias leti'.[2] Again in the first book, after a brief explanation of the barbarous method by which Mettius Fufetius was executed, Livy simply adds: 'All turned their eyes from the utter grisliness of the sight.' But Dionysius is inhibited by no such delicacy or restraint.[3]

Emphasis is however often laid on the terror experienced by individuals in fearful situations, even at the price of distortion of the facts.[4] Perhaps the outstanding example of Livy's evocation of such terror and awe is his description of the Carthaginians when confronted with the towering Alps. The effect of ἐνάργεια is conspicuously achieved here:

Then, though the actuality had been anticipated by rumour, by which things unknown are often exaggerated, the sight from near at hand of the height of the mountains, the snows almost mingling with the sky, the unsightly huts perched on the rocks, the cattle and mules shrivelled with cold, the inhabitants unshaven and unkempt, all things alive and inanimate alike stiff with frost—these and other sights grislier to behold than to describe revived their panic.[5]

---

[1] xxv, 26, 7 ff.   [2] xxxi, 18, 7; compare Pol. xvi, 34.
[3] I, 28, 10; Dionys. III, 30, 5. Burck, *Die Erzählungskunst*, 206 f., contrasts prevalent Hellenistic practices with Livy's less sensational narrations of the capture of cities and camps.
[4] Above, 162 f.
[5] xxi, 32, 7. For a similarly powerful picture see xxi, 53, the attempted crossing of the Apennines, an excellent example of the 'pity and fear' sought in such passages.

Also frequent is the depiction of joyful emotions, as at the Corinthian games at which Flamininus announced the liberation of Greece. Here Livy has lent enhanced dramatic effects to the version of his source. Polybius says that such a din arose at the beginning of the announcement that 'some did not hear it, others wished to hear it again, whilst the majority were incredulous, and thinking that they heard the announcement, as it were, in a dream because of the unexpected nature of the event, demanded that the herald should advance and repeat the proclamation'. Livy's version ignores those who had not heard the message, and concentrates the attention on the psychological impact felt by those who did hear it: 'At the words of the herald, their joy was too great to contain in its entirety. Each one could scarcely believe that he heard aright; they looked at each other in wonder as though they had seen the unsubstantial figure of a dream; every individual, unable to trust the evidence of his own ears, questioned his neighbours.'[1] This stunned reaction of silent joy underlines the astonished gratitude of the Greeks to the Romans in an effective and quite unhistorical manner. Later, where Polybius is content to remark that when the tumult had subsided no one paid further attention to the athletes, Livy claims that 'the games were hastily concluded, for no one was concentrating eyes or mind on the performance'. Minor inaccuracies are condoned to accentuate the dramatic effect.

Livy evokes this atmosphere of stunned joy on numerous occasions. When the result of the battle of the Metaurus is announced at Rome, the inhabitants 'received the news with their ears rather than with their minds at first, for it was greater and more joyful than they could imagine or sufficiently believe'.[2] Livy also describes how, after the battle of Pydna in 168, the rumour of victory reached the city during the celebration of public games.

[1] xxxiii, 32, 6 ff.; compare Pol. xviii, 46, 6.   [2] xxvii, 50, 7.

There is a sudden concerted murmur; then the din increases, and finally shouting and clapping breaks out. When the news is confirmed thirteen days after the battle, a high proportion of the spectators abandon the games and bear the joyful news to their wives and children.[1] Similar, too, is the scene in the camp of Tiberius Gracchus after his successful battle with Hanno, when the freedom of the slaves is announced: 'Now they embrace and congratulate each other, now they raise their arms to heaven, and pray that every blessing may attend on the Roman people and on Gracchus himself.'[2]

In such episodes, then, and likewise in such scenes of grief and anger as were mentioned in the previous chapter,[3] Livy seeks to portray emotional reactions by a vivid, imaginative and often imaginary reconstruction of crowd scenes. How is the graphic effect achieved? Especially conspicuous are the uses of asyndeton, short clauses, accumulation of words and expressions, historic presents and historic infinitives. The swift enumeration of successive events in pithy, staccato clauses builds up a vivid portrait of hasty action or overflowing emotion: 'signum ex arce dare iubent. itaque ad portas, ad muros discurrunt'.[4] Or again, Livy's delineation of a settlement of domestic differences at Rome, when *equites* and *plebs* promise voluntary service; the senators parade the forum, 'voce manibusque significare publicam laetitiam, beatam urbem Romanam et invictam et aeternam illa concordia dicere, laudare equites, laudare plebem, diem ipsum laudibus ferre, victam esse fateri comitatem benignitatemque senatus. certatim patribus plebique manare gaudio lacrimae....'[5]

Very often the pictorial effect is assisted by an account of an assembly, a town under assault, or an army in action

---

[1] XLV, I.　　　　　　　[2] XXIV, 16, 10.
[3] Above, 170f.　　　　　[4] XXXI, 24, 5.
[5] V, 7, 9–11.

depicted not in general terms but by the description of the
reactions of individuals or small groups. As Quintilian
puts it, 'minus est tamen totum dicere quam omnia'.[1]
This technique of 'division' of a crowd is especially frequent in scenes of disorder or confusion. Note how Livy
depicts the haste of the Roman fleet at Teos in 190 when
enemy fleet movements were reported: 'There was panic
similar to that in a sudden fire or a captured city; *some*
rushed to the city to summon back their comrades, *others*
made for the ships at full speed....'[2] This device is continually found with such combinations as *alius...alius,
partim...partim, alibi...alibi, nunc...nunc*.[3]

By the use of such stylistic techniques Livy seeks to
lend vividness and greater dramatic force to the material
found in his sources. But it is not merely a question of
stylistic arrangement; he often adds imaginative touches
which enhance the pictorial quality of his writing. For
example, he read in Polybius that, at the battle of Cynoscephalae, Philip in his advance 'found the summits of the
hills deserted' by the Romans; his own version pic-
turesquely adds that 'there lay upon the hills a few enemy
corpses and scattered arms'.[4] (One is powerfully reminded here of the description of the scene after the battle
at Lake Trasimene: 'As the sun's heat grew and the mist
was dispelled, revealing the light of day, the mountains
and plains in the bright sunshine exposed to view the
defeat, the repulsive sight of the Roman line mown to the
ground.'[5]) Or again, observe how he elaborates on
Polybius' description of the misty scene before the engagement at Cynoscephalae. Polybius tells us that 'at
dawn all the mist from the clouds came down to ground
level, so that the prevailing darkness made it impossible

---

[1] *Inst. Or.* VIII, 3, 70.   [2] XXXVII, 29, 4.
[3] E.g. XXXI, 3, 5; 35, 5; 39, 8; 41, 10; XXXII, 22, 1; XXXIII, 46, 8.
[4] XXXIII, 8, 9: 'iacentibus ibi paucis armis corporibusque hostium...', and
Pol. XVIII, 24, 3: ...ἐρήμους κατέλαβε τοὺς ἄκρους.
[5] XXII, 6, 9.

to see even those close at hand'; Livy's imaginative version recounts how 'a mist so thick had blotted out the daylight that the standard-bearers could not see their way, and the soldiers could not sight the standards. The line of march wandered in the direction of vague shouts, and disorder ensued such as if they had lost their way at night.'[1]

Skilful choice of words is prominent in the achievement of this pictorial effect. Where Polybius describes the Aetolians as *deriding* a peace offer, Livy's phrase, 'clam mussantes carpebant', illustrates vividly (if inaccurately) the people whom he continually characterises as ineffectual grumblers.[2] Again, during the Roman invasion of Gallograecia in 189, Polybius tells us, some priests of the cult of Cybele approached Manlius Vulso, saying (φάσκοντες) that the goddess prophesied a Roman victory. Livy's account portrays them as chanting the message, 'vaticinantes fanatico carmine'.[3] Perhaps most striking of all is Livy's description of the Gaul who fought the duel with Manlius Torquatus. According to the traditional version as reflected by Claudius Quadrigarius, he is naked (*nudus*), but Livy decks him out in bright garments and gleaming arms—'versicolori veste pictisque et auro caelatis refulgens armis'.[4]

Such comparisons with the source-material elaborated by Livy best demonstrate his constant preoccupation with ἐνάργεια. A second feature of which such systematic comparison makes us aware is his technique of compression (συντομία). He had of course set himself definite limits in his history by the avowed intention of omitting anything irrelevant to Roman affairs; he speaks of the plan 'by which I decided not to touch upon external topics save where they are concerned with Roman

---

[1] xxxiii, 7, 2; Pol. xviii, 20, 7.
[2] xxxiii, 31, 1; Pol. xviii, 45, 1: κατελάλουν τὸ δόγμα.
[3] xxxviii, 18, 9; Pol. xxi, 37, 5.
[4] vii, 10, 7; Claudius' version is at Gell. ix, 13.

matters'.[1] With this rule he is not fully consistent. Where an event has surpassing human interest, or sheds discreditable light on Rome's enemies, he cannot resist including it. He records the circumstances of Philopoemen's death in view of the hero's fame and the strange circumstances; for a similar reason the incredible adventures of Masinissa, before Scipio Africanus' arrival in Africa, are included for their dramatic and romantic content; and the heroism of Theoxena, who tried with husband and children to escape from the Macedonians to Euboea, is unfolded—a story which depicts in terms of human suffering the evil Macedonian menace once again confronting Rome.[2]

In his description of external affairs relevant to Roman interests, Livy sifts from events or discussions the topics of more absorbing interest for his audience. For example, in a description of a visit to Antiochus of embassies from Elea and Epirus, Polybius allots to each a similar length of account; Livy dismisses the Eleans in a few words, and devotes a longer account to the Epirotes, presumably because of the closer proximity of that state to Rome.[3]

Livy's technique of compression has an obvious connection with his dramatic presentation. Thus in describing the conference between the Romans and Antiochus at Lysimachia in 196, where he is at pains to focus attention on the antithetical speeches of the two sides, he omits all mention of the remarks of the representatives of Smyrna and Lampsacus which followed the main speeches. To have included them would have drawn the reader's attention from the clash of the main contestants, and from that

---

[1] XXXIX, 48, 6; compare VIII, 24, 18; XXXIII, 20, 13.

[2] XXXIX, 49–50; XXIX, 30ff.; XL, 4.

[3] XXXVI, 5; Pol. XX, 3. Note also at XXXVII, 25, 9 how Livy omits mention of Pleuratus of Illyria and expands the comment on Masinissa, who was better known to his readers (contrast Pol. XXI, 11, 1 (the source), where both are mentioned). Precisely the same technique is found at XXXVII, 53, 21 f. (Pol. XXI, 22, 2–5).

atmosphere of implacable enmity which he seeks to achieve in describing conferences of this type.[1]

Above all, it is in his episode construction[2] that his compression of his sources for artistic purposes is to be found, for he lends prominence to a particular event by summarising or omitting all occurrences immediately prior or subsequent to it. In addition to this general aim, the different types of narrative have their stock techniques of συντομία. We shall see, for example, how in accounts of troop movements Livy abbreviates the source-content without loss of clarity; or again, how in dialogue scenes he eliminates all topics that impede the incisive progress of the discussion.[3]

Another literary principle constantly in Livy's mind, and adopted from Hellenistic procedure, is his aim of clarification (σαφήνεια).[4] He constantly seeks to clarify points of geography or history, local custom or recondite terms, the knowledge of which his source assumed in the reader. Especially common are insertions of geographical detail, clarifying the topography of battles, cities, and natural features.[5] Elsewhere there is parenthetic historical information; when he discusses occurrences in the area of Amphilochia and the Dolopes in 189, he recounts recent events there—information of which there is no trace in his source.[6] In his account of the struggle with the Samnites he outlines the site of Palaeopolis and the origin of its inhabitants.[7] He is careful to explain such specialised Greek terms as *hemerodromos* and *apocletoi*.[8] He shows an intelligent interest in the clarification of procedure in city councils and assemblies, as in his description of the entry of Attalus into Athens. Polybius is con-

[1] XXXIII, 39f.; Pol. XVIII, 50–2. (For a similar example of a conference symbolic of national enmity see XXXI, 18, 1–4, and the comment of A. H. McDonald, *PCA* (1938), 25.)   [2] Above, 178f.
[3] Ch. VIII.   [4] Above, 38.
[5] Above, 156f.   [6] XXXVIII, 3, 4.
[7] VIII, 22, 5.   [8] XXXI, 24, 4; XXXV, 34, 2.

fused here; he suggests that the Athenians voted the king extraordinary honours immediately upon his arrival, before the assembly was convened. Livy transposes the ceremony to a later point in the proceedings, when the reception of the king in the streets was over; the privileges are bestowed in the assembly, the obvious place for the conferment of such honours.[1] Similar procedural clarification is achieved in Livy's account of the election of the Boeotarch Brachyllas in 196.[2]

The other main principle observed by Livy in transcription of his sources is credibility in narration (πιθανότης). This affects him as historian rather than literary artist, and accordingly need not detain us here.

Livy's literary approach can thus be summarised as follows. He utilises one main source, reorganises the structural arrangement, and introduces new material to achieve more dramatic effects. He compresses or omits the less interesting content, using as criteria the purpose of his work and the interests of his audience. Then, in addition to these literary aims of ἐνάργεια and συντομία, he seeks to fulfil his historian's duties of σαφήνεια and πιθανότης. The literary techniques appropriate to different types of episode can now be examined in the light of this general procedure.

---

[1] XXXI, 15, 6; Pol. XVI, 25, 8; 26, 1.
[2] XXXIII, 27, 8; Pol. XVIII, 43, 3. For other examples of σαφήνεια see H. Nissen, *Kritische Untersuchungen*, 74f.

VIII

THE NARRATIVE: LITERARY
GENRES

IN the previous chapter, the principles of Livy's
literary art were outlined in general terms. But it is
important to realise that, following a procedure well
established amongst some Hellenistic historians, he had
developed stock methods of describing particular types of
episode. Especially notable is his tendency towards uni-
formity of treatment of sieges, battle accounts, dialogues
between leading personalities, conferences in general, and
'human' situations of a dramatic or pathetic kind.

I

In ancient warfare, and especially in such offensive operations as Rome undertook overseas, sieges and blockades
were a feature of virtually every campaign. For the historian like Livy, whose aim was not merely to instruct
but also to engage his readers, they posed a difficult
problem, for unless there were some unusual method of
attack or other distinguishing feature, the narrative of
stereotyped operations would quickly become monotonous. Livy solves the problem by the general expedient
of focusing the attention on the persons under siege. He
thus exploits that facility for psychological observation
which is always so prominent in his writing, and here
especially demonstrates his affinities with the 'tragic'
approach so popular in Hellenistic historiography. Nor
should this be construed as mere sensationalism; the
increasingly humanitarian spirit of the Augustan age, like

the Athens of Menander, is reflected in this compassionate approach.

This emphasis on the courage, anguish, uncertainty, and desperation of the besieged enables Livy largely to ignore the technical devices used by both sides. Such lack of interest in siege machinery detracts from the historical value of his narration, as in the siege of Syracuse,[1] where there is no mention of the *sambucae*, or of the machines used by the defenders for dropping stones and lead on the attacking ships, or of the wickerwork covers with which the Roman ships were shielded. Instead, the reader is made to relive the emotional experiences of the persons under siege, and to achieve this effect Livy usually makes the briefest mention of the attacking party first, and then gives an extended account of the defenders, especially commenting on their state of mind. His narration of the siege of Ilorci in Spain by Scipio Africanus is an apposite example:

Fired to enthusiasm after this exhortation from their commander, the Romans allotted the ladders to men specially chosen from each maniple, and the army was divided into two sections, one of which was under the legate Laelius; they attacked the city from two places simultaneously, affording a double terror to the inhabitants.

No single commander or group of leaders incited the townsmen to an energetic defence of the city, but their own fear born of awareness of their guilt. They both recalled and warned each other that they were the target not for victory but for execution. The question was where each man should seek his death—whether in the conflict of the battle-line, where the fortunes of war which both sides shared often exalted the conquered or humbled the conqueror, or whether they should breathe their last a little later, when the city had been dismantled and burnt, after suffering every kind of foul and humiliating treatment, bound and scourged before the eyes of their captured wives and children. So it was that not merely those

---

[1] xxiv, 33 ff.; Pol. viii, 4. Above, 158.

of military age and not merely the men, but the women and the boys lent their spirit and strength to the resistance; they handed weapons to the fighters, and piled up stones on the walls for the builders. The issue was not merely freedom, a cause which incites the hearts of brave men only; before the eyes of all was the final punishment of ignominious death. Their spirits were roused not only by the contest of toil and danger, but also by the very sight of each other, so that they joined the struggle with such enthusiasm that the renowned army which had subdued the whole of Spain was on several occasions driven back from the walls by the youth of a single city, and showed panic in this most unedifying engagement.[1]

There is no doubt that here Livy feels a lively sympathy for the besieged, though the Romans are the attackers; he seems to relish this unexpected reverse for 'the conquerors of the whole of Spain'. He constantly identifies himself with defenders in this way, describing the Romans on numerous occasions as 'the enemy', as at the siege of Veii and that of Heraclea.[2] And repeatedly, when he draws attention to the defenders, it is to comment on their state of mind rather than their methods of resistance. It is interesting to observe how frequently the word *repente* occurs in siege descriptions, emphasising the suddenness of the onset of madness and desperation after a period of unnerving strain. 'Such madness entered the common folk', he writes of the astonishing events of Abydus after its fall, 'that *suddenly* they all rushed in different directions to slay their wives and children, and to kill themselves by every form of suicide.'[3] Similarly at the siege of Saguntum, as Alorcus makes his speech urging surrender, '*suddenly* the chief citizens withdrew before an answer could be given, and collecting in the forum all the silver and gold from private and public sources, they threw it

[1] xxviii, 19, 9–15.
[2] v, 21, 12; xxxvi, 23, 6. Other examples: ii, 17, 3; xxxviii, 6, 6; 29, 2, etc.
[3] xxxi, 18, 6; see Pol. xvi, 34, 9 for proof that Livy has introduced the emphasis on suddenness.

on a fire speedily kindled for that purpose; several hurled themselves on it as well'.[1]

Livy's accounts of the fall of cities have often a generic resemblance, largely because he pays most attention to those sieges of a pathetic and psychologically interesting kind. The well-known narratives of the sieges of Saguntum and Abydus have many features in common; as Livy says, the Abydenes *ad Saguntinam rabiem versi*, and it is notable that he has made additions to Polybius' version of Abydus which increase its resemblance to Saguntum. Polybius states that the Abydenes left fifty chosen men in the city to murder the wives and children, and to throw into the sea all the gold and silver if the city fell; Livy adds to this catalogue of injunctions an instruction to burn as many private and public buildings as possible, just as at Saguntum the townsfolk, 'enclosed with wives and children, burnt the houses over their heads'.[2]

Still more striking is the similarity between the capture of Astapa in Spain by the Roman L. Marcius and that of Abydus by Philip. At Astapa, the besieged heap up their most precious possessions in the forum, make their wives and children sit on them, and throw wood all around, leaving *fifty guards* (the same number as at Abydus) to set fire to all should the city fall; they beg them by the gods to leave nothing to the savage mockery of the enemy, and 'to this exhortation is added a grim curse if hope or cowardice should turn any man from his purpose'. (At Abydus too the chosen fifty are bound by oath, 'praeeuntibus execrabile carmen sacerdotibus'.) After the soldiers have perished in suicidal attacks on the Romans, there was a further slaughter in the city, when the crowd of women and children, too weak for war, was cut down by their own citizens, who threw the bodies, many of them still alive,

---

[1] XXI, 14, 1. For similar uses of *repente* and *subito* see XXI, 9 1; 57, 7; XXIII, 26, 8; XXXVIII, 7, 7, etc.

[2] XXXI, 17, 8; XXI, 14, 4. See Quint. VIII, 3, 68 on the suitability of this topic in descriptions of captured towns.

on the burning pyre. The torrent of blood quenched the rising flames; finally the men, tired by the wretched slaughter of their kin, threw themselves arms and all into the midst of the blaze.[1]

Here the correspondence with the equally dramatic recital of the fall of Abydus is very close. It is not merely that the inhabitants 'obéissent à ce code des vaincus héroïques',[2] and that the two are described in a similar manner. Marcius' obscure Spanish campaign, of which Astapa is an episode, has been filled out, either by Livy or earlier in the source-tradition, with details gleaned from Polybius' version of the siege of Abydus.

Such sensational detail of the fall of cities is however exceptional. Often Livy ignores the topic completely, especially in the early books, as in Romulus' capture of Caenina: '...urbem primo impetu cepit. inde exercitu victore reducto...'. On other occasions, as in the assault on Fidenae, there is a bald statement: 'urbs castraque diripiuntur'. Even in the dramatic account of the fall of Veii, the distress of the women and children is described only during the fighting; after the capture of the city, the plundering and sale of the citizens is only mentioned. A phrase used by Livy in his account of the fall of Victumulae may indicate his purposeful restraint in contrast to the sensationalism of others: 'No harm which under such circumstances historians think noteworthy was left unperpetrated.'[3]

The construction of siege descriptions generally in Livy repays inspection. The shorter narrations form typical examples of the 'episodes' mentioned in the previous chapter. For example, the fall of Sutrium twice in one day, first to the Etruscans and then to Camillus, begins with the 'pluperfect' introduction ('...aliam in partem

---

[1] XXVIII, 23. [2] L. Catin, *En lisant Tite-Live*, 102.
[3] Caenina, I, 10, 4; compare I, 11, 2; 14, 11, etc. Fidenae, IV, 34, 3; compare Anxur, IV, 59, 7. Veii, V, 21, 11 ff. Victumulae, XXI, 57, 14: 'neque ulla, quae in tali re memorabilis scribentibus videri solet, praetermissa clades est'. See E. Burck, *Die Erzählungskunst*, 206 f.

terror ingens ingruerat'). The central description—
Camillus' dramatic arrival and recapture of the town—is
described with a wealth of short clauses, historic presents,
historic infinitives, and the 'division' technique (*alii...
alii*); and the conclusion duly rounds off the episode.[1]
The more protracted sieges, such as those of Saguntum
and Abydus, are allotted a greater length of description
than is compatible with the usual 'episode', so Livy
artistically divides the narration into sections, interposing
events not directly relevant to the siege. After describing
the first attacks on Saguntum, he recounts the visits of
Roman legates first to Spain and then to Carthage, where
a long speech is delivered by Hanno on the menace afforded by Hannibal. There follows the second section of
the siege, in which the citadel is partly captured; now a
speech urging surrender (delivered by Alorcus) follows,
and only then is the third and final stage of the siege recounted. By such piecemeal description the reader is not
confronted with a concentrated version of the warfare, and
is kept in suspense as the climax develops in three separate
acts.[2] Similar effects are achieved, under the influence of
Polybius, in the account of Abydus, where the siege and
capture are separated by a dialogue between Philip and
the young Marcus Aemilius.[3]

In brief, Livy's narration of sieges, constructed for the
most part in episodes, aims at a more dramatic and pathetic
treatment than that found in his source. This effect is
gained by excluding extended mention of attackers and the
technical apparatus employed; instead he concentrates
the attention on the situation of the besieged, assessing
the effects of the attack in terms of human emotions and

[1] VI, 3. For other examples of sieges constructed in this fashion see XXXI, 23 (Chalcis), where the central description is of burning buildings, indiscriminate slaughter, seizure of booty, liberation of prisoners, and destruction of
statues of Philip; XXXII, 17, 4ff. (Atrax); XXXII, 23, 4ff. (Corinth); XXXVI, 22, 5ff. (Heraclea), etc.
[2] Part I: XXI, 7-9, 2; II: 11, 3-12, 3; III, 14, 1-15, 2.
[3] XXXI, 18; Pol. XVI, 34.

sufferings, and thereby affecting his audience with that 'pity and fear' at which the 'tragic' historians of the Hellenistic period had aimed. Yet this psychological approach is not allowed to deteriorate into mere sensationalism, for Livy is more concerned with the motives and emotions of the besieged when under attack than with harrowing accounts of their fate at the hands of the aggressors.

II

The general deficiencies of Livy's battle accounts have already been outlined.[1] These are attributable to the inadequacy of the annalistic source-material in part; but also to the fact that scientific disquisitions on warfare were not considered by the Romans appropriate to *historia*. Livy's aim is to produce a clear, uncomplicated account by embracing the Ciceronian canons of chronological sequence, topographical elucidation, and explanation of strategy; there must be no obscurity in the sequence of events or in the tactics employed. In addition to this primary requisite of clarity, the interest of the reader is to be engaged by such unusual features as distinguished a particular conflict, by attempts to describe the course of a battle dramatically, and above all by constantly depicting the mental attitude of the participants—the feature looming so large also in sieges.

To achieve his primary aim of clarity, Livy regularly unfolds battles in phases of distinct chronological sequence; in large-scale engagements, the operations of the various sections of the army or fleet are recounted separately. Even when these sections are engaged in the same struggle, or simultaneously in different struggles, he tends to relate them in turn as if they were in action separately or at different times. Thus standard methods of battle disposition are imposed on virtually every narration;

[1] See Ch. vi.

and above all, there is the division into stages by use of such adverbs as *primo, mox, deinde, postremo*.

Many of these accounts accordingly reflect an identical pattern.[1] In the first stage, the commencement of the engagement, there is a regular analysis of the psychological reactions of the protagonists. 'They hesitated for a time (*parumper*), waiting for each other to begin the conflict; then (*deinde*) shame stirred the line to action.' 'They remained inactive, as though numb with reciprocated fear; then (*dein*) they no longer held back.'[2] Once the contestants have recovered from their fear, and the battle commences, Livy portrays the approach of victory. It is noteworthy how often this stage is depicted from the viewpoint of the defeated, an interesting illustration of Livy's sympathies consistent with his approach to siege narrations. Here too his preoccupation is with the unfortunates.

To begin with (*primo*) the onset of the battle was sustained with constancy and without flinching; then (*dein*) when the massed enemy bore heavy on them, they began gradually to withdraw...; finally (*postremo*), since there was now more danger in delay than protection in maintaining ranks, they all rushed into scattered flight.[3]

The Macedonians thronged around the standards in greater numbers than the others, and for a long time (*diu*) made the hope of victory uncertain; finally (*postremo*), exposed by the flight of the rest,... they first retreated and then were driven back and fled.[4]

In many engagements there is no intermediate resistance; panic and flight ensue immediately after the attack. 'They were immediately confused, and first (*primo*) produced disorder amongst themselves, then (*deinde*) turned, and

[1] K. Witte, *RhM* (1910), 392 ff.
[2] II, 10, 9; XXXIII, 7, 5. Other examples: IX, 32, 5; XXXI, 36, 7; XXXVII, 43, 4; XL, 32, 3, etc.
[3] XXXVIII, 25, 12.
[4] XXXIII, 15, 10. Other examples: XXIX, 34, 12; XXXIV, 28, 11; XXXVI, 9, 11; XLI, 26, 3, etc.

finally (*postremo*), throwing away their arms, they rushed into headlong flight.'[1]

These are typical examples of the stock techniques in the descriptions of short engagements. In more extensive battles, as has been demonstrated,[2] it is his practice to discuss successively the operations of right wing, left wing, and centre, and to impose this mould even on battles not contested with such formations. This fixed narrative form for battles is also to be observed in Livy's depiction of sea engagements, and especially those of the fourth decade;[3] they are constructed identically and their terminology is markedly similar. In the first stage, the preparation for battle, the enemy fleet (of Antiochus) is invariably mentioned first, beginning with details of his left wing and then of his right. Livy then depicts the reaction of the Roman or Rhodian fleets. The battle itself in each case has as its main feature clashes between individual ships and small groups, and the main engagement is described baldly, with emphasis duly laid on the courage of the Roman forces and the superior naval skill of the Rhodians. The third stage, the flight, is described in each case briefly and with similar terminology. It is quite obvious that these battles are written to a stereotyped pattern which makes the operations easily apprehended by the reader.[4]

One device employed to simplify army operations is the technique of 'combined description'; Livy succeeds in combining in a single narration the separate descriptions of the movements of opposed forces recorded by his source. By this exercise of brevity (συντομία) the historian incidentally allows the reader a bird's-eye view of

---

[1] XXXIII, 18, 18. Other examples: VI, 32, 8; VII, 8, 3; XXXIII, 36, 11; XXXVIII, 41, 7, etc.

[2] Above, 161f.

[3] XXXVI, 43–5 (off Cissus); XXXVII, 23–4 (off Phaselis); XXXVII, 29–30 (off Myonnesus).

[4] For further detail see below, 252f. Some sea battles previous to the fourth decade, notably those at XXI, 49, 12ff., XXII, 19, 11ff. and XXVI, 39, also contain some of the features mentioned here.

both armies together. Such a technique is used in the narrative of manœuvres before Cynoscephalae, as comparison with Polybius reveals.[1] Livy's account is certainly neater and simpler, without loss of any vital information, and the device can be observed elsewhere.[2]

Clarity, then, at all costs is Livy's primary aim, but also notable is his brave attempt to introduce an individual colouring into each battle. This is the reason for the recurrence of a number of motifs, especially in the early sections of the *Ab Urbe Condita* where the battles have little historical content.[3] There is the 'cavalry fighting as infantry' motif, or again, the intervention of mist or rain; there is the 'I told you so' variation, where an impulsive soldiery fights against the wishes of its commander, and then has to be rescued by him. Fabius Cunctator's alleged experiences with his *magister equitum* Minucius and the troops who followed him are thus visited upon Camillus and C. Sulpicius.[4]

But the most popular of these motifs is the duel between a champion of each side, symbolic of the struggle between nations, for it demonstrates 'which race is superior in war'.[5] In such passages as the duel between Manlius Torquatus and the Gaul, or that between Badius the Campanian and Crispinus the Roman,[6] Livy does not introduce much fictional material; but by emphasis on the national characteristics of each side through the medium of the duel, he seeks to invest them with a wider significance. On other occasions, when a battle is marked by none of these distinguishing features, he has recourse to hyperbole to lend uniqueness to a particular engagement. 'They fought with greater spirit and greater numbers

[1] Pol. XVIII, 19, 2 and 5; 20, 2–3; Livy XXXIII, 6, 4–9.
[2] XXVII, 2, 12; XXVIII, 14, 4 (see Pol. XI, 22, 2–3); XXXI, 33, 8–9.
[3] Above, 159.
[4] XXII, 29, 1 ff. (Fabius); VI, 24, 1 ff. (Camillus); VII, 14–15 (Sulpicius).
[5] VII, 9, 8: 'ut noster duorum eventus ostendat utra gens bello sit melior'.
[6] VII, 10; XXV, 18.

than had ever been seen before.' 'Rarely at any other time is so loud a shout said to have been raised at the beginning of a battle.' Phrases such as *raro alias* mushroom forth in such profusion that the historian almost defeats his own purpose—exceptional features in a battle become the rule.[1]

Of outstanding interest is the frequent attempt to make a battle more dramatic by the unexpected intervention of an ambushing force or a relieving body at the vital point of a struggle. This might be labelled the '*deus ex machina*' technique, an apt title if one recalls Livy's comment on Fabius Cunctator's sudden appearance to save Minucius: 'Fabius' battle-line appeared in support *suddenly, as though let down from heaven.*'[2] This is Livy's favourite dramatic device. In his account of the battle of Thermopylae he describes how at the outset Cato and Flaccus were dispatched with chosen forces to try to outflank the enemy; then, ignoring their progress, he turns to the narration of the main battle—the preliminary success of Antiochus' forces, the later advance of the Romans, the ensuing stalemate. At this stage, with the Romans in an unenviable position ('*They would either have retired with their attempt unachieved, or more soldiers would have fallen*'), the victorious Cato is suddenly introduced in the rear of the king's forces. In Appian's account (like Livy's, drawing upon Polybius) no such arrangement is sought.[3]

Another typical example of a task force similarly springing up in the rear is found in the description of a battle in Epirus:

While the enemy fought outside the fortifications, driven on by their enthusiasm for battle, the Romans were considerably superior;...but when, after the loss and wounding of many men, the king's army retired to positions defended by fortifications or by nature, the danger swung against the Romans;... and *they would not have retired from that position with their rashness*

---

[1] IX, 39, 5; XXXIII, 9, 2. Also IX, 32, 9; 37, 2; XXVII, 49, 5.
[2] XXII, 29, 3: 'repente, velut caelo demissa'.
[3] XXXVI, 15 ff., esp. 17, 1; 18, 8; App. *Syr.* 17–20.

unpunished had not a cry been heard in the rear, and then the commencement of battle affected the king's troops, maddened by this sudden terror.[1]

Three points are noteworthy here. In each description there is initially a bare mention of the ambushing force; the surprise attack is related in the form of a conditional clause; and the suddenness of the attack is stressed. These features emerge again in the description of a battle between Hannibal and Claudius Nero. Livy mentions that Nero laid some men in ambush by night, but subsequently the *insidiae* are ignored until the critical moment: 'Hannibal *would have succeeded in drawing up his men in the panic and confusion*, had not the shouting of the cohorts and the maniples running down over the hills been heard in the rear....'[2] Or again, in the preliminary stages of the Roman attack on Locri, Livy mentions the Locrian element suborned by the Romans to assist against the Carthaginian garrison. There follows the main description, and its climax: 'The Romans *would have been overwhelmed* because of their considerable numerical inferiority, had not a shout been raised by those outside the citadel.'[3] This technique of *peripeteia*, achieved by drawing the reader's attention to the sudden appearance of the ambushing or rescuing force, hitherto kept carefully in the background, is quite cinematographic in its effect, especially in such descriptions as that of the fall of New Carthage to Scipio Africanus, in which the defenders know nothing

[1] 'repentino terrore' (XXXIII, 12, 4). In Plutarch, *Flam.* 4, 6, there is far less emphasis on the danger confronting the main force, and no indication of the sudden, opportune arrival of the task force.

[2] XXVII, 41-2 (esp. 42, 4).

[3] XXIX, 6, 13. Burck, *Die Erzählungskunst*, 215 f., notes many passages in the early books with this *peripeteia* achieved by use of the conditional sentence, and compares similar techniques of ἔκπληξις attempted by Clitarchus, Duris, and others. The passages in Livy: II, 47, 3 and 8; 48, 5; 50, 10; 51, 2; 56, 14; III, 1, 4; 5, 8, etc. R. Jumeau, *Rev. Phil.* (1939), 41, in citation of three examples from XXX, 18, suggests that this formula of the conditional is reproduced from an annalistic source. This is an unlikely suggestion, for the device is freely used whatever the source.

of the surprise attack by way of the lagoon 'until spears rained on their backs'.[1]

The influence of Caesar's *Commentarii* is noteworthy in another method by which Livy seeks to make his battle narrations more dramatic. Caesar almost invariably refrains from stating in detail the instructions given to subordinate commanders or particular contingents. With a phrase such as 'He told them of his requirements' or 'He gave them their orders', he passes directly to the account of the operations themselves, which as they unfold indicate what his instructions had been. Obviously such a narration becomes more vivid by concealing from the reader the plan of campaign.[2] Livy occasionally makes use of this device. For example, Polybius narrates the method by which the Ambracians were to smoke out the Roman attackers from their tunnel in the form of *a suggestion* made by someone—that is, in what might be called the didactic manner. Then he explains how the event accorded with the suggestion. Livy has avoided the preliminary narration of the suggestion, and describes the operation as it actually happened; thus his version is more lively than that of Polybius.[3] Precisely the same difference is to be observed between the two accounts in their descriptions of how Scipio Africanus dealt with the mutiny of his troops in Spain. Polybius recounts Scipio's instructions to the non-revolting troops at New Carthage to move out their baggage from the town before dawn, to march out at daybreak, and to seal off the exits to prevent any of the mutineers from leaving. All this is described by Livy as it actually happened.[4]

By such methods Livy seeks to impress upon the traditional account a more dramatic quality. Above all,

[1] xxvi, 46, 5.
[2] C. E. Moberly's note at *Bell. Civ.* iii, 62, 3 (Oxford, 1925) adverts to this point. [3] xxxviii, 7; Pol. xxi, 28.
[4] xxviii, 26, 11 f.; Pol. xi, 27, 1 f. For an additional example see xxv, 9, 10, and compare Pol. viii, 28, 1.

in his description of warfare as of all else, he seeks to achieve 'tragic' effects by engaging the reader's interest in and sympathy for the thoughts and emotions of the contestants, especially if they are enduring defeat and humiliation. Typical is his psychological portrait of the Romans when they were obliged after the disaster near Caudium to submit to the Samnite yoke:

They looked at each other, and eyed their weapons soon to be surrendered, their right hands now to be stripped of arms, their bodies exposed to the foe; and each man pictured before his eyes the yoke of the enemy, the jeers and arrogant looks of the conquerors, and their own unarmed progress through armed ranks; then the wretched journey of the shameful column through the cities of their allies, and the return to their own fathers and to that city to which they and their forbears had often come in triumph. Of all the Romans they alone had been defeated without wounds, without weapons, without an engagement; they alone had not been permitted to draw their swords, to grapple with the enemy: in vain had they been endowed with arms and strength and spirit.[1]

To sum up, Livy's narrative of battles and troop movements is written to appeal to a non-specialist audience, so that the refinements of strategy and tactics are sacrificed in favour of a clear, easily followed exposition. In addition, the interest of the reader is aroused by original or striking features and by dramatic effects. Above all, there is that preoccupation with psychological considerations—the joy, spirit, and determination of the victors, the depression, fear, and madness of the defeated—which holds so high a place in Livy's conception of the historian's craft.

III

Apart from the narration of warfare, the dramatic sections of the *Ab Urbe Condita* are chiefly to be found in descriptions of meetings and discussions, whether between

---

[1] IX, 5, 8–10.

individuals, or at councils and assemblies. With all the Roman historians the composition of speeches was a major preoccupation, and they are set within a carefully constructed framework.

Livy's first aim here was to set the scene clearly, in accordance with Hellenistic rhetorical theory, by an indication of the occasion, the site, and the circumstances. One notes, for example, the attention devoted to his introductory comment before the narration of how the freedom of Greece was proclaimed in 196. The occasion was the Corinthian Games, and he remarks on the popularity of such contests in Greece, on the central position of Corinth, and on the particular significance of this occasion. Again, the conferences at the river Aous and at Nicaea between Flamininus and Philip V of Macedon are prefaced with picturesque details of the scene.[1]

Attention is also paid to dramatic structure. Livy's experience in writing philosophical dialogues on the Ciceronian pattern was of service here. The most obvious structural device is his method of artistic division between sections of a discussion. Livy's introduction of *a silence* between speeches is especially noteworthy for its dramatic possibilities. At the Nicaea conference, for example, he has invented a silence. Polybius, after his narration of the preliminary remarks made by Philip and Flamininus, states that the two leaders bade each other speak first; Livy converts this into an embarrassing silence, which effectively breaks up the continuous conference.[2] Still more effective are the silences introduced into the informal trial at the court of Macedon, when Perseus indicts his brother Demetrius before their father Philip. The king's reproachful speech to both sons is followed by the words: 'Tears welled up in the eyes of all, and *for a long time a grim silence prevailed.*' Then, after Perseus' long accusation of his brother, '*there was a long silence*, for it

---

[1] XXXIII, 32; XXXII, 10; 32.   [2] XXXII, 33, 1; Pol. XVIII, 1, 10.

was clear to all that Demetrius was choked with tears and could not speak'. One notes silences inserted for dramatic effect in the dialogues of Cicero; and they are a commonplace in historians reflecting 'tragic' influence. Dionysius, for example, on one occasion records that 'so profound a silence overcame the assembly that the place was quiet as a desert'.[1]

Many of these conference scenes are constructed around antithetical speeches—a device to which many ancient historians are addicted.[2] In such scenes the speeches are the most important feature, and little attention is devoted to the incidental narrative. But in other episodes the attention is focused on the behaviour of the spectators present, and *oratio obliqua* is unobtrusively employed to delineate their attitudes. Livy's exploitation of the crowd scene is one of the most consciously dramatic features of his writing.[3] Always he attempts to probe below the surface, to seek the psychological reasons for mass behaviour, often attempting to convey by this method a picture of national temperament. Almost invariably he embellishes his source in these descriptions, as in his account of the liberation of Greece by Flamininus.[4]

Nor is Livy content with the reproduction of assemblies recorded in his sources; there are occasions when he has introduced fictitious ones to give play to such psychological considerations, as a comparison with Polybius reveals. In 191 B.C., the Aetolians had been attempting to obtain peace from the Romans, who were, however, uncompromising in their demand for unconditional sur-

---

[1] The Macedonian court, XL, 8, 20; 12, 2. Other dramatic silences, III, 47, 6; IX, 4, 7; XXX, 30, 2; XXXII, 20, 1; XXXIV, 59, 1. On this topic see E. Dutoit, *Mél. J. Marouzeau* (Paris, 1948), 141–51. For such silences in Cicero see *De Or.* III, 143; *De Rep.* II, 64. The passage of Dionysius, VI, 83, 2.

[2] For Tacitus' use of the technique see P. Fabia, *Les Sources de Tacite* (Paris, 1895), 285 f.

[3] W. Kroll, *Studien zum Verständnis der röm. Literatur*, 356: '...einen der wichtigsten Kunstgriffe des Livius, der ihm, soweit wir sehen können, eigentümlich ist'.

[4] Above, 184.

render. Polybius states that when the Roman reply was noised abroad the Aetolian reaction was so savage that they would not even assemble to discuss it. Livy changes this version, and the 'coacta omnis multitudo' hears of the interview of the Aetolian legates with the Roman commander Glabrio. The imaginary assembly is described vividly: 'They were so nettled by the harshness of the command and by mental anger that if they had been at peace they could have been roused to war by that onset of indignation.' Livy delineates their anger, their helplessness at being unable to comply with the Roman instructions, their wild hope of a miraculous intervention by king Antiochus, to whom Nicander, one of their legates, had been sent. In Polybius Nicander reports back to the Apocleti, the deliberative council, but in Livy he returns to find the *assembly* discussing the Roman peace terms.[1]

In view of the numerous examples of crowd descriptions in earlier chapters,[2] it would be superfluous to examine Livy's techniques here. As one scholar aptly summarises them: 'la foule, dont le rôle est d'exprimer les sentiments qui meuvent de loin en loin la communauté humaine, colère, terreur, espoir, allégresse...'.[3] One further example will suffice to illustrate his portrayal of the atmosphere of a conference by describing the thoughts and uncertainties of the participants:

A council was granted to them at Sicyon. But the Achaeans' attitude of mind was by no means one and the same. The Spartan Nabis, an oppressive and unremitting enemy, was a source of fear; they were apprehensive of Roman arms; they were bound by the Macedonians' kindnesses, both recent and long-standing; they were suspicious of king Philip himself because of his cruelty and deceit, and, ignoring his immediate attitude, they realised that after the war he would be a sterner master. Not only had they no idea of the opinions passed in

[1] xxxvi, 29, 1-11; Pol. xx, 10.   [2] Above, 170f., 184f.
[3] Catin, 153; compare Burck, *Die Erzählungskunst*, 229ff.

individual states or in general councils; they themselves as they pondered the question could not express their decisions or desires.[1]

Under the heading 'conferences', then, there are two types of episode differently treated. In the first the set speeches are of primary importance; outside them Livy's sole artistic concern is the setting of the scene and the structural division. The second type comprises crowd descriptions, for which Livy, like Tacitus, has an inordinate fondness because of the scope for psychological interpretation.

IV

The dialogue form, as an artistic feature of historical narrative, obviously claims descent from Homeric epic, and is observable early in the Greek historiographical tradition. In Herodotus there is the lengthy conversation recorded between Croesus and Solon, and the exchange of views between Xerxes and Demaratus—both serving an important characterising function. In Thucydides one recalls the renowned Melian dialogue, in which national attitudes are effectively portrayed.[2]

Livy's treatment reflects the development of this art form in Hellenistic historiography; this is perhaps the most rigid of the narrative genres in technique, as can be observed by comparison with his sources. Characterisation of the participants remains the ultimate purpose; invariably some noteworthy person is involved, whose character is illuminated not merely by the views expressed, but also by his reactions when faced with diplomatic situations of an unexpected and exacting kind. Livy also seeks to recount attitudes expressive of national characteristics, so that a dialogue may be symbolic of antipathy between nations.[3]

[1] XXXII, 19, 6.   [2] Her. I, 30; VII, 101; Thuc. V, 85.
[3] See Ch. VII, 189 n. 1.

Because of this usefulness for delineation of character and the inherently dramatic nature of this medium, Livy occasionally constructs fictitious dialogues. An interesting example is the adaptation of the conversation (recorded by Polybius) between Philip and the Roman commissioners after Philip's revengeful attack on the town of Maronea in 184. In Polybius, the conversation extends over two days. On the first day, Philip pleads as defence that the Maronean factions have harmed themselves, and asks the Romans to invite any townsman to lay an accusation against him; Appius Claudius Pulcher sternly replies that they know who is guilty. On the next day, Philip is ordered to send Onomastus and Cassander (his agents in the outrage) from Maronea to Rome so that the facts can be ascertained beyond Philip's reach—a master-stroke of Roman tactics that causes Philip acute dismay. Livy reports the conversations of two different days as a single dialogue. The Roman *coup de grâce* is delivered not as the result of overnight deliberation as in Polybius, but suddenly and at the very time when Philip is answering the Roman complaints with the greatest confidence. This air of assurance in the first stage is thus sharply contrasted with his obvious confusion later—the basis of Livy's dramatic effect. Further, Polybius' comment, 'Philip was taken aback and for some time discomfited', becomes in Livy: '...adeo turbavit ea vox ut non color, non vultus ei constaret'. His face falls and loses colour—an embellishment of the ἀπορία mentioned by Polybius.[1]

This dialogue aptly illustrates Livy's favourite dialogue structure. There are two statements on each side. *A* makes a statement which causes *B* no concern whatsoever; it may even encourage a certain complacency, and *B* replies with assurance. *A* then makes the vital comment—an unexpected demand which causes the utmost fear, anger, or confusion in *B*; this emotion is then reflected in the words

[1] xxxix, 34, 3 ff.; Pol. xxii, 13, 8 ff. See Witte, *RhM* (1910), 288.

which *B* finally brings himself to speak. This effect of
peripeteia often exists in the source, and Livy merely
embellishes it to accentuate the contrast; this is true of the
Maronea dialogue. Another apposite example is the conversation between Philip and Flamininus which took
place across the river Aous. First Flamininus demands
that Philip should remove his garrisons from Greek
towns. Philip in reply distinguishes between conquered
cities, which he agrees to cede, and hereditary possessions.
He further suggests that disputes could be referred to a
neutral arbitrator. Flamininus then demands that the
Thessalians be first freed. This provokes an outburst of
anger from Philip, who storms away from the conference.
Now Diodorus, who follows Polybius closely in such
dialogues, makes no mention of the Thessalians. It is
tempting to believe that this, and the more forceful
expression of Philip's anger, are imaginative details
supplied by Livy himself.[1]

Not all dialogues, however, contain the germ of drama
on which this technique of *peripeteia* depends. For the
rest, Livy constructs a lively conversation free of wordy
connections and explanations; if possible, the discussion
is confined to the most important topic, with the omission
of side issues. One notes, for example, a drastic pruning
of the Polybian account of a dialogue between Philip and
Aemilius Lepidus at Abydus. In Polybius, Aemilius
begins by reciting a Senatorial decree requesting Philip
not to attack any Greek state nor to seize any of Ptolemy's
possessions, and to submit to a tribunal the question of
compensation for his attacks on Attalus and the Rhodians.
Compliance with these instructions would mean peace,
non-compliance war. This important historical material
Livy blithely sweeps aside; his twelve-word version
contains only a hint of what was said ('He complained

[1] XXXII, 10, 3 ff.; Diod. XXVIII, 11. For greater detail, Walsh, *RhM* (1954),
107 f. For other dialogues of the *peripeteia* type, XXXVI, 28; XXXI, 25.

of the attacks made on Attalus and the Rhodians, and especially of the present attack on Abydus').

Livy's aim is here to concentrate the attention solely on Abydus. In Polybius, after Philip's claim that he had been attacked by the Rhodians, Aemilius interjects: 'What then of the Athenians, Cians, and Abydenes? Did any of *them* attack you first?' But Livy ignores the reference to Athenians and Cians, and writes: 'num Abydeni quoque, inquit, ultro tibi intulerunt arma?' Livy's dialogue is in fact a series of brief statements on each side devoted solely to Abydus, and for this purpose he has completely remodelled the factual version of Polybius.[1]

One outstanding method by which incisive brevity is achieved is the use of *oratio recta*, connected with simple words like *inquit*, for the clumsier *oratio obliqua* of the source. The conversation preliminary to the Nicaea conference is so constructed:

'If you were to disembark', said Flamininus, 'we could speak and listen to each other more conveniently.'

When the king refused, Quinctius asked: 'Whom then do you fear?'

Philip, with proud and kingly spirit, replied: 'None save the immortal gods, but I do not trust the good faith of your companions, least of all the Aetolians.'

'But', said the Roman, 'this is a danger common to all who hold conversation with the enemy, should there be an absence of good faith.'

'Yet, Quinctius,' said he, 'Philip and Phaeneas would not be an equal prize for treachery, if there were deceitful conduct, for it would not be so difficult for the Aetolians to find another leader as for the Macedonians to put a king in my stead.'

The sequence of simple verbs here (*inquit...negaret... inquit...ait...inquit*) replaces much longer conjunctive expressions in Polybius: τοῦ δὲ Τίτου κελεύοντος...τοῦ δὲ πάλιν ἐρομένου...τοῦ δὲ τῶν 'Ρωμαίων στρατηγοῦ

---

[1] XXXI, 18; Pol. XVI, 34. See Witte, 304. Further examples of such concentration on a single topic, XXXII, 36, 4ff. (Pol. XVIII, 9, 4); XXXVII, 52 (Pol. XXI, 18).

θαυμάσαντος καὶ φήσαντος. . . .[1] Such incisiveness is a feature common to all Livy's dialogues, with the discussion repeatedly centred on a single topic. The same conference at Nicaea later contains an exchange between Philip and the Aetolian Phaeneas illustrative of the point. In Polybius there is a long defence by Philip of his actions; in Livy this becomes merely: 'orsum eum dicere in Aetolos maxime...', and again he betrays that his interest is in the form of the dialogue rather than in accurate reproduction of the content.[2]

The frequent introduction of *oratio recta* into these dialogues seeks to produce a livelier conversational effect, and to concentrate attention on a particular speaker, the person particularly characterised. Sometimes both parties in the dialogue use it, but more often it is reserved for the final comment, thus adding emphasis to the explosive indignation so frequently expressed.

One can thus summarise Livy's dialogue techniques: he adopts every possible means to render a discussion brief and addressed to a single issue, and in many cases seeks to achieve an effect of *peripeteia*—in Aristotle's definition 'a change to the reverse of what was expected'—in depicting the reduction of a protagonist from confidence to perplexity and dismay.

V

Livy's psychological preoccupations lead him to pay close attention to events with conspicuous 'human' interest. The approach of many Hellenistic historians, with their enthusiasm for incidents of a pathetic, horrific, heroic, or romantic nature, is reflected here.

In the earlier books, with their wealth of legendary content, there are numerous descriptions built around such personalities as Horatius Cocles, Mucius Scaevola,

[1] XXXII, 32, 13 ff.; Pol. XVIII, 1, 6 ff.
[2] XXXII, 34, 2 ff.; Pol. XVIII, 4, 1 ff.

Verginia, the Decii. The literary treatment of these legends embodies motifs popular in some Hellenistic writing. So the conflict of the *trigemini fratres*, Romans against Albans, which ends when the one surviving Horatius dispatches successively the three Curiatii, produces an effect of *peripeteia*; and the same is true of the account of Coriolanus' sudden retirement from the environs of defenceless Rome, halted not by arms but by maternal entreaty. The heroism of Cloelia in leading a band of maidens out of Lars Porsena's clutches and swimming with them across the Tiber is an exemplar of female valour (παράδειγμα γυναικείας ἀρετῆς), a theme beloved of many Greeks, including Plutarch. The Scaevola anecdote, the intrepid thrusting of the hand into a furnace to demonstrate Roman fortitude, has the element of the unexpected, τὸ παράλογον. Horatius on the bridge projects the epic prowess, the ἀριστεία, of the authentic warrior.[1]

In the later books, when the source-material presents more continuous and coherent historical content, there are fewer of these picturesque anecdotes, but Livy takes the opportunity to include any matter of this type relevant to Roman affairs, and indeed some which is irrelevant,[2] which appeared in his sources. A good illustration, already briefly mentioned,[3] concerns the barbarian princess Chiomara. The depiction of her female valour, surviving both in Polybius and in Livy,[4] allows one to observe Livy's refinements. The most significant aspect of his treatment is the increased emphasis on Chiomara's *pudicitia* in her relationship with the centurion who violated her; Livy invents a stage prior to the assault, in which the centurion seeks her voluntary co-operation, and is rebuffed. The description in stages ('is primo animum temptavit; quem cum abhorrentem a voluntario videret

---

[1] So Kroll, 353. Horatii and Curiatii, I, 25; Coriolanus, II, 40; Cloelia, II, 13; Scaevola, II, 12; Horatius Cocles, II, 10.
[2] Above, 188.   [3] Above, 76.
[4] XXXVIII, 24; Pol. XXI, 38.

stupro, corpori...vim fecit') is a technique regularly employed in such accounts of *pudicitia* by Livy. It is found in the narration of Appius' evil designs on Verginia, and again in the attempted assault of Lucius Papirius on the youth C. Publilius.[1] Livy also introduces into the Chiomara episode this edifying conclusion: 'She is said to have preserved to her final day the glory of this matronly deed by her general piety and sobriety of life.'

Another point worthy of note in Livy's edifying stories of young women is his insistence on their beauty, a feature which demonstrates the romantic facet of his character. Chiomara has a *forma eximia*: so has the girl presented to Scipio Africanus by his troops in Spain: Verginia is *forma excellentem*: it is Lucretia's *forma* which provokes the lust of Sextus Tarquinius. This 'fair maid' motif is also to be observed in Livy's anecdote of an affray at Ardea, where a dispute about a girl ('virginem... maxime forma notam') coveted by both a nobleman and a commoner leads to faction.[2] This romantic approach is perhaps partly explicable by the influence of New Comedy on the traditional material, but Livy's personal attitude is also to be taken into account; like Ovid in the *Amores* and *Ars Amatoria* he clearly anticipates the chivalry popularly associated with medieval times. Like Ovid, too, he takes more than a passing interest in female psychology. One thinks especially of his wise comments on the fracas preceding the passing of the laws of Licinius and Sextius, which according to the tradition were precipitated by the marriages of Fabius Ambustus' daughters at different social levels. Livy's picture of women who spend their time in gossip, who hate to be laughed at, and who above

---

[1] III, 44, 4: 'hanc virginem adultam forma excellentem Appius amore amens pretio ac spe perlicere adortus, postquam omnia pudore saepta animadverterat, ad crudelem superbamque vim animum convertit'. VIII, 28, 3: 'florem aetatis eius fructum adventicium crediti ratus, primo perlicere adulescentem sermone incesto est conatus; dein, postquam aspernabantur flagitium aures, minis territare...'.

[2] XXVI, 50, 1; III, 44, 4; I, 57, 10; IV, 9–10.

all are indignant if their relatives fare better in the marriage stakes, is humorously and shrewdly drawn.[1]

More common than this gentle humour are the portraits of a pathetic kind. The court case following upon the attempted abduction of Verginia by Appius Claudius contains obvious traces of such pathetic treatment. Verginius, father of the girl, is 'sordidatus': Verginia is clad 'obsoleta veste': Icilius is earlier moved to tears by the warmth of the crowd's support. And after Verginia is slain by her father to preserve her chastity, and Appius and his henchmen have suffered exile or chosen suicide, the whole episode is rounded off in poetic language accentuating the drama of the situation: 'The shades of Verginia, who was happier in death than life, had wandered through many homes in pursuit of vengeance, and now at last sought rest, for no guilty man remained.'[2]

Again, there is the pathetic description of the daughter of Hiero of Syracuse, Heraclia. She was married to Zoippus, who had sought voluntary exile rather than serve Hieronymus, the new tyrant. We read how she took refuge with her household gods and her two virgin daughters, 'resolutis crinibus, miserabilique alio habitu'. Sympathy for the victims is especially engaged by the stress on the psychological factor—how the girls, after their mother's throat was cut, were entered by a madness which lent them strength to resist:

They then attacked the maidens, who were sprinkled with their mother's blood. But they, mentally maddened with grief and fear, were overcome with a kind of wildness, and burst forth from the shrine at such speed that had escape into the streets been open they would have filled the city with uproar. Even as it was, though there was not much room in the house, they evaded their innumerable armed pursuers for some time without injury, and tore themselves from the grasp of their oppressors, in spite of the numbers and the strength of the hands

[1] VI, 34.   [2] III, 47, 1; 46, 8; 58, 11.

with which they had to struggle. At last, overcome with wounds and covering everything with blood, they sank lifeless to the ground.[1]

But perhaps the most famous and the most dramatically moving 'human' situation described by Livy is in his account of the violation and suicide of Lucretia. Due emphasis is laid on her chastity and on her oppressor's lust, a vice inevitably followed by the expulsion of the Tarquinii. Here is the supreme example of γυναικεία ἀρετή. Livy first describes how Lucretia was visited by her husband Collatinus and by Sextus Tarquinius in her home at Collatia. The rest is worth quoting in full.

After the lapse of a few days, unknown to Collatinus, Sextus Tarquinius came to Collatia with one companion. There he was received hospitably, for his design was unknown, and after dinner he was taken to the guest-chamber.

When all seemed to be asleep and all about him secure, burning with love he drew his sword and approached the sleeping Lucretia. Pressing his left hand on her breast, he said: 'Be quiet, Lucretia: it's Sextus Tarquinius: one sound, and you die.' When Lucretia awoke in panic, and saw no help at hand but death overhanging her, Tarquinius confessed his love, besought her, mingled threats with prayers, and sought to affect her woman's heart by every means. When he saw that she was unyielding, and moved not even by the fear of death, he reinforced fear with dishonour, and said that he would place by her dead body a naked slave with throat severed, so that men would say that she had been killed in squalid adultery. His lust thus prevailed as though by force over her unyielding chastity by this fearful threat; and then he left the house, insolent from his victory over a woman's honour.

Lucretia, heart-broken by this great outrage, sent a messenger to her father and then to Ardea to her husband, bidding them each come with a trusty friend, for there was need of action and haste; a foul crime had occurred. Spurius Lucretius came with P. Valerius, son of Volesus, and Collatinus with L. Iunius

[1] XXIV, 26, 12–14.

Brutus, for his wife's messenger had met them as they chanced
to be returning together to Rome.

They found Lucretia sitting sadly in her bed-chamber, and at
their approach her tears welled up. Her husband asked: 'Is
everything all right?' She answered: 'By no means, for what
can be right for a woman who has lost her chastity? In your
bed, Collatinus, are the traces of another man. But my body
alone has been outraged; my mind is inviolate, and death will
be my witness. But give me your right hands, your pledge that
the adulterer will get his deserts. It was Sextus Tarquinius who
last night came armed, an enemy in the guise of a friend, and
wrested from here a joy which will bring destruction not only
on me, but also, if you are men, upon himself.' One after
another they give their pledge, and console her in her sickness
of mind, absolving her reluctance from guilt and blaming the
instigator of the crime. The mind was the source of guilt, they
said, and not the body, and there was no guilt where there was
no intention. She replied: 'Do you arrange to requite Tarquinius; though I absolve myself of sin, I cannot free myself of
punishment, for no unchaste woman will live on with Lucretia
as precedent.' She plunged into her heart the knife she had
kept hidden beneath her robe, and slipping forward on her
wound she fell dying to the ground.[1]

Successive examination of these various types of narration—sieges, battle accounts, conference scenes, dialogues, 'human' situations—brings increasing awareness
of the extent to which literary considerations impinge on
Livy's conception of *historia*. In sieges and battles there
is the preoccupation with dramatic effects, and the prominence given to psychological factors. In his reporting of
conversations, Livy 'edits' them to achieve a more incisive and arresting version. His descriptions of deeds of
individual heroism and suffering are suffused with a
pathetic colouring. In all these scenes Livy's debt to the

---

[1] I, 58. Burck, *Die Erzählungskunst*, 170ff., 202, well compares with Dionys.
IV, 64ff., to show how Livy concentrates the interest on Lucretia, and lays
additional stress on *pudicitia*.

practitioners and techniques of 'tragic' history is seen to be considerable.

To what extent do such literary aims militate against the historical accuracy of Livy? Remembering that his work is one of synthesis rather than of original research, that it was addressed to a wide audience and not to specialists, one must applaud the attempt to make the *Ab Urbe Condita* a genuinely memorable work of literary value. But in so far as he falsifies military detail, suppresses or over-abbreviates topics of importance in diplomatic exchanges, and invents accounts of meetings in further-ance of purely artistic and dramatic ends, one must stig-matise his approach as wrong-headed. Clearly these occasions neither recur habitually nor result in major distortion; but it must none the less be understood that Livy is willing to waive accuracy of detail to achieve en-hanced literary effects. To this extent his basic attitude is unhistorical.

IX

THE SPEECHES

THOUGH Livy took considerable pains with the artistic arrangement of his narrative, even more attention was paid to the composition of his speeches, on which his literary reputation at Rome above all rested. Quintilian, Tacitus, Seneca all pay eloquent tribute to them; and a remark of Suetonius suggests that they were published and studied separately in Domitian's day,[1] as they have been in France up to recent times.

This enthusiastic reception is not echoed by many modern scholars, who are rightly censorious of the practice of composing speeches rather than reproducing the actual words uttered.[2] But it is vital to remember here that Livy is an exponent of Isocratean theories of 'rhetorical' history, in which historiography is regarded as 'opus oratorium maxime'. Further, the insertion of composed speeches, a convention as old as Herodotus, is ingrained in Roman history-writing. Just as Sallust composed the speeches of Caesar and Cato in his *Catiline* although the original versions were accessible for reproduction, just as Tacitus redrafted a speech of the emperor Claudius in a style markedly more elegant than the original,[3] so Livy's speeches differ invariably in presentation (and occasionally in content) from the versions he read in his sources. But the purpose of these composed speeches is not an empty demonstration of rhetorical virtuosity; Livy attempts to

[1] Quint. x, 1, 101; Tac. *Ann.* iv, 34; Sen. *De Ira* i, 20, 6; Suet. *Dom.* x, 3.
[2] E.g. H. Nissen, *Kritische Untersuchungen*, 25 ff.
[3] Sall. *Cat.* 51 ff.; Tac. *Ann.* xi, 24 and *CIL* xiii, 1668 (Dessau, 212).

'get inside' the speaker, and to present, through the words attributed to him, a psychological portrait of his qualities. In short, in Livy 'les discours historiques sont avant tout des études de caractères sous une forme empruntée à la rhétorique';[1] and whilst one may regret that such speeches are unhistorical in a literal sense, the psychological insight which they reflect makes Quintilian's praise, 'cum personis tum rebus accommodata sunt', most apt.[2]

The form and division of the speeches are greatly influenced by Greek rhetorical theory, which is most clearly formulated by Aristotle, and which is analysed at Rome chiefly by the author of the treatise *Ad Herennium*, by Cicero and by Quintilian. The ancients distinguished three types of oratory—the *genus iudiciale*, the type appropriate to the law-court; the *genus demonstrativum*, the epideictic oratory suited to a formal ceremony (Pericles' funeral speech is an obvious example); and the *genus deliberativum*, comprising speeches delivered in councils, assemblies, and on the battle-field. As Aristotle remarks,[3] the three are distinguished by their aims; the first embodies accusation or defence, the second praise or censure, the third exhortation or dissuasion. Livy's history contains speeches exemplifying each of these genres, thereby showing a range wider than the work of any previous historian. Naturally enough, however, the *Ab Urbe Condita* is rarely

[1] R. Ullmann, *La technique des discours dans Salluste, Tite-Live et Tacite* (Oslo, 1927), 6.

[2] Quint. x, 1, 101. For a good discussion of this 'imagination psychologique' see H. Taine, *Essai sur Tite-Live*[6], 288 ff. Some scholars have taken Livy to task not because his speeches are fictitious, but because they are insufficiently instructive. On this view Livy, in his ignorance of political and legal evolution, and in his failure to propound fundamental truths of human nature, compares badly with Thucydides (see Hesselbarth, 692 f.; W. Soltau, *Livius' Geschichtswerk*, 15 f.). One may question this allegation of crass ignorance of political and legal evolution (above, 165); it would have been unhistorical to credit protagonists in their speeches with an awareness of such evolution, apprehended only by later analysis. And a preoccupation with alleged 'laws' of human behaviour carries the danger that the facts may be moulded to conform with the laws. See R. G. Collingwood, *The Idea of History*, 26 f.

[3] *Rhet.* I, 3 ff.; compare Quint. III, 4, 15.

concerned with law-courts or with formal ceremonial, so that almost all the speeches fall into the deliberative category.

The theorists of rhetoric formally divided the judicial speech into five or six sections. Such a complex arrangement was not sought in deliberative orations,[1] and their structure in Livy is always simple. Sometimes there are four divisions—introduction (*exordium* or *prooemium*), statement of the theme (κατάστασις), discussion of the theme (*tractatio*), and conclusion (*conclusio*); but often the statement of the theme can be omitted. This simple structure is well adapted to achieving the three aims posited by Cicero—*delectare, docere, movere*. Initially the speaker strives to *gratify* his audience to gain its good-will: the kernel of the speech *instructs* on the policy to be adopted: and the peroration contains the impassioned exhortation which *moves the emotions* of the hearer.

All the extensive speeches in the first and third decades are constructed according to this clearly observed oratorical design. It is interesting to compare the versions of Livy and Polybius recounting the same speeches made during the Hannibalic War, for this demonstrates the skill with which Livy rearranged the traditional material.[2] But in the fourth and fifth decades Livy does not always make a rearrangement according to the rules of rhetorical division, but is often content to transcribe speeches in the order of topics followed by Polybius. Each speech has a suitable *exordium* and *conclusio*, but beyond that no major stylistic change is made.[3] Livy does not, then, devote the same creative effort to many of these later speeches. Nor is he equally anxious to seize every apposite opportunity

---

[1] Quintilian (III, 8, 10ff.) does not apply these divisions to deliberative speeches.
[2] E.g. Pol. III, 62ff., Livy XXI, 40ff.; Pol. XI, 28f., Livy XXVIII, 27ff.; Pol. XV, 6, 4ff., Livy (following Pol.) XXX, 30.
[3] Compare, e.g., XXXVII, 53f. with Pol. XXI, 19ff., and note the absence of rhetorical divisions at XXXIV, 31f.; XXXIX, 36, 6ff.; XLI, 23; XLII, 40; XLIV, 22; XLV, 22ff.

for oratorical composition; on three occasions he refers the reader to speeches of Cato then extant, without troubling to compose an embellished version or to transcribe the actual words spoken.[1] Naturally enough, Livy feels the anticlimax after the crises and triumphs of the Hannibalic War. Many personalities whose speeches the historian conscientiously records have little appeal for purposes of characterisation; hence, with some notable exceptions, he composes these speeches more hastily and less artistically.

Of the surviving books, however, by far the greater number of speeches is constructed according to the divisions of rhetorical theory. There is always a formal *exordium*, inserted by Livy himself if his source has plunged abruptly *in medias res*.[2] The various methods of capturing the good-will of an audience (*captatio benevolentiae*) can all be exemplified. A common form is a speaker's concentration of attention upon himself (*principium a nostra persona*), as when Camillus, in his speech opposing the projected transference of the capital to Veii, states in commencement that his return from exile is not from personal motives but to oppose the abandonment of Rome.[3] Frequently the speaker adverts first to his audience (*principium ab auditoribus*), as when the praetor Aristaenus chides the Achaean council for its craven silence.[4] When a proposed measure is meeting resistance, a speaker may use a forensic technique, and attack his opponents (*principium ab adversariis*); so Appius Claudius begins by imputing to the tribunes self-interest as the sole motive for their agitation.[5] Finally, the *exordium* may refer to the topic of the speech (*principium a re*), as

---

[1] XXXVIII, 54, 11; XXXIX, 42, 6; XLV, 25, 3.

[2] Livy's insertion of *exordium* and *conclusio*, XXXIII, 39–40 (compare Pol. XVIII, 50, 5 ff.); XXXVII, 53 (Pol. XXI, 19), etc.

[3] V, 51, 1 f.; see also IX, 4, 8; XXII, 59, 1, etc.

[4] XXXII, 21, 1; also VI, 18, 5; XXII, 39, 1–3, etc.

[5] V, 3, 2; also XXII, 60, 6 f., etc.

in the speech of the consul on the scandal of the Bacchanalia in 186 B.C.[1]

Little need be said of the κατάστασις; it is brief, and often inseparable from the third section, the *tractatio*.[2] Here the spokesman discusses the projected course of action not merely from the aspect of expediency, but also with regard to what is honourable.[3] Quintilian adds a third basic criterion, the *possibile*. He also lists various subdivisions of the *utile* and the *honestum*. The honourable can embrace *fas*, *iustum*, *pium*, *aequum*, *mansuetum*; the expedient incorporates *facile*, *iucundum*, *magnum*, and *sine periculo*. These τόποι, and their opposites, form the staple content of the *tractatio* in Livy's speeches; and here above all, in the τόποι allotted to a speaker, the historian can introduce characterising elements. According to Quintilian, 'all will admit that the counsel given is in accordance with the speaker's character';[4] the reader makes his assessment by the types of argument used. Note, for example, the contrast between the speeches of Scipio and Hannibal in Book XXI. Scipio's arguments stress not merely the *facile* and *possibile*, but also the *religiosum*, the *pium* and the *dignum*, as is consonant with a god-fearing, highly serious Roman; Hannibal emphasises more materialistic motives—the *necessarium*, the *utile*, the *facile*.[5]

The closing section of the speech (*conclusio*) aims to move the emotions of the audience towards acceptance of the viewpoint proposed. Here too Livy introduces characterising elements. The wisdom and maturity of a statesman can be suggested by apposite generalisation.

[1] XXXIX, 15, 2; also XXXI, 7, 2; XXXIV, 2, 1.
[2] Ullmann, *La Technique*, confidently separates κατάστασις (or *propositio*) from *tractatio*, as at V, 51, 3; XXII, 39, 4–8, etc. But such division can become a very subjective process.
[3] Cic. *De Inv.* II, 156: 'in deliberativo autem Aristoteli placet utilitatem, nobis et honestatem et utilitatem'.   [4] 'secundum mores' (III, 8, 13).
[5] XXI, 40–4; compare Pol. III, 63–4. See also 232f. Mr R. M. Ogilvie notes the influence here of the schools of rhetoric; a speech like III, 67f. is full of τόποι traceable to Demosthenes and other authors.

So Fabius Cunctator advises L. Aemilius Paulus: 'veri-
tatem laborare nimis saepe aiunt, exstingui nunquam.
gloriam qui spreverit, veram habebit...omnia non pro-
peranti clara certaque erunt; festinatio improvida est et
caeca.'[1] A similar characterising effect is achieved by
citation of *exempla*, which Aristotle suggests are apt in
the peroration;[2] when Q. Caecilius Metellus in 179
moralises on the need for concord, he cites the salubrious
precedent of Titus Tatius and Romulus, and the peaceful
incorporation into the Roman state of Albans, Latins, and
Sabines.[3] But the peroration is chiefly marked by impassioned language (*amplificatio*) expressive of hauteur,
indignation, or lamentation; and having thus roused the
audience to enthusiastic support, the speaker closes with
an exhortation, or more concretely with a specific pro-
posal. Where Livy's source contains no rhetorical peroration, the entire *conclusio* is fittingly composed by him.

This rhetorical pattern of the deliberative speech
is best observed by summary of a typical example—the
speech of the Campanian envoys in the Roman Senate in
343 B.C.:[4]

Exordium: The fact that we seek help from you will ensure our
permanent friendship. (*Principium a nostra persona.*)
Tractatio: iustum. Though you are allied to our foes the Samnites,
there is no stipulation that you should undertake no new
alliances.

utile. We have rich resources to offer, and a strategic base
against your perennial foes, the Aequi and the Volsci.

aequum. It is right that you should help, since we are
facing destruction through aiding the weaker Sidicini; the
Samnites aim not at mere reprisal but at destruction or
occupation.

facile. You need only indicate your help; no war will be
necessary.

[1] XXII, 39, 19–22. [2] *Rhet.* III, 17, 5.
[3] XL, 46, 10–12. [4] VII, 30, 1–23.

utile. Capua will be your most splendid, fertile, and faithful colony.

Conclusio: The plight of our civil population is grievous; we exhort the Senate to urgent deliberation.[1]

Within this *genus deliberativum* certain types of speech have a stereotyped presentation. One such is the application for a triumph—a type much favoured by the late annalists.[2] But the outstanding example is the *hortatio* on the battle-field, with the emphasis almost invariably on the ease with which victory will be won (*facile*), the advantages accruing from victory (*utile*), the glory to be acquired (*gloriosum*). The speech of M'. Acilius Glabrio before Thermopylae in 191, that of Hannibal in XXI that of Valerius Corvus before engaging the Samnites, the words of Cn. Manlius before the conflict with the Tolostobogii, all have an identical ring.[3] But these facets of the *utile* are in the case of the great Romans reinforced by nobler sentiments in the interests of characterisation so a speech of Scipio Africanus to his troops in Spain discusses not merely the *possibile* and the *facile*, but also the *religiosum*.[4]

There are several speeches which might appear, from the circumstances in which they occurred, to approximate to the *genus iudiciale*. For example, there is the controversy between Papirius Cursor and Fabius Rullianus, after Fabius had fought in defiance of the dictator's orders: the court case involving Verginia, victim of Appius Claudius' lust: and the condemnation at Rome of Pleminius, the rapacious governor of Locri. But in the first two episodes no extended speech is recorded; and the

---

[1] Weissenborn rightly notes that this speech contains reminiscences of Thuc. I, 32 ff. (the Corcyreans seeking aid against the Corinthians).

[2] So Nissen, 92. Examples in Livy, XXXVIII, 47, 6 ff.; XLV, 37 ff.

[3] XXXVI, 17, 2–6; XXI, 43–4; VII, 32, 6 ff.; XXXVIII, 17, 2 ff. See also VII, 35, 2 ff. The *hortatio* (παρακέλευσις) was a traditional feature of Greek historiography.

[4] XXVI, 41, 3–25. Note also the speech of Scipio at XXI, 40–1.

speech made by Locrian envoys against Pleminius is not marshalled with judicial argumentation.[1]

The only definite examples of the judicial type are the speeches of Perseus and Demetrius before their father Philip at the Macedonian court, in which Perseus alleges that Demetrius has tried to assassinate him, and Demetrius denies the charge. In fact, this was not an official trial, but Livy has accentuated the features which lend the scene a judicial appearance.[2] Accordingly the speeches in accusation and defence are constructed according to the scheme tabulated by the theorists.[3] Perseus' speech begins with an *exordium*, in which he laments his dilemma; his father will not believe the plot until it is successfully accomplished. There follows the *narratio*, the account of the circumstances of the attempted assassination. In the *probatio*, Perseus speaks at length on the motives of Demetrius—his design to obtain the kingship, supported by Roman arms: he outlines his brother's attempt to seize the opportunities offered for the assassination: and demands that Demetrius' companions be called as witnesses. There is a close correspondence here with the εἰκότα, σημεῖα, τεκμήρια of Aristotle.[4] The conclusion comprises an exhortation (προτροπή) to Philip to punish the guilty. Livy allows Demetrius a speech in defence one-and-a-half times as long. The *exordium* begins with a *principium ab adversariis*, a stock judicial technique. The main section of the speech, as is apposite for a defendant, is a detailed *refutatio* of the threefold allegation of Perseus; and the long peroration is a *commiseratio* (again characteristic of a defendant's speech), bewailing Demetrius' lack

---

[1] VIII, 30 ff.; III, 44 ff.; XXIX, 17 f.

[2] XL, 8, 7 ff.; see 234 f.

[3] *Auct. ad Her.* III, 4, 7 ff. lists six divisions: *exordium, narratio, partitio, refutatio, confirmatio, conclusio*. But Quintilian (reasonably) denies a separate section to *partitio*, which is merely an aspect of general arrangement (III, 9, 2). Aristotle groups *confirmatio* and *refutatio* under the single heading of 'proof' (*Rhet.* II, 26). Thus the most simply stated scheme is *exordium, narratio, probatio, conclusio*.

[4] *Rhet.* I, 2.

of a skilled advocate, his lack of time to prepare his case, his distress at hearing the charge, his fears for when Perseus becomes king.

Examples of the *genus demonstrativum* are similarly rare. The speech of Aemilius Paulus shortly after his triumph hardly falls into this category, unless self-praise is a qualification for admission; this is not a funeral speech pronounced over his adopted sons so much as a catalogue of his own recent military successes, supplemented by a pathetic reference to his childlessness.[1] The speech of the Saguntine ambassadors in which they extol the altruism of Rome is a clear-cut example, for cities no less than men can be the recipients of such panegyric.[2] There is much to be said for including the attack on Pleminius under this head, for the *genus demonstrativum* embraces not only praise but also denunciation.[3]

Though there is this distinction in rhetorical theory between the three types of speech, Livy does not embody any conscious differences of style such as the fourth-century Athenians manifest. Logographers would consciously employ a more poetic language and a more high-flown style in epideictic oratory than in speeches composed for the Pnyx or for the law-court,[4] and judicial speeches were often given a deliberately unsophisticated form to characterise the speaker as a man of plain words and unsubtle mind. In this sense, the Roman historians show a lesser sense of refinement and discrimination, adopting an argumentation appropriate to the particular genre, but seeking no consistent variation of style or diction.[5]

---

[1] xLV, 41; against Ullmann, *La Technique*, 194, and Bornecque, 159f.
[2] See Quint. III, 7, 26.
[3] *vituperatio*: Quint. III, 7, 19ff.
[4] See J. D. Denniston, *Greek Prose Style* (Oxford, 1952), 18.
[5] The criticism should be qualified by the realisation that the only extant judicial speeches in Livy hardly allow of simple and unstudied language (see Quintilian's comment, VIII, 3, 14). But the criticism holds for some deliberative

All three types, deliberative, judicial, and epideictic, contain argumentation in the central section and emotional fervour in the *conclusio* which are the media for Livy's attempts at characterisation. Such portrayal is in exclusively moral terms—one recalls Tacitus' avowal not to record speeches save those 'insignes per honestum aut notabili dedecore'.[1] Compare the versions of Livy and Dionysius of a speech made by Icilius after the scandalous abduction of Verginia by Appius Claudius. In Dionysius, Icilius speaks with sophisticated irony, bidding Appius make off with all the womenfolk he requires; Livy depicts a more moral and dignified stand—'saevite in tergum et in cervices nostras; pudicitia saltem in tuto sit'.[2] The speeches of Camillus underline his altruistic patriotism, his proud independence when exiled, his dignity and perspicacity. The dignified, restrained tone of the plebeian P. Decius Mus is contrasted with the impetuosity and violence of Appius Claudius. Africanus' speech to his mutineering troops has a higher moral fervour than the traditional version of his words. Cato's speech on the *lex Oppia* characterises him as an idealistic moralist and patriot, as well as an orator of vehemence, candour, and biting sarcasm.[3]

Livy's speeches befit not only the speaker but also the occasion. Notice how, when M. Valerius Corvus addresses some seditious Roman troops marching upon the capital, he ignores arguments of expediency, and emphasises the *pium, aequum*, and *honestum*. When Hannibal confers with Scipio before Zama, bidding him use his

---

speeches demanding a less sophisticated tone. Note, for example, the speech of an honest-to-goodness sergeant-major, Sextus Tullius (VII, 13), which any practised orator would have been proud to own. But more moderation is shown at XLII, 34, where the centurion Sp. Ligustinus makes a patriotic speech in homely language.

[1] *Ann.* III, 65.

[2] III, 45, 6–11. Compare Dionys. XI, 31, 4.

[3] Camillus, V, 44, 51–4; Decius Mus, X, 7–8; Africanus, XXVIII, 27 (compare Pol. XI, 28–9, and see above, 99f.); Cato, XXXIV, 2–4.

success with moderation, the words are appropriate to the fading of the Carthaginian's fortunes.[1]

Yet however apposite many such speeches are, the preoccupation with rhetoric which so dominated Roman historiography, the desire frequently to adorn the narrative with oratorical display, leads Livy to introduce speeches on occasions quite inapposite. Presumably he was well aware of these absurdities, but believed that his contemporary audience would conspire with him to forget the manufactured occasion in its delight at the oratorical performance. One such speech is made by a delegate of the disgraced survivors of Cannae before Marcellus in his winter quarters. Nothing could be more incongruous than this theatrical display before a single man, with all its emotive overtones and wealth of rhetorical figures. In anticipation of such criticism, the spokesman says: 'I seem to be gazing upon both consuls and upon the whole body of the Senate when I look upon you, Marcus Marcellus.' The speech is even marked with a salutation to quite imaginary *patres conscripti*![2]

On another occasion we read of an attack to be launched in the middle of the night by Publius Decius from a hill overlooking the enemy. Secrecy is essential, so the soldiers are bidden not to applaud. Instead of whispered instructions the commander exhorts his men with an imposing oration, long enough not merely to have roused the enemy but also to have allowed them to overwhelm the bemused Romans.[3] The same incongruity is to be observed in a speech delivered by Manlius Capitolinus to plebeian leaders at dead of night behind closed doors, for there is nothing furtive or conspiratorial about the form

---

[1] VII, 40; XXX, 30. See also 232f.

[2] XXV, 6, 5: 'ambo mihi consules et universum senatum intueri videor cum te, M. Marcelle, intueor'. For a further example see the highly elaborate oration addressed by the Campanian Pacuvius Calavius to his son, the would-be assassin of Hannibal, at XXIII, 9, 1–8.

[3] VII, 35, 2–12.

of a speech which contains every rhetorical figure in the manual, and which was better suited to the open forum.[1]

Equally inapposite but equally effective as a rhetorical *tour de force* is the speech uttered by Queen Sophoniba on the threshold of the palace at Cirta, when Masinissa gallops up to seize this potential centre of resistance. He stands at the porch in statuesque immobility, his arms and princely robes conspicuous amongst his supporters, whilst Sophoniba, grovelling at his knees, utters this dramatic *supplicatio* with its wealth of adjuration:

The gods, your merits, and your happy fortune have bestowed on you utter power over us. But if a captive woman can utter a suppliant word before the lord of her life and death, if she can touch the victor's knees and his right hand, I pray and beseech you by that regal majesty which we too but recently enjoyed; by the name of the Numidian race, which you have shared with Syphax; by the gods of the palace (may they receive you with omens more favourable than those with which they dispatched Syphax!): grant to my supplication the mercy of the disposal of your captive according to your own inclination, and do not permit me to pass into the haughty, cruel dominion of any Roman. Had I been merely Syphax's wife, I should yet have preferred to entrust myself to a Numidian, one born, as I was, in Africa; but as I am a Carthaginian and daughter of Hasdrubal, you see what I must fear from a Roman. I beg and beseech you to preserve me by death, if no other way is possible, from the dominion of the Romans.[2]

Yet if by modern standards Livy is to be condemned for such imaginative and inapposite compositions, it is salutary to examine by comparison the speeches in Dionysius' *Roman Antiquities*. Judged by this criterion, Livy is to be applauded for his moderation. Apart from a few orations delivered at critical points in early Roman history, the speeches attributed by Livy to Roman leaders have a brevity far more in keeping with the characters of the

[1] VI, 18, 5-15.   [2] XXX, 12, 12 ff.

spokesmen than have the interminable compositions of Dionysius. Compare, for example, the two versions of the negotiations following upon the secession to the Mons Sacer. Livy is content with a few lines of *oratio obliqua*; Dionysius records no fewer than ten speeches, covering thirty-eight chapters.[1] It is noteworthy that, proportionately speaking, Livy's speeches are less extensive than Sallust's, and occupy only half as much of the whole work as do those of Thucydides; the number of lengthy speeches is small, and such judicious husbanding of his resources enhances his rhetorical effectiveness.[2]

So far as content is concerned, comparison with extant source-material suggests that Livy does not personally introduce many fictitious topics. But he willingly incorporates from untrustworthy sources matter transparently suspect from an historical viewpoint. It can truthfully be claimed that he suspends his standards of integrity and accuracy on many occasions through such docile reproduction. For example, he is perfectly willing to take from Antias the reports of speeches allegedly uttered by Terentius Varro, Fabius Cunctator, and Aemilius Paulus before the battle of Cannae. The eloquent and prophetic oration attributed to Fabius and the fatalistic words of Aemilius were clearly composed long after the battle in denigration of Varro; Polybius has no mention of these forebodings, and Livy is acquainted with his version. It is hard to avoid the conclusion that a love of oratory has contributed to Livy's decision to prefer the false account incorporating these utterances.[3]

Frequently, too, the content of the sources is augmented

---

[1] II, 32, 5–12; Dionys. VI, 49–86. For general assessments of this episode see E. Burck, *Die Erzählungskunst*, 232 f.; Ullmann, 19 f.

[2] The proportion of speeches to the whole extant work is about twelve per cent; by comparison, Sallust's is fifteen per cent, Thucydides' twenty-four per cent. Of the 407 extant Livian speeches, only sixteen extend beyond one hundred lines of the Teubner text. For an exhaustive (and exhausting) statistical analysis see O. Kohl, *Über Zweck und Bedeutung der liv. Reden*, 2 ff.

[3] XXII, 38, 6 ff.; Pol. III, 108 ff.

or reduced from artistic motives, especially in those conference scenes constructed around antithetical speeches. Livy goes to extraordinary lengths to balance such speeches in length and in order of topics. The accounts of the conference at Lysimachia in 196, as recorded by Polybius and Livy, are instructive. Polybius records a speech of Antiochus two-and-a-half times as long as that of the Romans which preceded it; Livy has effectively reduced the one and expanded the other to lessen the disparity. An *exordium* and *conclusio* are inserted into the Romans' speech, as well as conventional argumentation. The speech of Antiochus is rearranged so that the points raised by the Romans are answered in the same order.[1] A similar balancing technique occurs in the description of a Roman assembly addressed by Eumenes and the Rhodians; Livy has reduced the length of the first speech and slightly expanded that of the Rhodians by the insertion of a few fictitious topics.[2] In some accounts of conferences, the balance is achieved by the insertion of identical τόποι in the *tractatio* of opposed speeches; so in the discussion on the *lex Oppia*, Cato and Valerius both discuss in the same order the *honestum, tutum, utile, necessarium,* and *aequum*.[3]

An especially apposite example from the third decade of such artistic editing is the balance between the speeches of Scipio (father of Africanus) and Hannibal before the first engagement on Italian soil. Polybius is not Livy's direct source here, but he gives us the traditional version, with which Livy's account stands in strong contrast. In Polybius both speeches are brief, but Scipio's is shorter than Hannibal's; the words of the Carthaginian are recounted first, and are partly in *oratio obliqua*, as indeed is the greater part of Scipio's speech. Livy has carefully

[1] xxxiii, 39–40; Pol. xviii, 50–1.
[2] xxxvii, 53–4; Pol. xxi, 18–24. Ullmann, 156, emphasises the patriotic motive behind such insertions, as at xxxvii, 54, 17–28.
[3] xxxiv, 2–7.

constructed the two to be of identical length; for this purpose the motifs of the *tractatio* of Scipio's speech are expanded to introduce the elements of piety and patriotism already mentioned.[1] Both speeches are greatly prolonged, so that the solemnity and significance of this moment before the great struggle may be apprehended. Scipio's speech is put first, because it forms a smoother transition from the previous narration; then Hannibal's harangue answers Scipio's point by point, as if he had been present at the Roman commander's speech. *Oratio recta* is employed throughout both speeches to achieve the maximum impact. In short, Livy has been concerned to arrange this scene in an artistic, antithetical, and dramatic way, and has effectively conveyed not merely the characters of the protagonists but also the importance of the occasion.[2]

Another interesting technique of speech construction is the method by which the historian draws together a number of separate speeches to form a single, coherent, non-redundant statement. In the description of a war conference held by Antiochus, Hannibal is represented as giving his views. In fact, he was not present at this conference; Livy has added his comments to those of the speakers who were there in order to include every element hostile to Rome.[3] A slightly different example can be found in the Aetolian attempt to obtain peace from Fulvius Nobilior; first one reads of the proceedings of the Aetolian council, and then of the supplication of the Aetolian envoys to the Roman consul. The reply of Fulvius answers not only the petition of the envoys, but also the points raised at the council at which he was not present.[4]

---

[1] Above, 223.

[2] xxi, 40–4; Pol. iii, 62–4. For detailed comments see Ullmann, 16 f.; Burck, *Einführung*, 71 f. Other examples of this balancing technique are at xxviii, 40 ff. (conflict between Fabius Cunctator and Scipio Africanus); xxxi, 29 ff. (Macedonian and Roman viewpoints at the Aetolian council).

[3] xxxv, 17–19; Witte, *RhM* (1910), 377.   [4] xxxviii, 8.

A distinctive feature of many of the speeches, for which the comments on Livy's 'tragic' effects will have prepared the reader, is the infusion of a more pathetic spirit and a more dramatic atmosphere. Nowhere is this more obvious than in the speech of Philip to his two sons, a considerable section of which is preserved in Polybius. From this it is clear that Philip actually spoke in a tone of brisk admonition:

You should not merely read tragedies, fables, and historical speeches, but know them well and reflect on such things. In all of them one can see that those brothers who abandoned themselves to overmuch reciprocated wrath and contention were not merely ruined, but also utterly destroyed their lives, their children, and their cities....

The thesis is continued to show that prosperity attends on mutual toleration and moderation, and Perseus and Demetrius are rebuked for ignoring the salutary examples of the Spartan kings and the brothers Eumenes and Attalus.

Livy's version introduces a note of anger and sorrow, stressing the pathos of Philip's dual role of father and judge: 'sedeo, inquit, miserrimus pater iudex inter duos filios...'. The pathetic atmosphere of the law-court is evoked by the skilful use of rhetorical figures. Philip describes his sons as 'accusatorem parricidii et reum'; he says that he is doomed to find amongst his own kin 'aut conficti aut admissi criminis labem'. Indeed, the opportunities for such telling antithesis are obvious. The effect of pathos is gradually supplanted by one of anger, until the climax is reached in a series of short sentences, culminating in rhetorical repetition of the imperative:

nec fratrem nec patrem potestis pati. nihil cari, nihil sancti est. in omnium vicem regni unius insatiabilis amor successit. agite, conscelerate aures paternas, decernite criminibus, mox ferro decreturi, dicite palam quicquid aut veri potestis aut libet

comminisci: reseratae aures sunt, quae posthac secretis alterius
ab altero criminibus claudentur.[1]

One sees a similar dramatic preoccupation in Livy's
version of the speech of Scipio Africanus when imposing
peace terms on Antiochus. Polybius shows that this
speech was merely a catalogue of instructions: Antiochus
must retire beyond Taurus, pay 15,000 Euboean talents,
and the rest. Livy never tires of bringing Africanus into
dramatic prominence, and formal rhetoric is employed to
emphasise the solemnity of the moment, and the majesty
of Roman power: 'postquam traiecimus Hellespontum,
priusquam castra regia, priusquam aciem videremus, cum
communis Mars et incertus belli eventus esset, de pace
vobis agentibus quas pares paribus ferebamus condiciones,
easdem nunc victores victis ferimus.' It is with surprise
that one reads the words as recorded by Polybius: 'The
same answer would now be given to them by the Romans
as they had formerly obtained, when they came to the
Hellespont before the battle.'[2]

In his speeches, then, Livy aims to evoke a more compelling and dramatic atmosphere, and on certain occasions
for purposes of characterisation and from artistic motives
makes changes or additions to the source-content.
Generally speaking, however, it is his custom to reproduce substantially the content whilst rearranging the form
according to the principles outlined, and he does not
scruple to change the order of topics to produce greater
cohesion and rhetorical force.[3]

But as Cicero and Quintilian emphasise, such invention
of content (*inventio*) and arrangement of topics (*dispositio*)
do not in themselves make for outstanding oratory;

---

[1] XL, 8; compare Pol. XXIII, 11.

[2] Pol. XXI, 17, 2: καὶ νῦν αὐτοῖς τὴν αὐτὴν ἀπόκρισιν δοθήσεσθαι παρὰ Ῥωμαίων ἦν καὶ πρότερον ἔλαβον, ὅτε πρὸ τῆς μάχης παρεγενήθησαν ἐπὶ τὸν Ἑλλήσ⟨ποντον⟩. The Livian passage is at XXXVII, 45, 13. See Ullmann, 149.

[3] As at XXXII, 34 (Pol. XVIII, 5); XXXIII, 31 (Pol. XVIII, 45); XXXVII, 36 (Pol. XXI, 15).

the third and most difficult attribute is *elocutio*, or style.[1] Fortunately we are able to compare a short address by Africanus as recorded by Valerius Antias with Livy's refined, embellished version; this gives a clear picture of Livy's stylistic preoccupations.

ANTIAS: memoria, Quirites, repeto diem esse hodiernum quo Hannibalem Poenum imperio vestro inimicissimum magno proelio vici in terra Africa, pacemque et victoriam vobis peperi insperabilem. non igitur simus adversus deos ingrati, sed censeo relinquamus nebulonem hunc, eamus hinc protinus Iovi Optimo Maximo gratulatum.

LIVY: hoc, inquit, die, tribuni plebis vosque Quirites, cum Hannibale et Carthaginiensibus signis collatis in Africa bene ac feliciter pugnavi. itaque cum hodie litibus et iurgiis supersederi aequum sit, ego hinc extemplo in Capitolium ad Iovem optimum maximum Iunonemque et Minervam ceterosque deos qui Capitolio atque arci praesident salutandos ibo, hisque gratias agam quod mihi et hoc ipso die et saepe alias egregie gerendae reipublicae mentem facultatemque dederunt. vestrum quoque, quibus commodum est, Quirites, ite mecum et orate deos ut mei similes principes habeatis, ita si ab annis XVII ad senectutem semper vos aetatem meam honoribus vestris anteistis, ego vestros honores rebus gerendis praecessi.

Apart from the last gratuitously added sentence, Livy seems to have tried to imitate the simplicity of the original,[2] at the same time adding several embellishments. The crudities are removed (one recalls Livy's unwillingness to reproduce the poem of Livius Andronicus for its archaic uncouthness).[3] 'diem esse hodiernum quo' becomes 'hoc die': 'in terra Africa' becomes 'in Africa': Livy omits 'non...simus'. But most notable is Livy's fondness for *congeries verborum*. 'tribuni plebis vosque

[1] Cic. *De Or.* I, 44; *Or.* 44; Quint. VIII, *pr.* 13 ff.
[2] Antias, *ap.* Gell. IV, 11, 4; Livy XXXVIII, 51, 7–11. See J. Marouzeau, *Rev. Phil.* (1921), 165 f.
[3] XXVII, 37, 13: 'abhorrens et inconditum si referatur'.

Quirites', 'cum Hannibale et Carthaginiensibus', 'bene ac feliciter', 'litibus et iurgiis', 'Capitolio atque arci', 'mentem facultatemque' all either replace a single expression or have no equivalent in Antias' version. If this is a typical example, as we can fairly assume, of Livy's regular treatment of the source-material, the time and care devoted to such stylistic transcription are obviously considerable. And when one sees a speech prefaced, as this is, by a phrase such as 'in hunc modum locutus fertur', 'in hanc sententiam locutum accipio', or 'tali oratione disseruit',[1] it is clear that such formulae conceal stylistic changes of a sweeping kind.

The most apposite method of examining the rhetorical elements of the speeches is by reference to Quintilian's analysis of the ingredients of *elocutio*.[2] After stressing the need for propriety of language and clarity of expression, Quintilian passes to rhetorical adornment (*ornatum*). Here he first discusses the general principles of ἐνάργεια (*repraesentatio*). Livy excels in such 'vivid description' no less in speeches than in his narrative,[3] achieving his effects by asyndeton, short clauses, rapid accumulation of expressions, and verbal figures: 'leur trait caractéristique est avant tout l'énumération rapide et le plus souvent asyndétique de faits qui se succèdent, pour former ensemble dans tous les détails une image vivante qui frappe l'imagination du lecteur'.[4] So the Campanian legates requesting Roman aid against the Samnites vividly portray the anxious anticipation of their people:

qua frequentia omnium generum multitudinis prosequente creditis nos illinc profectos? quam omnia votorum lacrimarumque plena reliquisse? in qua nunc expectatione senatum

---

[1] III, 67; XXII, 60, 5; XXXVII, 45, 11; XLII, 34, 2, etc.
[2] Quint. VIII–IX. The method was first adopted by H. V. Canter, *AJP* (1917), 125 ff.; (1918), 44 ff. R. Ullmann, *Étude sur le style des discours de Tite-Live* (Oslo, 1929), extended the scope of the discussion.
[3] Above, 181 ff.
[4] R. Ullmann, *Étude*, 17.

populumque Campanum, coniuges liberosque nostros esse? stare omnem multitudinem ad portas viam hinc ferentem prospectantes certum habeo.[1]

As Quintilian suggests, one obvious method of achieving *repraesentatio* is the use of similes; but if it is to illuminate, the subject chosen 'should be neither obscure nor unfamiliar'.[2] Livy's similes are restricted to such familiar topics as the sea, disease, animal life, and fire. Vibius Virrius the Capuan, in his tribute to Roman constancy in the blockade of Capua, remarks: 'One can divert wild beasts, roused to blind onslaught and madness, to lend help to their own by attacking their haunts and lairs; when Rome was blockaded their own wives and children did not divert the Romans.'[3] Consistently with his free stylistic arrangement Livy inserts his own similes, excises others, or seeks to refine on them. On one occasion such refinement is carried too far. In Polybius, a speech by the Athenian Leon compares the Aetolians when roused by irresponsible demagogues to the tranquil sea stirred by the winds. Livy introduces into the simile Antiochus as the rock on which the Aetolians are tossed—forgetting that they are being compared with the sea, and not with ships or sailors![4]

The author of the treatise *Ad Herennium* suggests that *exempla* perform a function similar to that of similes.[5] Here Livy's historical studies are usefully employed. Often he introduces additional *exempla* when a speech in his source contains the citation of inspiring or deterrent precedents. In the speech of Philip already mentioned, where Polybius' version cites as examples of harmonious brotherhood Eumenes and Attalus, and the Spartan

---

[1] VII, 30, 21 f. Other examples, XXV, 6, 20 f.; XLV, 39, etc.

[2] Quint. VIII, 3, 73. He adds that the precept was frequently ignored in the schools of rhetoric, with disastrous results.

[3] XXVI, 13, 12. Other beastly similes, XXXV, 18, 6; XXXVIII, 17, 5.

[4] For omission of a simile, XXXVII, 54, 10 (Pol. XXI, 22, 13). The unfortunate over-elaboration, XXXVIII, 10, 5 f. (Pol. XXI, 31, 6 ff.). Other sea similes, V, 52, 1; XXIV, 8, 12; disease, V, 5, 11; XXXIV, 4, 8; fire, XXI, 10, 4 and 11; XXVIII, 42, 10.

[5] *Auct. ad Her.* IV, 49, 62.

kings, Livy cites in addition Titus and Lucius Quinctius Flamininus, and Publius and Cnaeus Cornelius Scipio. It is no coincidence that these are Roman *exempla*, for it is part of Livy's purpose to demonstrate that the Romans of old possessed such virtues.[1] Amongst non-Romans especially notable is Masinissa, repeatedly cited as the supreme example of the faithful ally fairly and generously treated by the Romans.[2]

Quintilian next briefly discusses the various methods by which amplification can be achieved, and then lists the various tropes and figures, rigorously distinguishing between them. Such schematic division verges on pedantry, as he himself admits; whatever their names, the effects are the same,[3] and it is more convenient to list them under two headings only—figures of thought and figures of speech.[4]

The verbal figure is that which 'attracts attention and arouses interest by similarity of words, or by words which are matched or contrasting'.[5] Perhaps the commonest is ἀναφορά (*repetitio*), the repetition of a word or phrase as in the Churchillian utterance: 'We will fight on the beaches. We will fight on the landing-grounds. We will fight in the hills.' There is surely no speech of Livy which does not contain such rhetorical repetition as: 'quid ab legionibus, quid ab iustis armis, quid ab animis fortissimorum militum expectari?' (The converse device, ἀντιστροφή (*conversio*), by which consecutive phrases or sentences *end* with the same word, is much less common.) *Antithesis*, the balancing of opposed ideas, is a central feature: 'an blandiores in publico quam in privato, et alienis quam vestris estis?' Such antithetical effect is often reinforced by the figure known as *isocolon*, the exact balancing of syllables numerically between the two contrasting parts

---

[1] E.g. xxviii, 29, 1; xxxix, 51, 11.

[2] xxxvii, 25, 9; 53, 21, etc.   [3] ix, 1, 8.

[4] Quint. ix, 1, 16: 'illa (*sc.* figura sententiae) est enim posita in concipienda cogitatione, haec (*sc.* figura verborum) in enuntianda'.

[5] Quint. ix, 1, 17.

of a sentence. It is astonishing to observe how frequently this is achieved, and it conspicuously demonstrates the artistry which lies behind Livy's composition: 'cum vincere cupimus / tum te duce vincere, tibi lauream insignem deferre / tecum triumphantes urbem inire'.[1] Another ally of antithesis is the figure known as *chiasmus*, the arrangement of words and phrases in an *a, b, b, a* pattern: 'a facinoribus manus, mentem a fraudibus abstinuissent' is a good illustration, showing the exactness of balance often achieved. Occasionally the pattern is more complex (*a, b, c, c, b, a*): 'ut nos virtute culpam nostram corrigere et abolere flagitii memoriam nova gloria patereris'. Another figure, *congeries verborum*, has already been observed in Livy's expanded version of a speech of Africanus; two or more words are used tautologically to attain increased emphasis, as in 'libertas nostra...hic quoque in foro obteritur et calcatur'.

These are the commonest of the verbal figures, but others occasionally employed are *adnominatio*, the juxtaposition of words of similar sound but dissimilar meaning ('velut hospitis non hostis adventu...'); *zeugma*, the use of a single verb expressing different senses with different objects ('Graeci suam fortunam, vestros animos gerunt'); and *homoioteleuton*, the rhyming effect produced at the end of clauses ('nunc imperare animo nequivi quin, priusquam perirem, cur periturus essem scirem').

Amongst the figures of thought, a less homogeneous group, it is notable that Livy's range of metaphor is bolder and wider than that of Cicero. Such expressions as 'clandestina concocta sunt consilia', 'libertatis desiderium remordet animos', and 'discordia ordinum est venenum urbis huius', reflect the natural development of the Latin language.[2] Next can be mentioned *irony*, an effect

---

[1] This refinement is from the speech of Sex. Tullius (see 227, n. 5).
[2] XL, 11, 2; VIII, 4, 3; III, 67, 6. Kühnast, *Die Hauptpunkte der liv. Syntax*, 301.

especially observable in the characterisation of die-hards like the elder Cato; it is usually heralded by *scilicet*. Also notable is *incrementum* (αὔξησις), the building up of a climax of words or expressions. Very common is *apostrophe*, the device by which the speaker enlivens his speech by turning aside to address gods or men. Frequently it is a mere phrase such as 'patres conscripti', but the more effective use is the direct appeal: 'Will Scipio, the famed conqueror of Africa, be trampled down by your feet, tribunes?' Other standard techniques of the orator's repertoire are *praeteritio*, the drawing of the audience's attention to a topic, and then passing over it ('sed omitto haec'); *reticentia*, a statement begun which leaves the rest to the audience's imagination; *praesumptio*, an admitted objection to an argument, usually introduced by *at, at enim, at hercule*, which lends an air of reasonableness to a speaker; *fictio personarum*, the momentary assumption of the identity of an opponent, which pretends to interpret the opposing view; and *exaggeratio*, the transparent hyperbole used to attract attention.[1]

But the commonest and most effective of the so-called figures of thought are *exclamatio* and *interrogatio*. The *exclamatio* can be a mere phrase like 'di immortales!' or 'pro deum fidem!', or it can extend over a whole sentence. The *interrogatio* embraces a number of refinements. It can be a rhetorical question, asserting the reverse of the expected reply; or the kind of question which elicits a reply, real or imaginary, from an opponent; or, most usually, a strong assertion put for emphasis in interrogative form. This figure is especially effective in repetition, as in the speech of Demetrius refuting Perseus' charge of attempted fratricide:

aut explica, utrum aperte an clam te aggressuri fuerimus. si aperte, cur non omnes ferrum habuimus? cur nemo praeter eos

---

[1] Examples of irony, IV, 5, 3; XXXII, 21, 28; *incrementum*, XXV, 6, 17–18; XLV, 24, 11 f.; *apostrophe*, XXXVIII, 53, 1 (quoted); IX, 8, 8–10; *praeteritio*, XXI, 43, 13; XXXIV, 32, 11; *reticentia*, VII, 30, 23; *praesumptio*, V, 52, 5; XXXVII, 53, 25; *fictio personarum*, V, 4, 7; XLV, 23, 6; *exaggeratio*, XXIX, 18, 7.

qui tuum speculatorem pulsaverunt? si clam, quis ordo consilii fuit? convivio soluto cum comisator ego discessissem, quattuor substitissent, ut sopitum te aggrederentur, quomodo fefellissent et alieni et mei et maxime suspecti, quia paulo ante in rixa fuerant? quomodo autem trucidato te ipsi evasuri fuerunt? quattuor gladiis domus tua capi et expugnari potuit?[1]

Also worthy of note as a rhetorical element is the abundance of *sententiae*; as Aristotle remarks, they lend character to a speech, and the listener feels pleasure at the exposition of a general truth already entertained.[2] Their employment in the *conclusio* has already been noted, but they are used more generally for purposes of characterisation. Cato's attack on the *lex Oppia* contains a number of them, but the speeches of the youths Perseus and Demetrius have none.[3] Such *sententiae* are regarded by Livy as part of the form of a speech, and he dispenses with those he found in his sources if he is so inclined.[4]

Such are the techniques affecting the form of the speeches. His general approach and purpose have been admirably summarised by a French scholar:

On constate que Tite-Live a fait subir à sa source des modifications très sensibles, abrégeant ici, développant ailleurs, contaminant deux ou trois discours, pour des raisons patriotiques... et surtout littéraires: il veut introduire plus de clarté dans la suite du raisonnement, plus de relief dans la marche du développement, plus de force convaincante dans le choix des exemples historiques, plus de variété dans la peinture des sentiments, et d'une façon générale, plus de vie, de mouvement, et de pathétique.[5]

Finally, one must advert to Livy's use of *oratio recta* and *oratio obliqua*. The first is obviously the more vivid and expressive medium, used especially for more imposing utterances at significant moments of history, and employed

---

[1] XL, 14.   [2] *Rhet.* II, 21, 15 f.
[3] Cato, XXXIV, 1–4; Perseus and Demetrius, XL, 12–13.
[4] See, e.g., the omission of two *sententiae* at XXXVII, 54 (compare his source, Pol. XXI, 22, 8; 23, 9).   [5] H. Bornecque, 174.

as an important element in the characterisation of major figures.

A surviving quotation from Livy's contemporary Pompeius Trogus, in which Sallust and Livy are censured for 'transgressing the bounds of history' by the introduction of *oratio recta*, suggests that the normal procedure in the annalists had been to reproduce speeches in *oratio obliqua*.[1] This accounts for the preponderance of reported speech in Livy; it has been computed that in the first six books there is almost four times as much indirect as direct speech.[2] This preponderance is more limited later, when Livy allows himself more scope for detailed characterisation; one notes that when following Polybius, who uses *oratio recta* freely, he not merely transcribes such speeches into the same medium, but also converts *oratio obliqua* in Polybius into *oratio recta* on several occasions.[3]

Whilst it is true that direct speech is often preferred to secure a greater rhetorical effect, it must not be assumed that there is no rhetorical embellishment in the medium of *oratio obliqua*.[4] On the contrary, examination of a typical passage illustrates a wealth of rhetorical figures— *antithesis, anaphora, interrogatio, congeries verborum*:

regem conspici, regem unum ducem, unum imperatorem videri debere. si classem, si exercitum amittat Hannibal, idem damni fore ac si per alium ducem amittantur; si quid prospere eveniat, Hannibalis eam non Antiochi gloriam fore: si vero universo bello vincendi Romanos fortuna detur, quam spem esse sub rege victurum uni subiectum qui patriam prope non tulerit? non ita se a iuventa eum gessisse, spe animoque complexum orbis terrarum imperium, ut in senectute dominum laturus videatur. nihil opus esse regi duce Hannibale: comite

[1] *Ap.* Iustin. 38, 3, 11.
[2] A. Lambert, *Die indirekte Rede als künstlerisches Stilmittel des Livius* (diss. Zürich, 1946), 10.
[3] E.g. in XXXVII, chs. 36, 45, 53 (compare Pol. XXI, 15, 16f., 19–21—this last a mixture of *oratio recta* and *oratio obliqua*).
[4] Against Ullmann, *La Technique*, 23: 'les discours sous forme indirecte n'ont pas d'intérêt pour la composition'.

et consiliario eodem ad bellum uti posse. modicum fructum ex ingenio tali neque gravem neque inutilem fore; si summa petantur, et dantem et accipientem praegravatura.[1]

Such passages as this clearly reveal Livy's habitual aims in his use of *oratio obliqua*. As historian, he reproduces the essential content of the source, but seeks to sharpen the elements of characterisation; from a literary viewpoint, there is constant attempt at stylistic variation.[2] One cannot state dogmatically the exact circumstances under which he prefers to use *oratio obliqua*,[3] or to have recourse to *oratio recta*; but certain valid principles can be posited. Direct speech is never used for mere repetition of content, for there is always stylistic embellishment for enhanced literary effect, and usually there is rearrangement, excision, and augmentation of the content. On occasion, indirect speech is used for mere repetition of content without embroidery, but this is in short statements mainly,[4] or in longer statements when the speakers are nonentities such as Livy does not desire to characterise.[5] But more frequently these longer speeches in *oratio obliqua* are treated so as to be interesting from a stylistic viewpoint.[6] In such extended usage, the aim of characterisation is foremost in Livy's mind, as in the passage just quoted, where the fears of Hannibal voiced by Thoas the Aetolian illuminate the speaker's fears and jealousy, and also portray the increasing influence of Hannibal over Antiochus. Above all, Livy artistically uses *oratio obliqua* to convey to the reader a psychological impression of the thought processes of groups of people witnessing an event or pondering a course of action.

[1] xxxv, 42, 9 ff. For another apposite example see Syphax's speech to Scipio Africanus at xxx, 13, 9 ff.

[2] So Kroll, quoted by Lambert, 19.

[3] Lambert, 17: 'habe ich keine Bemerkung gefunden, die uns Aufschluß geben könnte, wann und wie die oratio obliqua anzuwenden sei'.

[4] As at xxxvi, 35, 9–10; xxxviii, 20, 8; xxxix, 54, 10–12, etc.

[5] xxxv, 35, 7–10; 46, 5–13; xl, 36, 1–4, etc.

[6] xxxiii, 12, 5–11; xxxviii, 22, 4–6; xxxix, 26, 1–10, etc.

X

LIVY'S LATINITY

ABOUT the middle of the first century B.C., a determined attempt had been made to define and observe strict standards of pure latinity. Three of Cicero's treatises[1] give some indication of the conscious effort made by the small group of Roman intellectuals to reject 'provincial harshness and foreign innovation', with the object not merely of establishing correct case usage and due regard for gender and tense, but also of restricting the literary vocabulary to words 'quae nemo iure reprehendat'.[2]

The result of this attempted reform is a latinity widely at variance with contemporary speech, and indeed with much of the earlier literature. For there is now a standardised grammar and syntax, with one correct form and gender for each word, and one correct construction for each kind of clause. By this achievement of the Roman purists, the language lost something in variety and flexibility, but there was a great advance in clarity, a concept with which the Romans, under the influence of Greek rhetorical theory, were closely preoccupied. The passion for clarity extended also to vocabulary, for intellectuals like Caesar not merely excised from their writing the 'inauditum atque insolens verbum',[3] but also sought to employ a single word to express a particular shade of meaning. In the pursuit of such *elegantia* there was thus

---

[1] *De Oratore, Orator, Brutus.*

[2] *De Or.* III, 44: 'neque solum rusticam asperitatem, sed etiam peregrinam insolentiam fugere discamus'. Compare III, 40; *Brut.* 171.

[3] See Gell. I, 10, 4.

created what we call classical prose, represented in ancient literature above all by Cicero and Caesar.

Where does Livy stand in relationship to such *urbanitas*, the prose of Cicero and Caesar? His own attitude proclaims that he is an enthusiastic supporter of Ciceronian latinity, for he bids his son read Demosthenes and Cicero, and then the authors who most closely resemble them.[1] One notes, too, that later Romans associate Livy with Republican prose rather than with the writers of the empire.[2] It is therefore surprising that many modern grammarians exclude him from the ranks of classical prose writers. A more intelligent view is that which sees him as in some ways forming a transition between the purists and the more decadent prose of the imperial period, but which groups him with Caesar and Cicero because on the whole his language conforms with theirs. Yet, as the best of the Livian grammarians comments, 's'il est permis de rattacher encore Tite-Live à l'époque classique de la prose, il faut avouer qu'il se trouve bien près de la limite, et que la langue a déjà changé d'une façon sensible depuis Cicéron et depuis César jusqu'à lui'.[3]

The specialised approach of the grammarian, however, may ignore a consideration vital in the assessment of the relationship between Livy's latinity and classical prose. *Historia* has its own literary canons which allow a greater licence than Cicero permits for the forum; as Quintilian comments, it is closely akin to poetry, and avoids wearying the reader 'with more unusual vocabulary and freer use of figures'.[4] It is precisely by such freedom of vocabulary (and of course by metrical differences) that Cicero distinguishes *poetry* from oratory, 'verborum...licentia

---

[1] Quint. x, 1, 39: '...legendos Demosthenem atque Ciceronem, tum ita ut quisque esset Demostheni et Ciceroni simillimus'.

[2] Tac. *Agr.* 10; Vell. Pat. 1, 17, 2.

[3] O. Riemann, *Études sur la langue et la grammaire de Tite-Live*² (Paris, 1885), 13.

[4] Quint. x, 1, 31: 'verbis remotioribus'.

liberior'.[1] Cicero, too, tells us that in *historia* and in epideictic oratory Isocrates and Theopompus should be the models.[2] It was in epideictic oratory above all that poetic language was permissible, so that its association here with *historia* is significant. One must therefore conclude that Cicero would have approved for Livy the use of a more poetic language than he himself employed in political and forensic assemblies. If Cicero's language is no criterion, neither is Caesar's. For Julius' account of his campaigns, though praised by Cicero for its latinity,[3] is only an intermediate stage between a diary of events and *historia* proper.

Livy's history, then, is legitimately coloured by poetic phrase and reminiscence, but his writing also reflects a decisive development away from classical prose. The influence of the schools of rhetoric is relevant here; the declamations practised were marked not merely by bizarre themes, but also by precious language disdaining the words of common speech. We all know how Tacitus could not call a spade a spade, and how he called a *spado* a man 'of deprived manhood'—typical examples of how the rhetorical schools, in Quintilian's phrase, 'cut out a large part of the vocabulary of everyday language'.[4] Inevitably this search for more exotic variation caused the language of literary prose to take on a more poetic colouring and to become 'like poetry freed of metre'.

Along with this increasingly precious nature of vocabulary, there comes what is undoubtedly syntactical degeneration. The standards of the purists had never obtained in the more colloquial media, as Cicero's letters testify. In Livy there are evident signs that this laxity is widespread in the literary Latin of Augustan Rome.

---

[1] *De Or.* 1, 70.   [2] *Or.* 207.
[3] *Brut.* 262: 'nihil enim est in historia pura et illustri brevitate perfectius'.
[4] Tac. *Ann.* 1, 65: 'per quae egeritur humus'; VI, 21: 'Abdus ademptae virilitatis'. For a good account of declamation in the Augustan age see M. L. Clarke, *Rhetoric at Rome* (London, 1953), ch. VIII.

This is an appropriate place to discuss a theory of Livy's latinity that has found wide acceptance. Its general thesis is the paradoxical one that in his first decade Livy reflects the Augustan urge to break from the fetters of classicism, but that by the third and fourth decades he is returning to the standards of Caesar and Cicero.[1] Such a retrogression, it is claimed, is attributable partly to a conscious attempt in the early books to lend poetic character to his language through imitation of and borrowing from the poets, and partly to his experimentation with an historical style which he later abandoned. The thesis is supported by a statistical survey of a large number of poetic words and expressions employed on a greatly decreasing scale as the history progresses.

Recently, however, these examples have been subjected to fresh scrutiny, as a result of which the thesis is no longer tenable in its entirety.[2] Some allegedly poetic usages are shown to have reputable antecedents in Caesar and Cicero; others, unsupported in classical prose, occur indiscriminately throughout the extant books. Where the statistics are valid, and show a less poetic vocabulary in the later books, one must take into account differences of content. The later decades contain ever-increasing detail of Senatorial business, the prosaic nature of which militates against poetic language. The truth must therefore lie not in the ingenious (but *a priori* unlikely) theory that an unsuccessful stylistic experiment has been abandoned, but in the more obvious claim that the content of the early books, 'poeticis magis decora fabulis', was more amenable to poetic colouring, was composed with echoes of the early poets in mind, and was affected by the

[1] S. G. Stacey, *Die Entwickelung des livianischen Stiles* (Leipzig, 1898), 118: 'Das Merkwürdige aber ist, daß Livius nicht im Haufe der Jahrzehnte die goldene Latinität zur silbernen umgeformt, sondern umgekehrt gerade in der ersten Dekade dem neuen Zeitgeiste am meisten gehuldigt hat, und später, d.h. schon in der dritten und noch mehr in der vierten Dekade, zu den strengeren Formen und Normen des Klassizismus zurückgekehrt ist.'

[2] K. Gries, *Constancy in Livy's Latinity* (New York, 1949).

use of sources similarly aware of the verse histories of the Roman state. Such poetic expressions become naturally rarer in the more sober transactions of later years, but they are employed when apposite events demand them. Finally, Livy's enthusiasm wanes after the third decade, when the subject-matter is less exciting, and his writing becomes more mechanical and less artistically creative.

All these factors mentioned—the natural development of the language, the licence conceded to *historia*, the indirect influence of the poet-historians, especially Ennius, and the effect of the sources—leave their impress on Livy's latinity. Thus whilst one recognises that he is a disciple of Cicero, reacting sharply against the Sallustian brevity with 'lactea ubertas',[1] one finds differences in many particulars.

Analysis of Livy's sentence arrangement in narrative (differing, naturally enough, from Cicero's because of the difference of literary genre) demonstrates his technique in choosing stylistic media apposite to subject-matter. There is a marked contrast between the formal annalistic sections, marking the turn of each year, and the more extended narration; and again, more dramatic events command a more urgent presentation.

The annalistic sections are often almost as jejune as the original chronicles: 'consules M. Valerius P. Postumius. eo anno bene pugnatum cum Sabinis. consules triumpharunt.' Or again: 'deinde M. Valerius Sp. Verginius consules facti. domi forisque otium fuit; annona propter aquarum intemperiem laboratum est. de Aventino publicando lata lex est, tribuni plebis idem refecti.' In prodigy lists a simple, paratactic sentence arrangement is adopted, though *variatio* is sought in the formulae of introduction: 'in Albano monte tacta de caelo erant signum Iovis arborque templo propinqua, et Ostiae lacus.... cruentam

---

[1] Quint. x, 1, 32.

etiam fluxisse aquam Albanam quidam auctores erant...
et Priverni satis constabat bovem locutum....'[1]

In his more extended narrative Livy devised a regular
periodic structure. This periodic style is adapted to his
technique of episodic narration; his individual sentences
interlock to contribute to the architecture of the whole
episode. Take for example the account of how the sacred
geese saved the Capitol:

[A]   dum haec Veiis agebantur, interim arx Romae Capito-
liumque in ingenti periculo fuit.

[B]   namque Galli, / seu vestigio notato humano qua nuntius
a Veiis pervenerat, seu sua sponte animadverso ad Carmentis saxo
in adscensum aequo, / nocte sublustri cum primo inermem qui
temptaret viam praemisissent, / tradentes inde arma ubi quid
iniqui esset, / alterni innixi sublevantesque in vicem et tra-
hentes alii alios, prout postularet locus, / tanto silentio in sum-
mum evasere / ut non custodes solum fallerent sed ne canes
quidem, sollicitum animal ad nocturnos strepitus, excitarent.

anseres non fefellere quibus sacris Iunonis in summa inopia
cibi tamen abstinebatur.

quae res saluti fuit;

[C]   namque clangore eorum alarumque crepitu excitus /
M. Manlius qui triennio ante consul fuerat, / vir bello egregius, /
armis arreptis simul ad arma ceteros ciens / vadit, / et dum
ceteri trepidant / Gallum qui iam in summo constiterat umbone
ictum deturbat.

cuius casus prolapsi cum proximos sterneret, / trepidantes
alios armisque omissis saxa quibus adhaerebant manibus
amplexos trucidat.

[D]   iamque et alii congregati telis missilibusque saxis proturbare hostes, ruinaque tota prolapsa acies in praeceps deferri.

[E]   sedato deinde tumultu reliquum noctis, quantum in
turbatis mentibus poterat cum praeteritum quoque periculum
sollicitaret, quieti datum est.[2]

First, the scene is set with a short, uncomplicated
sentence [A]. Then comes a typically Livian period—

---

[1] II, 16, 1; III, 31, 1; XXVII, 11, 2 ff.   [2] V, 47, 1–6.

a skilfully contrived complex of participial and adjectival phrases combined with subordinate clauses, which gradually builds up to the climax of the main verb. This variation in the expression of the subordinated ideas is typical of historical narrative in Latin, and reflects the influence of the Caesarean period:[1] to suggest that the lack of a logical relationship between subordinate clauses impairs the lucidity of the Latin is absurd.[2] Here the whole of the Gallic attempt to seize the Capitol is embraced in a single sentence. With impressive economy Livy narrates how they found the path, sent forward a man to reconnoitre, avoided the clashing of arms, helped each other up and arrived unperceived [B]. The Latin appropriately reflects the stages of the climb. When they reach the top, they disturb the geese; a simple sentence suffices for this climax. The focus now switches from attackers to defenders. To balance the long sentence describing the Gallic activity, Manlius' reactions are similarly recounted in a period-sentence [C]; and a short statement, balancing 'anseres non fefellere...', suffices for the slaughter of the leading Gauls. Note how Manlius' haste, in contrast to the Gauls' stealth, is depicted by historic presents ('vadit...deturbat...trucidat'); and this dramatic presentation continues with historic infinitives when Manlius' comrades join him [D] ('proturbare...deferri'). Finally, the conclusion of the episode is narrated in a simple sentence [E].

Conspicuous here is the balance achieved by describing the action successively from the viewpoint of attackers and defenders. 'This alternation of action, represented syntactically, is the key to much of Livy's "periodic"

[1] E.g. *B.G.* v, 3, 5: 'sed postea quam non nulli principes ex ea civitate / et familiaritate Cingetorigis adducti et adventu nostri exercitus perterriti / ad Caesarem venerunt et de suis privatim rebus ab eo petere coeperunt, / quoniam civitati consulere non possent, / veritus ne ab omnibus desereretur, / Indutiomarus legatos ad Caesarem mittit'.
[2] As L. R. Palmer, *The Latin Language* (London, 1954), 137, suggests.

composition.'[1] There are numerous engagements in the later books with such presentation within the composed episode. Here, for example, is the identical structure in three naval battles, showing how rigid the stylistic formulation has become. Note how in each case the enemy arrival is first cited.

Battle A (off Cissus) Polyxenidas, ut appropinquare hostes adlatum est, occasione pugnandi laetus sinistrum ipse cornu in altum extendit, dextrum cornu praefectos navium ad terram explicare iubet, et aequa fronte ad pugnam procedebat.

Battle B (off Phaselis) ab regiis sinistro cornu, quod ab alto obiectum erat, Hannibal, dextro Apollonius purpuratorum unus praeerat: et iam in frontem derectas habebant naves.

Battle C (off Myonnesus) et regia classis, binis in ordinem navibus longo agmine veniens, et ipsa aciem adversam explicuit, laevo tantum evecta cornu, ut amplecti et circuire dextrum cornu Romanorum posset.

Next are narrated the reactions of the Romans or the Rhodians:

[A] quod ubi vidit Romanus, / vela contrahit malosque inclinat, et simul armamenta componens opperitur insequentes naves....

[B] Eudamus postquam hostium aciem instructam et paratam ad concurrendum vidit, / et ipse in altum evehitur.

[C] quod ubi Eudamus qui cogebat agmen vidit, / ...concitat naves....

Eventually the main fleets join:

[A] Et iam classes quoque undique concurrerant....

[B] Sed momento temporis et navium virtus et usus maritimae rei terrorem omnem Rhodiis dempsit.

[C] iam totis classibus simul ab omni parte pugna conserta erat....

In each case Livy's arrangement plunges the reader into the middle of the battle. In two of the battles, the

---

[1] A. H. McDonald, *JRS* (1957), 165, who exemplifies the point with Livy's account of the theft of Hercules' cattle at 1, 7, 4–7.

result is clear-cut, and the close of the episode depicts the flight:

[A] ...sublatis dolonibus effuse fugere intendit (*sc.* Polyxenidas). [C] (naves) sublatis raptim dolonibus... capessunt fugam.[1]

This pattern illustrates above all how Livy has geared his periodic style to the service of the composed episode, and how the principle of alternation between opposed viewpoints is conceived as vital for a harmonious whole.

Within the composed episode the more complex period-sentence is used sparingly. Livy was well aware that a dramatic effect is heightened not by such an artificial, sophisticated structure, but by a profusion of verbs unconnected by particles. ('Longinus', commending such repetition and asyndeton, quotes the effective sentence of Xenophon: 'Locking their shields, they thrust, battled, killed, died.'[2]) Livy's use of such devices, already noted,[3] excludes the longer period-sentence from the centre of dramatic action; he employs it more usually when recounting a number of preparatory events in an economical way as the prelude to more exciting narration.

Within this 'periodic' organisation a major distinguishing feature is the effect of poetic influences—attributable, as has been noted, partly to the change in cultured prose generally in the Augustan age, partly to a deliberate colouring allowed to composers of *historia* proper. Though the early books are more poetically tinted than the later, throughout the extant work one readily finds more poetic rhythms, more poetic diction, and more poetic constructions than in classical prose.

Livy's opening words, 'facturusne operae pretium sim', form four feet of a dactylic hexameter, as Quintilian duly

---

[1] xxxvi, 44f. [A]; xxxvii, 23, 7ff. [B]; xxxvii, 29, 8ff. [C].

[2] *De Subl.* xix, quoting *Hell.* iv, 3, 19: καὶ συμβαλόντες τὰς ἀσπίδας ἐωθοῦντο, ἐμάχοντο, ἀπέκτεινον, ἀπέθνησκον.

[3] See Ch. vii.

noted.[1] It has been suggested that this is a phrase 'which no one thinks of attributing to the imitation of a poet rather than to chance'.[2] The proposed alternatives are unsatisfactory. The story of the discovery, after Plato's death, of a tablet with the four opening words of the *Republic* written with variations of the word order upon it[3] aptly illustrates the care with which such an exordium was phrased. Livy's word order was equally deliberate; not that he was imitating any particular poet. Such dactylic effects were a feature common in Roman historiography. This is probably a relic of the influence of Ennius and the other verse historians who wrote in hexameters. The fragments of Sisenna and Coelius Antipater, as well as the extant writings of Sallust, also attest to the propriety of dactylic and spondaic rhythms in *historia*.[4] It was likewise no accident when Tacitus began his *Annals* with a complete hexameter: 'urbem Romam a principio reges habuere'.[5] Tacitus immediately establishes the line of descent of *historia*, especially in its connection with the early history of Rome.

Livy's narrative contains numerous phrases which are either dactylic in rhythm, or which fall into dactyls with the minimum of rearrangement. Some of these are reminiscences of Ennius, deliberately employed to evoke the atmosphere of the original verses. So the escape of Sempronius Tuditanus, a military tribune, after the disaster of Cannae, falls directly into dactyls:

> haec ubi dicta dedit, stringit gladium, cuneoque
> facto, per medios (vadit hostes...).[6]

A battle with the Umbrians contains the phrase

> scutis magi(s) quam gladiis geritur res,

---

[1] Quint. IX, 4, 74.   [2] Gries, 40.

[3] Quint. VIII, 6, 64. The story may not be genuine, but its existence reflects the ancients' preoccupation with stylistic features.

[4] See R. Ullmann, *Symb. Osl.* (1932), 72–6; (1933), 57–69.

[5] Against R. Syme, *Tacitus*, 357.   [6] XXII, 50, 10.

regarded by some as a conscious echo of Ennius.[1] This type of *Quellenforschung* has, however, been overdone. Livy employs such rhythms, in conjunction with a poetic vocabulary, to achieve his own poetic effect. But it is notable that few of these clausulae are fully Vergilian in form. There are some examples, such as

> parcere lamentis Sutrinos iussit; Etruscis
> se luctum lacrimasque (ferre...)

and

> ...imperat ut legionum signa sequantur,[2]

but these are rare. It has even been suggested that Livy's readers would not have noticed many dactylic clausulae, or regarded them as such, because they were schooled to the niceties of Vergil's hexameter ending.[3] This is to underestimate the attention paid by the ancients to the form of artistic prose.

The speeches are a different matter. As part of the oratorical genre the clausulae continue for the most part with the Ciceronian canons; the sentence endings chiefly employed are the double spondee (by far the most common), the double choree, and the spondee/peon.[4]

What of Livy's poetic diction? One is constantly made aware of his attempt to infuse both colour and variation into his narrative. He writes *ad primam auroram* for the more prosaic *ad primam lucem*; *sopor* as a variant of *somnus*; *molimen* for *conatus*, and other forms in -*en* common in poetry, such as *cacumen, hortamen, regimen*. The poetic *amnis* appears as a variation for *fluvius* and *flumen*. He

---

[1] IX, 41, 18 (Ennius, *Ann.* 269 (Vahlen³): 'vi geritur res'). See first E. Wölfflin, *RhM* (1895), 152.

[2] VI, 3, 4; XLII, 65, 12.

[3] So Gries, 41 (Vergil's fifth foot avoids commencement of a word with the first short syllable).

[4] R. Ullmann, *Symb. Osl.* (1925), 65 ff., computes the clausulae in the speeches as follows: double spondee 32 per cent, spondee/peon 11 per cent, double choree 11 per cent, dactyl/trochee 8 per cent, cretic/trochee 5 per cent, double cretic 4 per cent, trochee/cretic 4 per cent, cretic/peon 4 per cent. The occasional occurrence of other combinations accounts for the other 21 per cent.

prefers the poetic *cupido* to the prose form *cupiditas*, and likewise uses *iuventa* and *senecta* on occasion for *iuventus* and *senectus*. He often seeks out compound adjectives such as *fatiloquus, sublustris, pernox, semianimis*—words earlier found only in poetry. There are numerous verbs of similarly poetic appearance, such as *avolare, adorare, prae-pedire, ingruere, remordere,* and other such unusual compounds, and a few simple verbs like *mussare* and *hebetare*.

A striking feature of such poetic diction is the high proportion of words used also by Vergil, and one scholar lists a number of adjectives (including *cristatus, effrenus, invius, semustus*) and of verbs like *abolescere, effulgere, hebetare, incessere* which he claims to be creations of Vergil.[1] But many of these words are used by Vergil solely in the *Aeneid*, which was not published until after the poet's death in 19 B.C., by which time Livy had published his first decade, in which many of them are found. It is *possible* that the historian heard recitations of the *Aeneid* before publication, as Propertius apparently did,[2] or that he read the work privately and made borrowings from it. But it is much more probable that both writers were drawing on the early verse historians for such striking vocabulary.

It is not merely in single words that Livy shows similarity with Vergil. Some of his memorable phrases find an echo in the *Aeneid*, and both undoubtedly stem from the early tradition. For example, Livy's 'vi viam faciunt' and Vergil's 'fit via vi'[3] have presumably a common source, and likewise the invocation by Horatius Cocles to Father Tiber and Aeneas' prayer to the river-god are both deliberate reminiscences of an extant line of Ennius.[4] Equally striking is the correspondence between the sack

---

[1] M. Müller, in his edition of Livy i (Leipzig, 1875).

[2] Prop. ii, 34, 66.

[3] Livy iv, 38, 4; *Aen.* ii, 494.

[4] Ennius, *Ann.* 54 (Vahlen³): 'teque, pater Tiberine, tuo cum flumine sancto'; Livy ii, 10, 11: 'Tiberine pater, inquit, te sancte precor, haec arma et hunc militem propitio flumine accipias'; Verg. *Aen.* viii, 72: 'tuque, o Thybri, tuo genitor cum flumine sancto / accipite Aenean et tandem arcete periclis'.

of Troy in Vergil, and the destruction of Alba Longa in Livy.[1] Now Vergil's second book draws upon Ennius' description of the fall of Alba Longa, and it would be surprising if Livy's account did not show traces of the same influence. Notice this striking similarity between Vergil's

> tum pavidae tectis matres ingentibus errant
> amplexaeque tenent postis atque oscula figunt,

and Livy's '...nunc in liminibus starent, nunc errabundi domos suas ultimum illud visuri pervagarentur'. This clearly reflects the use of Ennius as common source.[2] But we should be chary of the tendency to ignore Livy's own creative powers. The search for poetic sources has been taken to absurd lengths, with the illustration of highly dubious parallels in Lucretius, Tibullus, Horace, and others, most of which prove only that all were writing in Latin.[3]

There is indeed a strong possibility that Vergil, the most derivative of poets, has been on occasion directly indebted to Livy.[4] Such dependence is the most obvious explanation for the remarkable verbal correspondence between the two versions of the theft by Cacus of the cattle of Hercules. Livy writes: (Cacus) 'aversos boves ...caudis in speluncam trahit'; Vergil: 'avertit...cauda in speluncam tractos'. And the correspondence is close later, when both describe Hercules' hearing the lowing of the oxen.[5] Other resemblances have been suggested, as in the accounts of the execution of Mettius, but none are so clear-cut as this.

---

[1] *Aen.* II, 486 ff.; Livy I, 29 (above, 171 f.).

[2] For Vergil's use of Ennius see Servius *ad Aen.* II, 486. The common use of Ennius by Livy and Vergil is well set out by E. Norden, *Ennius und Virgilius* (Leipzig–Berlin, 1915). For other Livian passages in which Norden demonstrates the influence of Ennius see V, 54, 4; XXI, 19, 6; XXII, 49, 6.

[3] See, e.g., Stacey, 52–6; Brakman, *Mnem.* (1925), 371 ff.; (1926), 29 ff.; (1927), 54 ff.

[4] So A. Rostagni, *Da Livio a Virgilio e da Virgilio a Livio* (Padova, 1942), 15.

[5] Livy I, 7, 5 ff.; *Aen.* VIII, 207 ff. Stacey suggests a common source.

So much for diction essentially poetic in itself. But as Horace points out, often it is not the words but the arrangement of them which achieves a poetic effect.[1] Much of Livy's narrative is poetic in this sense, as in his portrait of the Alpine scene which first met the eyes of the Carthaginians: 'montium altitudo nivesque caelo prope immixtae, tecta informia imposita rupibus, pecora iumentaque torrida frigore, homines intonsi et inculti, animalia inanimaque omnia rigentia gelu'.[2] Or take his description of a falling town: 'cum...clamor hostilis et cursus per urbem armatorum omnia ferro flammaque miscet'.[3] Or the account of panic caused by elephants (though here there is a poetic element in the diction): '... ubi ad invia venerant, deiectis rectoribus cum horrendo stridore pavorem ingentem, equis maxime, incutiebant...'.[4]

The rhetorical colouring introduced into the more dramatic scenes is also redolent of the poetic works of the Silver Age. An alliterative effect is occasionally sought, especially in character sketches. Camillus' mental powers are depicted with the words: 'sed vegetum ingenium in vivido pectore vigebat virebatque integris sensibus'.[5] Hannibal is said to have a 'perfidia plus quam Punica'.[6] Another favourite device is that of *adnominatio*: words of similar sound but dissimilar meaning are juxtaposed: 'parendum atque imperandum', 'hostis pro hospite', 'perdere aut perire'. The central descriptions of dramatic episodes can indeed contain all the verbal figures which were noted in the speeches.[7] The account of the destruction of Alba Longa, for example, contains such figures as *chiasmus* and *congeries* ('silentium triste ac tacita maestitia'), *anaphora* and *isocolon* ('quid relinquerent, quid secum ferrent').[8] Such rhetorical treatment, in common with the

---

[1] *A.P.* 47f.
[2] XXI, 32, 7.
[3] I, 29, 2.
[4] XLIV, 5.
[5] VI, 22, 7, reminiscent of Lucr. v, 991: 'viva videns vivo sepeliri viscere busto'.
[6] XXI, 4. Other examples: I, 31, 2; XXI, 7, 5, etc.
[7] Ch. IX.
[8] I, 29.

poetic colouring, becomes progressively less marked as the work advances.

Livy's diction is also noteworthy for the occasional use of archaisms. It is logical to assume that this is chiefly attributable to the reproduction of words found in his annalistic sources;[1] his condemnation of the Sallustian style proves his opposition to conscious archaising tendencies. On several occasions he used *occipere* where *incipere* would be the classical usage, and *indipisci* is similarly found as a variant of *adipisci*. Classical words are occasionally employed with obsolete meanings; like Sallust, he uses *supplicia* for 'acts of worship', and *tempestas* with the sense of 'time'. Many of such features in the first decade—the use of words like *sospitare*, and forms like *ausit, faxo, duit*—are incorporated in quotations from legal and religious formulae, or from speeches deliberately accorded an archaic flavour. The archaic atmosphere of the early period leads Livy also to employ the old form *-ēre* (avoided by Caesar) in the third person plural of the perfect indicative active. It has been computed that in the early books *-ēre* is used three times as frequently as *-ērunt*, but by the fifth decade the position is reversed.

More consistent throughout the work is the appearance of certain colloquialisms avoided by the purists. Abbreviated forms like *satin'* (for *satisne*), and *forsan* are used, on some occasions with the object of depicting an incident in a homely way. So when Fabius Cunctator meets his son the consul, he says: 'experiri volui, fili, satin' scires consulem te esse'.[2] Further, pleonastic phrases like *itaque ergo* and *tum inde*, which must have been familiar in common speech, appear from time to time. Livy also uses *oppido* (for example, 'oppido adulescens') where Cicero in formal prose used *admodum*,

---

[1] So Riemann, 18, n. 1.

[2] XXIV, 44, 10; compare I, 58, 7. (Perhaps, as Mr R. M. Ogilvie suggests, this is an *archaic* colloquialism deliberately used.)

and *en umquam* ('did you ever?') is found on four occasions in quotation. Other colloquial usages include *qua...qua* for *et...et*; *aeque quam* for the more correct *aeque ac*; *si* for *num* in indirect questions ('...nihil aliud locutum ferunt quam quaesisse si incolumis Lycortas...equitesque evasissent').[1] Certain other picturesque expressions, such as 'coquere bellum', 'to cook up war', are also redolent of conversational Latin. And there are a large number of occasions on which frequentative forms, such as *imperito*, *clamito*, *agito*, *rogito*, are employed without refinement of meaning beyond that of the simple verbs—a particularly apt example of how the precision of the purists' diction has been gradually abandoned.[2]

Our final concern under the heading of diction is neologism and change in word meaning, the natural result of the development of the language. *titulus*, for example, is found with the sense of 'pretext', a meaning which it certainly does not bear before the Augustan period. And whereas *celeber* is frequently applied to impersonal nouns in classical prose, it is now used with reference to persons in the sense of *praeclarus*. A few words, such as *assuetudo*, now appear for the first time in extant literature.

But the field in which Livy's latinity contrasts most decisively with that of the classicists proper is syntax. The cumulative effect of archaism, colloquialism, poetic influences, and the movement of Augustan letters away from the rigid canons of classicism is so considerable that there seems to be scarcely a law of case usage or clause

---

[1] XXXIX, 50, 7; also XXIX, 25, 8; XXXIV, 3, 5, etc. H. J. Roby, *Latin Grammar*, §1754, claims this to be a conditional usage. But there is obviously a distinction between Caes. *B.G.* II, 9, 1: 'hanc (*sc.* paludem) si nostri transirent hostes expectabant', where there is no element of interrogation, and the Livian example cited.

[2] Stacey's claim for a return to the standards of classicism rests to some extent on the statistics of frequentatives; e.g. *agito* is found forty-seven times in the first decade, twenty-five in the third, seventeen in the fourth, four in the fifth. Such statistics mislead. These words are appropriate to dramatic contexts, not to details of Senatorial administration, which are increasingly prominent as the work progresses.

construction which Livy does not at some time contravene. But there are two factors here which will usefully be borne in mind. First, there was so wide a gulf between the literary language of the purists and everyday speech that an occasional lapse is not unduly surprising; and secondly, most of the peculiarities noted here are not consistent usages, but are exceptional not merely in classical prose generally but in Livian latinity in particular. These peculiarities can be examined under four headings —case usage, prepositions, conjunctions, and clause constructions.

Livy's use of the accusative case shows above all the influence of poetry. There is occasionally an accusative after a past participle in imitation of the Greek 'middle' voice ('virgines longam indutae vestem'),[1] and also the so-called 'retained' accusative after a passive verb ('adversum femur...ictus').[2] The reader of Vergil is sufficiently familiar with these, as also with the use of *cetera* with adjectives in an adverbial sense ('cetera egregium', 'cetera tereti').[3] Another construction hitherto rare in prose is the accusative after adjectives with the termination -*bundus*, which thus have a participial force; so Hanno the Carthaginian leaves Bruttium, 'vitabundus castra hostium'.[4] Some such adjectives occur in early poetry, but there are some not found in extant literature before Livy—for example, 'haec contionabundus'.[5] Another non-classical use is the direct accusative after verbs prefixed by *in*-, such as *invadere, incedere, invehi*, for Caesar invariably employs *in* with the accusative here. This simplified construction is to be attributed to a natural development of the language.

Of the usages of the genitive, the most important innovation is the poetic construction with adjectives.

---

[1] XXVII, 37, 12. [2] XXI, 7, 10.
[3] I, 32, 2; XXI, 8, 10. [4] XXV, 13, 4.
[5] III, 47, 2.

Horace's 'integer vitae scelerisque purus' is paralleled by such expressions as 'incertus animi', 'feracior virtutum', 'vini capacissimum', as many as fifteen different adjectives being employed in this way.[1] Another tendency rejected by the purists is the use of *urbs, flumen, mons* and similar words with a name in the genitive, like 'ad Asturae flumen';[2] this definitive genitive is common in both poetry and colloquial speech,[3] though the classicists would insist on 'ad Asturam flumen'. In another use of the genitive the influence of Greek is perhaps discernible; Cicero follows *opus est* with ablative or nominative, but Livy sometimes writes the genitive: 'ad consilium pensandum temporis opus esse'.[4]

The dative case is often employed after verbs of motion like *incurrere* and *inferre*, a construction also to be found very occasionally in Caesar and Cicero, though *in* with the accusative is regular. This too is to be attributed to natural development already beginning in Cicero's time, Livy uses such phrases as 'incidens portis exercitus' and 'levi armaturae hostium incurrere'.[5] *fretus* is found with the dative on several occasions, a usage peculiar to Livy: 'multitudo nulli rei freta'.[6]

Certain uses of the ablative have a poetic flavour. In such phrases as 'portis ruere', and 'crebri cecidere caelo lapides',[7] the more normal *e* or *a* is omitted in favour of a simple ablative of separation. Locatival ablatives are also more common than in Caesar and Cicero, who restrict them to a small group of words like *parte, regione, loco, proelio, terra, mari,* and to nouns with *totus* or *medius,* and even these were felt to be poetic in tone.[8]

---

[1] I, 7, 6; IX, 16, 19 and 13. Gries, Part II, *s.v.* 'Genitive with Adjectives', gives further examples.   [2] VIII, 13, 5.

[3] E.g. Verg. *Aen.* VII, 714; Cic. *Ad Att.* V, 18, 1.

[4] XXII, 51, 3; also XXIII, 21, 5.

[5] V, 11, 14; XXII, 17, 6.

[6] VI, 13, 1; also IV, 37, 6; VI, 31, 6, etc.

[7] XXVII, 41, 8; I, 31, 2 (perhaps a conscious reminiscence of early poetry).

[8] Cic. *Fin.* V, 4, 9: 'caelo, mari, terra, ut poetice loquar'.

Cicero would certainly never have written 'ei carpento sedenti' as Livy does.[1]

Of the variations from standard usage in Livy's employment of prepositions, the most notable is the inclusion of them in denoting movement towards and away from towns and small islands. He can write 'ab Roma legatos venisse' and 'ad Veios exercitus ductus'.[2] *domus* is likewise prefaced with a preposition of motion on several occasions.[3] Secondly, *a* or *ab* is frequently used in a causal sense in place of the simple ablative: 'non a cupiditate solum ulciscendi', or again, 'ab superbia et odio'.[4] Other unusual features are the use of *circa* both in a temporal sense and in numerical designation,[5] for both of which Cicero would have written *circiter*; the occasional prepositional use of the adverbs *palam* and *procul* with the ablative;[6] *sub* with the accusative meaning 'immediately after'—a colloquial use ('sub hanc vocem clamatum est');[7] *super* with the ablative in the colloquial sense of 'concerning' ('litteras super tanta re expectare') and with the accusative meaning 'besides' ('super morbum etiam fames');[8] and *tenus* with the genitive, not with the more normal ablative—a construction also found in the poets.[9]

Livy's use of conjunctions reflects the desire of Augustan letters for greater flexibility and variety, and hence rigid rules of word order are now abandoned. Though *itaque* is usually placed first in the sentence, there are numerous occasions when it is in a postpositive position, perhaps because the first word is to be emphasised.[10] Similarly the position of *namque* is varied, and contrary to the convention observed by Cicero and Caesar

[1] I, 34, 8.
[2] XXI, 9, 3; V, 19, 9.
[3] IX, 22, 2; XXVII, 16, 2, etc.
[4] V, 5, 3; IX, 40, 17 (but Walters–Conway read 'ad superbiam', unjustifiably).
[5] E.g. XLII, 57, 10; XXVII, 42, 8.
[6] VI, 14, 5; III, 22, 4.
[7] XXI, 18, 13; also XXXV, 31, 13.
[8] XXVI, 15, 5; XXVIII, 46, 15.
[9] XXVI, 24, 11; XLIV, 40, 8.
[10] Gries computes that *itaque* comes first 538 times, later 54 times.

it is found after one or more words in a sentence some twenty-seven times. On the other hand *igitur*, normally (but not invariably) postpositive in Cicero, is quite commonly placed first by Livy. He also revives the use of *quippe* as an alternative to *nam*, and its frequent occurrence in comedy suggests that it is drawn from common speech.[1]

Some Livian constructions also suggest an increasing indifference to Ciceronian canons. Whereas Cicero is careful to use *coepi* with active infinitives, and *coeptus sum* with passives, Livy often ignores such discrimination.[2] On one occasion he writes 'ne timete' for the regular 'nolite timere'.[3] Prolate infinitives are used much more freely, for example after *restat* (where Cicero would have *ut*) and after nouns like *copia* and *potestas*, where Caesar would use the gerundive construction.[4]

In some noun clauses there are clear signs of a degeneration of language. *forsitan* is in the classicists followed by a subjunctive because it introduces an indirect question (*fors sit an...*); Livy uses the indicative frequently, regarding it merely as a variation of *fortasse*.[5] On several occasions verbs of fearing are followed by the accusative and infinitive.[6] Most commonly of all, the use of *quin* after negative verbs of doubting is often ignored; the classical construction is used forty-three times, but avoided on thirty occasions.[7]

The same signs of licence are observable also in adverbial clauses. In temporal sentences, for example, one can point to five distinct non-classical usages. *cum* is found with an historic infinitive (though only where no strong temporal idea is present); *cum* meaning 'whenever' is

---

[1] E.g. Ter. *Phormio* 362; *Heaut.* 539.   [2] II, 29, 6; XXIV, 19, 6, etc.

[3] III, 2, 9. Servius, commenting on a similar construction at *Aen.* VI, 544, states that this use of *ne* with imperative is archaic. Livy may have used it for purposes of characterisation.

[4] XLIV, 4, 8.   [5] *Praef.* 12; XXI, 40, 11; I, 53, 9, etc.

[6] II, 7, 9; VII, 39, 4; X, 36, 3.

[7] So Gries, *s.v.* 'Non-classical usages'.

followed by the subjunctive; so also is the 'inverse' *cum*; *dum* in the purely temporal sense of 'while' is followed by an imperfect subjunctive; and *priusquam* is also followed by a subjunctive though no element of anticipation or purpose is present.[1] Noteworthy here is Livy's reflection of the Silver Age tendency to increased use of the subjunctive. In causal clauses, on the other hand, he has used the indicative with *non quia* for a rejected reason, where Cicero would have *non quod* with the subjunctive, and on six occasions the causal relative *quippe qui* governs the indicative, though the subjunctive is regular in classical prose.[2] He reacts against the rigidity of the purists in concessive clauses also by using *quamvis* with the indicative and *quamquam* with the subjunctive.[3] Another slight variation is the use of *ut* in consecutive clauses after *dignus* where Cicero invariably writes *qui*. And in clauses of comparison, the more exact *velut si*, *tamquam si*, and similar phrases now increasingly drop *si*, a simplification of language already beginning in Cicero's day.[4]

Livy also deviates from Ciceronian usage in his treatment of *oratio obliqua*. After a secondary, or historic, tense he freely employs the primary tenses of the subjunctive—a device known as *repraesentatio*—to lend greater vividness to the words spoken; he writes in the tenses actually used by the speaker. There is some evidence of systematic procedure in this treatment. Where there are subordinate clauses depending *directly* on the introductory verb of saying (that is, when they are *in the same sentence* as the

---

[1] *cum* with infinitive, II, 27, 1; III, 37, 5; *cum* meaning 'whenever' with subjunctive, II, 27, 8; XXI, 28, 10; 'inverse' *cum* with subj., XXIII, 27, 5; *dum* meaning 'while' with the subj., II, 47, 5; X, 18, 1 (Walters–Conway resolve this difficulty by reading *cum* in the first case, the indic. in the second); *priusquam*, XXV, 31, 12.

[2] *non quia* and the indic., VII, 30, 13; *quippe qui* with the indic., III, 6, 6; XXVI, 41, 8; XLII, 18, 1, etc.

[3] *quamvis* with the indic., II, 40, 7; *quamquam* with the subj., XXXVI, 34, 6.

[4] *dignus...ut*, XXIV, 16, 19; *indignus...ut*, XXII, 59, 17; omission of *si* in clauses of comparison, II, 36, 1; XXIX, 22, 1; XLI, 24, 3 (compare Cic. *In Verr.* II, 4, 49).

introductory verb), the rule of sequence is followed by the use of secondary subjunctives. But subsequent to that sentence, wherever the words originally spoken have *a corresponding tense of the subjunctive*, such a tense is retained; otherwise he reverts to the secondary tenses. Thus *facit* becomes *faciat*, and *fecit*, if it is perfect with 'have', becomes *fecerit*; but *fac*, *faciet*, and the future perfect *fecerit* become respectively *faceret*, *faceret*, *fecisset*.[1] There are inevitably exceptions to this scheme, when Livy (doubtless seeking *variatio*) intersperses primary with secondary subjunctives, but the pattern is sufficiently common for it to be regarded as a conscious technique. In classical prose, it is permitted to employ *repraesentatio* where the introductory verb is in the historic present tense; Livy has expanded the practice to include passages introduced by a secondary tense. Consistently with such *repraesentatio* he often retains the adverbs *nunc* and *adhuc*, and the pronoun *hic*, which classical prose excludes from clauses after a secondary tense in *oratio obliqua*.[2]

Livy also introduces a freer use of the participle. The past participle frequently stands as the sole component of an ablative absolute, or with a noun clause in place of noun or pronoun; *inexplorato*, *inaugurato* and a few others are found without a noun, and elsewhere there are such expressions as 'edicto ut...hostem haberent'.[3] One also notes the passive use of past participles of some deponent verbs. This is already a current practice in classical prose with a few words like *comitatus*, *meditatus*, but Livy extends the usage to *ultus*, *abominatus*, *expertus*, and others.[4] His use of the future participle is extended to embrace an idea of purpose, which Caesar would have rendered with

[1] See R. S. Conway's Pitt Press edn. of Livy II, App. II.
[2] For such tenses see e.g. II, 48, 2; III, 34, 2–5; X, 13, 6–7; XXVII, 5, 4ff. For *nunc*, *adhuc*, *hic*, etc. see V, 2, 3; IX, 45, 2, etc.
[3] XXI, 25, 9; XXIII, 42, 9; X, 36, 7, etc. This usage extends even to adjectives, e.g. XXVIII, 36, 12: 'incerto quid...peterent'; XXVIII, 17, 14: 'haud cuiquam dubio...'.
[4] XXXI, 12, 8; III, 44, 3, etc.

in animo habeo; so the consul Publius Cornelius '. . . ad castra hostium venerat, nullam dimicandi moram facturus'.[1]

Cicero and Caesar restrict the use of the gerund and gerundive in the ablative to the expression of instrument or means. Livy employs it more loosely. When he writes 'quieti, rem nullam nisi necessariam ad victum sumendo, per aliquot dies. . .sese tenuere',[2] the gerund is used with a mere participial sense; Caesar would have written *sumentes*. The gerund and gerundive are also found after *inter*, a usage familiar from Ennius and Terence; but in classical prose the accusative of the gerund is rarely found with prepositions other than *ad* or *in*. This use of *inter* appears so commonly in Livy that he must have drawn it from common speech.[3]

This brief survey of Livian syntax has incidentally noted a few usages influenced by Greek constructions. Another Graecism worthy of mention is relative attraction. This is not wholly absent from classical prose; Caesar can write 'cum essent in quibus demonstravi angustiis. . .'[4] rather than 'in eis quas', but such instances are rare. Livy employs them more frequently.[5]

It is clear, then, that Livy deviates to a considerable extent in diction and in syntax from the canons of classical prose, though the listed irregularities are greatly outnumbered by the occasions on which he conforms. This is an appropriate place to discuss the probable meaning of *patavinitas*, the alleged fault which Asinius Pollio found in Livy's writing. It should be stressed that Pollio was a harsh critic, and Livy was doubtless consoled that Sallust and Cicero had also been the victims of his strictures.[6] If the taunt of *patavinitas* were

---

[1] XXI, 32, 1. [2] II, 32, 4; also XXII, 14, 7, etc.
[3] VI, 39, 10; XXXIV, 25, 6; XL, 42, 1.
[4] *B.G.* III, 15. [5] I, 29, 4; IV, 39, 9; X, 40, 8, etc.
[6] For a good account of Pollio's exacting standards of latinity see J. F. D'Alton, *Roman Literary Theory and Criticism*, 257ff.

explicit and fully understood, the sneer might well be dismissed as pedantry. But the element of mystery, the opportunity for ingenious speculation, has given the criticism an importance it scarcely deserves. The pun of the seventeenth-century German scholar Morhof sums up the matter succinctly: 'It is a hard matter to decide whether there is more patavinity in Livy or more asininity in Asinius.'[1]

Two passages from Quintilian make it clear that that critic regarded Pollio's rebuke as directed against Livy's latinity, though he cannot illustrate precisely what Pollio meant.[2] As this is the only direct evidence of the meaning of the word, one must be suspicious of the interpretation which regards it as a criticism of his historical sense. This view has received much support in recent years, and is therefore worthy of detailed quotation:

A critic armed with the acerbity of Pollio must have delivered a more crushing verdict upon a historian of Patavium than the obvious and trivial comment that his speech showed traces of his native dialect....Nor was the judgement one of style.... The original sin of Livy is darker and more detestable. The word *Patavinitas* sums up, elegantly and finally, the whole moral and romantic view of history. Pollio knew what history was. It was not like Livy.[3]

This Pollio is something of a nineteenth-century figure, condemning 'the whole moral and romantic view of history'. Such a criticism would have a partial relevance to Sallust, whose prefatory remarks in his *Catiline* and *Jugurtha* likewise betray concern for a moral view of history, to Coelius Antipater, to Sisenna, to the whole Roman annalistic tradition. Why then call the fault *patavinitas*?

[1] D. G. Morhof, *De Patavinitate Liviana* (1685), cited by Bornecque, 203.
[2] Quint. I, 5, 56: 'taceo de Tuscis et Sabinis et Praenestinis quoque; nam ut eorum sermone utentem Vettium Lucilius insectatur quemadmodum Pollio reprehendit in Livio Patavinitatem...'. A second mention of the word at VIII, I, 3 is to be found in a discussion of non-Roman vocabulary.
[3] R. Syme, *The Roman Revolution* (1939), 485.

The fact is that this view underestimates the fanaticism of Pollio in regard to purity of language; he was notorious for his critical comments on this score.[1] Nor was Quintilian so obtuse as to be unaware that Livy's interpretation of history was under criticism both during and after his life; yet his comments clearly record that the criticism of Pollio was solely stylistic. What precise facet of Livy's Latin was attacked? The question cannot be finally decided. One interesting and well attested fact to remember is that Livy wrote *sibe* and *quase* for *sibi* and *quasi*[2]— a peculiarity apparently common in Patavium.[3] A more hypothetical suggestion is that the historian had a Venetic accent. Now the purists were very insistent on correct pronunciation, as Cicero's comments reveal on such matters as the sounding of the final -*s* and the aspiration of consonants.[4] Cicero also tells his friend Brutus that when he goes to Gaul, he will hear 'words not in use at Rome, but these can be changed and unlearnt. What is of greater importance is the fact that the voices of our (Roman) orators have a more elegant ring and sound.'[5] Quintilian, too, deprecates provincial pronunciation of Latin, such as that of the man of Placentia who pronounced *pergula* as *precula*.[6] Livy could not of course have been as rustic as this, but in general peculiarities of spelling, of pronunciation, and perhaps of intonation offer the most satisfying answer if Pollio's taunt of *patavinitas* has any literal significance. The jibe is trivial and esoteric.

Another view is probable if the word is regarded as having no peculiarly local significance, but as denoting

---

[1] See Sen. *Suas.* II, 10; *Contr.* II, 3, 13; IV, *pr.* 11; Quint. IX, 3, 13; Gell. x, 26, 1; Suet. *De Gramm.* 10.

[2] Quint. I, 7, 24: 'sibe et quase scriptum in multorum libris est, sed an hoc voluerint auctores nescio: T. Livium ita his usum ex Pediano comperi, qui et ipse eum sequebatur'.

[3] *CIL* v, 2960 (found at Padova) contains *sibe*. Other inscriptions from N. Italy have *nise* for *nisi*, *coniuge* for *coniugi*. See J. Whatmough, *HSCP* (1933), 95 ff.　　　　[4] *Or.* 160f.

[5] *Brut.* 171.　　　　[6] Quint. VIII, 1, 3; I, 5, 12.

provincialism in general as opposed to *urbanitas*. It can be claimed that Pollio's refined ear rejected turns of phrase and expression which lacked the finesse and precision of the best Roman diction; and that in calling these peculiarities 'Patavine' he was merely following the contemporary Greek convention of attaching outlandish labels, bearing no topographical connotation, to solecisms and verbal barbarisms.[1] Now Pollio was a protagonist of the Plain Style; as Quintilian remarks, 'tristes ac ieiuni Pollionem aemulantur'.[2] He undoubtedly viewed with distaste Livy's *lactea ubertas*—the admixture of poetic diction, the dactylic rhythms, the abundance of poetic constructions, and above all the elaborate architecture of the 'periodic' style. It is just possible that Pollio regarded such floridity as symptomatic of the oppressive worthiness of Cisalpine manners. But the obloquy of 'provincialism', viewed in a first-century literary context, was more probably an animadversion upon Livy's numerous departures from the canons of Ciceronian grammar and syntax.

The problem of *patavinitas*, then, is a problem of style. Its solution hinges on whether Pollio was alluding literally to the peculiarities of Patavians' Latin, or censuring Livy's *rusticitas* in general. On the first interpretation, the word is a reflection on the historian's spelling and pronunciation; on the second, it censures the many divergences from Ciceronian usage which this chapter has earlier illustrated.

[1] This is the persuasive thesis of K. Latte, *CP* (1940), 56–60, who quotes some interesting Greek parallels in such literary polemics.
[2] Quint. x, 2, 17.

XI

CONCLUSION: LIVY AS THE HISTORIAN OF ROME

As conclusion, the vital question must be posed: what value have Livy's writings for the study of Roman history? Some general observations, in review of the foregoing chapters, may first be made before a scrutiny decade by decade.

First, the influences on the *Ab Urbe Condita* of Livy's Patavian origin and the background of Augustan Rome are to be assessed. These would have emerged most relevantly in his analysis of first-century history, and in the extant books their importance is not conspicuous. The historian's upbringing in Cisalpine Gaul brought intensified emphasis on the traditional interpretation of history in moralistic terms; and the idealised picture of the *priscae virtutes* of the Romans of the early Republic is heightened by the pessimism with which he views the contemporary Roman scene at the beginning of the Augustan age. The label 'Augustan historian' is not so meaningful as some scholars maintain. Livy's friendship with Augustus does not mean that he was suborned to serve the new regime as official historian. The Princeps is given little prominence. All that can be said is that Livy's fundamental attitudes—his deep-seated religious feeling, his profound patriotism, his concern for sound morality—were nurtured by the prevailing climate of the early years of the principate. Yet at the very time when Augustus' studied moderation was causing an upsurge of optimism in Republican breasts, Livy was explicitly stating his scepticism of a return to Republican greatness.[1]

In fact, Livy is completely Ciceronian in his political attitudes—in his advocacy of the rule of law, in his doctrine of *concordia*, in his hatred of Roman kingship, in his defence of Pompey and Brutus and his coldness towards Julius. He is to be regarded, then, as pre-eminently a traditionalist, only superficially affected by the Augustan *Zeitgeist* and motivated chiefly by the Republican patriotism which his formative years in Patavium fostered. The general presentation of Roman history would not have been vastly different if Livy had written thirty years earlier.

Secondly, Livy's philosophical and religious preconceptions must be taken into account. There is considerable evidence of a Stoic interpretation of the earlier period. He attributes the foundation of Rome to the guidance of the gods and the fates, and depicts the providential help lent to the city in its early growth. The fabulous stories associated with the early period are 'rationalised' in a manner typical of neo-Stoicism. In the third decade, he retains the framework of ethical determinism within which Rome's disasters were traditionally recounted; impiety, injustice, lack of *fides* or of *prudentia* are visited by inevitable disaster. Subsequently, under the influence of Polybius, this theological interpretation is less in evidence. But the religious framework within which he presents early Roman activities and much of the Hannibalic War considerably diminishes the value of the *Ab Urbe Condita* as scientific history.

Thirdly, Livy's views on the aims and methods of history-writing are conspicuously affected by the treatises of Cicero, which in their turn are inspired especially by the theories of Isocrates. The repercussions are not merely literary. If history is to be *opus oratorium maxime*, it must

[1] Above, 18.

revolve around the personalities to whom speeches are allotted, and the selection of material for narrative is regulated accordingly. Further, the purpose of *historia* for Livy is didactic, to expound the *bonae artes* of earlier communities and to demonstrate the disastrous effects of the abandonment of them; in Bolingbroke's phrase, 'history is philosophy teaching by examples'. Thus the *Ab Urbe Condita* is centrally concerned with the characterisation of individuals. It is idle to deplore the absence of discussion of social and economic factors, for *historia* at Rome had no direct concern with such topics.

Livy's personal deficiencies as historian are considerable —weaknesses of geography, ignorance of military matters, lack of acquaintance with politics. He is thus incapable of rigorous evaluation or original interpretation in these fields. The main conclusion stands out inescapably: *Livy's value for Roman history varies according to the source followed.* Unfortunately, this is not all. The evidence which he reproduces is occasionally vitiated by mistakes in transcription, by his inability to expunge obvious errors in his sources, and by his failure to reconcile the various sources followed on questions of chronology and factual information.

Yet though he is too uncritical of his sources, Livy has higher standards of honesty and impartiality than his Roman predecessors. 'Povero sempre nella critica, ma amico sincero della verità.'[1] Such impartiality is however at Rome relative rather than absolute, and Livy is by no means guiltless of patriotic distortion in his delineation of the conduct of Roman armies and leaders. But Livy's manifest pride in their achievements and sympathy in their difficulties bring compensation for these drawbacks, in the sensitive insight with which he views human predicaments and suggests the psychological motivations behind particular decisions and acts.

[1] De Sanctis, *Storia dei Romani*, III, 2, 182.

Finally, he had not only historical but also literary purposes. The stream of would-be historians at Rome essayed their tasks in the belief that 'they would either produce more definite historical knowledge, or prove superior to unpolished antiquity in the art of writing'.[1] Livy's talent lies essentially in the second of these aims. The topics selected for dramatic interest—sieges of cities, dialogues, assemblies, acts of individual suffering or adventure—demonstrate the influences of Hellenistic historiography, whose fundamental spirit of compassionate humanitarianism now increasingly pervades Augustan Rome. The encasement of these dramatic descriptions in the framework of the composed episode, the embellishment of the source-material to produce a more lively or pathetic effect, and the adaptation of the style which achieves the requisite emotional pitch all reflect these influences.

Livy's narrative style is by no means uniform,[2] and must to some extent be affected by the source currently under scrutiny; but the typical composed episode skilfully combines extended 'periods', with their elaborate complex of subordinate clauses and participial phrases, with the sequences of short sentences so effective in depicting dramatic action. His literary genius also shows itself in the versatility with which he passes from this narrative style to the more antithetic latinity of the speeches. In these he is completely Ciceronian in the balance of clauses and phrases, and in the free use of rhetorical figures. Here and in his occasional digressions his latinity is at its richest and most diffuse. The discerning reader of the Preface, for example, cannot fail to note the subtlety of word order not merely to achieve specific rhythmical patterns, but also to evoke alliterative effects, the careful choice of diction arranged to achieve Gorgianic

[1] *Praef.* 2.
[2] In general, see Ch. x. For a stylistic analysis of xxx, 18–26, see R. Jumeau, *Rev. Phil.* (1939), 21–43.

antithesis, and the skilful use of figures which reinforce the achievements of vocabulary and word order.

Such stylistic considerations have not merely a literary but also an historical import. 'Livy was the master, the techniques his servants';[1] it is wrong to assume that his selection and treatment of material proceeded by purely artistic criteria. The vital lesson which extended comparison with his sources teaches is his faithful reproduction of the content. One observes here none of the excesses of a Duris or a Phylarchus, concerned to root out arresting topics whatever the cost, and to invent them when they cannot be found. Livy uses his dramatic techniques moderately, and only on the incidents to which his sources attest. Yet it must be noted that on several occasions he eschews strict historical accuracy in pursuance of enhanced dramatic or pathetic effects.

In short, Livy is heavily dependent on his source-material. But in transcribing this content he introduces his own motivation—religious and political, patriotic and moral. His emphasis is pre-eminently on psychological factors, and his literary techniques assist in the achievement of this aim.

Perennial controversy has centred on the value of the first decade (753–293 B.C.) as an historical document. Livy was himself under no illusions about the earlier elements of this period, and must be given credit for his explicit warnings that little factual detail was available for the years before 390 because of the paucity of authentic records.[2] The first systematically recorded priestly documents may have dated from about 300; yet the *annales maximi* must have incorporated genuine documentary detail from the fourth and even the fifth century.[3] The question must none the less be faced—how could

[1] A. H. McDonald, in *Fifty Years of Classical Scholarship*, 397.
[2] VI, 1, 2.　　　　　[3] Above, 111.

reliable traditions concerning the Regal period (753–510) and the early Republic be preserved over such an extent of time? One cannot totally discount the possibility of family records having dated from an era sufficiently early to contain factual information beneath the gilt of ancestral glorification. Secondly, there is the 'ballad' theory, usually attributed to Niebuhr;[1] ballads sung at banquets some generations before Cato's day celebrated the deeds of famous men. It has been inconclusively argued that these ballads were committed to writing.[2] But whether transmitted orally or by the pen, they furnished a basis, together with family material, on which the third-century historians retrospectively built. These sagas were augmented by speculative Greek accounts, and by literary motifs and techniques borrowed from Hellenistic historiography. Thus the annalistic tradition was born, the 'authorised version' of Roman history—a farrago of patriotic distortion, political animosity, and family chicanery. This is the source-material on which Livy depends, and the disastrous results are patent.

In view of this paucity of reliable information, it is tempting to discount (as Mommsen did) Livy's entire portrait of the political and military history of the Regal period. Yet archaeological evidence stresses the danger of such indiscriminate dismissal of the tradition. The sane procedure is to accept the broad outline of that tradition in so far as it is consonant with the limited archaeological information. On this basis one must abandon the legendary narrative of Rome's foundation, but affirm the existence of Numa Pompilius, Tullus Hostilius, and Ancus Marcius, especially as these gentile names recur in the consul lists of the early Republic. Again, though patriotic distortion has concealed the period of Etruscan

---

[1] But Niebuhr was anticipated by a seventeenth-century Dutch scholar Perizonius: see A. Momigliano, *JRS* (1957), 104 ff.
[2] By L. Pareti in his *Storia di Roma* (1952–   ).

dominance, tomb-inscriptions confirm the existence of the names Tarquinius and Tanaquil. The alternative tradition (unmentioned by Livy) which substitutes the Etruscan Mastarna for Servius Tullius indicates that there were other kings besides those listed by Livy. But the existence of Servius Tullius should not be questioned in view of his importance in the traditional saga of Roman achievement. As for the institutions traditionally assigned to the Regal period, such as the inauguration of religious ritual and the initiation of the 'Servian' reforms, there is no compelling reason to disqualify the general validity of such claims.[1] In short, Livy's first book, if one ignores the fictitious narrative of the foundation, reflects a selective version of tenacious folk-tradition, the bare outline of which may be accepted as an authentic part (but only a part) of Roman history under the kings.

The earliest section of Republican history—the exile of Tarquinius Superbus and the repulse of Lars Porsena—must be regarded in Livy's version as fabulous. It is virtually certain that an Etruscan occupation of Rome has been excised from the tradition, and though there is no need to deny the existence of such heroes as Horatius Cocles and Mucius Scaevola, there is no doubt that such legends in Book II have been developed according to Greek literary motifs.[2]

To what extent do Books II–X incorporate authentic magistrate lists? As has been noted, Livy's annalistic sources drew chiefly on the *annales maximi* but partly on the *libri lintei*. The list in the *annales maximi* may well have been based on genuine records not only for the fourth-century entries, but also for much of the fifth century. The *libri lintei* are a more uncertain quantity, but they are

---

[1] On this large subject see H. Last, *CAH* VII, 374 ff. (religious innovation); 432 ff. ('Servian' reforms). Chapters XII and XIII of this volume (by Last and H. Stuart Jones respectively), and the first volume of De Sanctis, *Storia dei Romani* (Turin, 1907), are the most valuable of modern analyses. For a recent brief survey of the problems see P. Fraccaro, *JRS* (1957), 59 ff. [2] Above, 212 f.

known to have been of great antiquity, and perhaps contained genuine fifth-century entries. Thus Livy's version contains a collation (perhaps made by Tubero) of two separate documents, which differed in some particulars from each other. The list preserved by Diodorus, on the other hand, which nineteenth-century scholars preferred, is based on a single documentary source. There are solid grounds for believing that the various extant magistrate lists (the *Fasti Capitolini*, and those which can be compiled from Diodorus, Dionysius, and Livy) are largely reliable, and that on the relatively few occasions on which they differ Livy's list is to be preferred: 'It is probable that Livy preserves the best record of the magistrates of the Roman Republic.'[1]

Such a reliable framework, which can be accepted from the early fifth century onwards,[2] is clearly of immense value. Within this framework, however, the 'authorised version' put out by Livy contains little detail which can be accepted without qualification. Of the two main themes of domestic struggles and external warfare, the first is in Livy's account the more valuable. The outline of the legislation which marks the milestones in the conflict of the orders can be accepted.[3] Undoubtedly this material was elaborated by sources preoccupied with the economic

---

[1] T. R. S. Broughton, *The Magistrates of the Roman Republic* I (New York, 1951), xii. [2] I follow Beloch, *Römische Geschichte*, 15 ff.

[3] It goes without saying that Livy's record of the constitutional changes of the fifth century contains little reliable *detail*, as can easily be established by noting the divergent versions of Diodorus, Cicero, Dionysius and Livy. Livy's use of Aelius Tubero in this decade is reflected in the legal purism with which such events as the establishment of the tribunate, the procedure of the Decemvirs appointed to codify the laws, and the like are recounted. For a modified defence of Livy's version of the Valerio-Horatian laws of 449 see H. H. Scullard, *Roman World*, App. 6. But Livy's version of one clause, 'ut quod tributim plebs iussisset, populum teneret' (III, 55, 3), should certainly have been more explicit in view of his account of later laws passed for the same purpose in 339 and 287. The fourth-century legislation presents fewer difficulties. But for varying views on Livy's version of the Licinian Rogations of 367 (VI, 35, 4–5) see Scullard, *Roman World*, 92, n. 1, 94. Unfortunately the loss of the second decade has deprived us of his account of the final six years which culminated in the *Lex Hortensia* of 287.

upheavals which troubled Rome after the activities of the Gracchi; undoubtedly, too, the roles of individuals and of families have been largely invented by annalists (from the third century to the first) who sought to laud their own names and to denigrate rival families.[1] Yet Livy's portrayal is of immense value not only for the factual information residing beneath the crust of such embellishment, but also for his psychological insight in evoking the atmosphere of the struggle. Though there are long extant extracts from Diodorus and Dionysius (and briefer items from others) on this subject, Livy's continuous narrative is the primary source.

Severe qualification is necessary before one can accept even the main outline of external operations from the fifth century to the beginning of the third. The exclusion of Rome from the Latin league, culminating in the battle of Lake Regillus, is obviously historical, though the clear-cut Roman victory is a patriotic fabrication.[2] There follows the century of continual warfare waged by the triple alliance of Romans, Latins, and Hernici against the mountain tribes, the Volsci, Aequi, and Sabines. Hardly any detail of the operations can be vouched for.[3] The same is true of Rome's engagements on her northern front. Though the initial warfare with Veii, the long period of peace, the capture of Fidenae about 425, and the final fall of Veii in 396 can be accepted in outline, most of the detail is highly dubious.[4] The 'authorised version'

---

[1] Above, 88 ff.

[2] II, 19–20. H. Last, *CAH* VII, 488 f., adds that the tradition of this war allows the acceptance of the genuineness of the *foedus Cassianum*.

[3] For the Volscian Wars, Livy and Dionysius (both dependent on the late annalists) are virtually the only sources. Coriolanus' name does not occur in the *Fasti*. The Livian date of the Volscian attacks (491–) is highly dubious (see Last, *CAH* VII, 499). But Livy's account of the attacks of the Aequi receives support from Diodorus; and though the operations of Cincinnatus (dictator traditionally in 462) are overlaid with sundry improbabilities, his *gens* is prominent in fifth-century history.

[4] The battle of Cremera, in which the Fabii were said to have shouldered the war for Rome in 477, has obviously an historical basis; perhaps Roman losses

of the Gallic capture of Rome, with its framework of divine anger and its detail of face-saving legend, need only be compared with the brief remarks of Polybius to demonstrate the extent of the patriotic distortion.[1]

Though Livy claims for the second pentad a surer historical basis ('clariora deinceps certioraque gesta domi militiaeque'[2]), the narrative of external events for the hundred years after the Gallic sack remains confused. Some would totally reject Livy's account of the fighting of the first thirty years against Gauls, Etruscans, Volsci, Aequi, Hernici, and Latins; Polybius explicitly states that the forays of the Gauls did not recur during this period, and the repeatedly large-scale fighting, which appeared suspicious even to Livy,[3] is too incredible to be remotely true. Presumably minor border raids and incursions have been grossly magnified to inflate the stature of Camillus, the central figure in the remarkable Roman recovery.[4]

Again, Livy's version of the so-called First Samnite War (343–341) is transparently suspect; Diodorus has no mention of it, and the defenders of the historicity of this episode have great difficulty in reconciling it with the subsequent revolt of the Latins, who are supported by the Campanians against Rome.[5] The narrative of the Great Samnite War (326–304) raises numerous per-

in this battle fell heaviest on the *Fabia gens*. Livy is intolerably vague about the reasons for the ensuing period of peace; his interest instead is centred on the domestic struggle. The capture of Fidenae is recounted twice; the first occasion, attributed to 435, is probably fictitious (so Last, *CAH* VII, 509). One cannot dismiss lightly the coincidence between the ten-year siege of Veii and that of Troy; and in this episode 'the details of Livy's story are in large part an unprofitable study' (Last, *CAH* VII, 512).

[1] Pol. II, 18, 2.   [2] VI, 1, 3.

[3] Pol. II, 18, 5; Livy's comment is at VI, 12, 2. See in general Beloch, *Römische Geschichte*, 314–19.

[4] For an acute analysis of the elements of the Camillus legend see A. Momigliano, *CQ* (1942), 111 ff. For a more conservative estimate see L. Homo, *CAH* VII, 566 ff.

[5] The tradition concerning this war appears also in Dionysius and Appian. For persuasive arguments against it see F. E. Adcock, *CAH* VII, 588. For a defence of the tradition see De Sanctis, II, 269 ff.

plexing problems. The first few years are 'the sport of rival traditions' reflected in the variants offered by Livy.[1] The great disaster near Caudium in 321 is fictitiously reconstructed with a face-saving theological framework and a structure more appropriate to drama than to historical narrative.[2] The five or six years of the Caudine peace humiliatingly imposed by the Samnites have been cloaked by fictitious detail of spirited Roman retaliation, and the chronological detail of subsequent operations must accordingly be revised. Finally, much of the geography of the final campaigns recorded in this decade is inaccurate.[3]

Livy's third decade, the account of the Hannibalic War, is greatly superior to the first as an historical document. The reasons are not merely that the facts of this more recent period were more easily accessible to his sources, or that his treatment is more thorough through his devoting ten books to the events of seventeen years. Also important is his use of different authorities.

Though the main theatres of the struggle were Italy and Spain, Sicily was also important, and the final campaign which decided the issue took place in Africa. For these Sicilian and African operations Livy relied on Polybius, 'a man who loves truth and sees things in perspective, who understands what he sees'.[4] Thus Livy's account is in these sections informative and accurate, if occasionally marred by well intentioned but disastrous attempts to improve upon the source.[5] Livy's testimony is all the more valuable because much of Polybius' record has been lost.

On the other hand, Livy's sections on the First Macedonian War in Books xxvi–xxix, where Polybius is again

[1] VIII, 30 ff.; Adcock, *CAH* VII, 598.
[2] See Ch. VI, 160, n. 1, and references there.
[3] Ch. VI, 154, n. 1; also Adcock, *CAH* VII, 602, n. 2; 603, n. 1.
[4] T. R. Glover, *CAH* VIII, 24.　　　　[5] See e.g. above, 157.

the main source, are not so satisfactory.[1] Livy has abridged Polybius' account—an unfortunate but inevitable feature since these Greek operations were only peripheral to the main struggle with Carthage. There are errors of chronology. Above all, Livy has at some points supplemented the Polybian narrative with detail taken from the late annalists, who in their treatment of Macedonian and Greek affairs can be highly unreliable. Yet because the account of Polybius has survived only fragmentarily here, Livy's history is the main authority for these operations, and hence is of considerable importance.

Secondly, the monograph of Coelius Antipater was extensively used, especially for the early years of the war. In spite of its sensationalism and rhetorical colouring, this work offered a better account of the military operations than did the late annalists. In particular, Coelius' use of Carthaginian sources has a beneficial effect on Livy's narrative, for much authentic detail of Carthaginian strategy and operations has been reproduced from this monograph.

Finally, Livy drew upon the late annalists, increasingly as the decade progressed, to fill in the picture of operations from a Roman viewpoint. The factual information which these authorities incorporated from documents allows Livy to give a detailed picture of political appointments and military movements. A complete table of the dispositions of legions and military commanders throughout the war (with the exception of those in Spain between 215 and 211) can thus be drawn up, though the entries for 217–216 are rather confused.[2] Again, there is full information on the yearly political and on the religious appointments, so that there is a sound framework within which the military and political events can be narrated.

---

[1] See M. Holleaux, *CAH* VIII, 116.
[2] See the lists compiled by De Sanctis, III, 2, 633 ff. B. L. Hallward, *CAH* VIII, 104, has produced a similar table.

Unfortunately, as has been noted, Livy had not the capacity fully to utilise the opportunities which these sources offered. His chronology is especially at fault in this decade, some errors being unwittingly reproduced from the sources, and others being caused by difficulties in passing from one authority to another.[1] His account of military operations is vitiated by the defects earlier exemplified. He is too credulous in reproducing the figures of battle accounts quoted by his sources;[2] there are numerous 'doublets' of battles in this decade caused by his recounting the same engagements from different sources;[3] his versions of several major battles are inadequate or inaccurate,[4] and he is content to reproduce the annalistic accounts of minor engagements without removing glaring patriotic distortion and without repairing the inadequacies in topography and tactics;[5] he omits essential technical detail in the siege of Syracuse, and has insufficient knowledge of battle strategy.[6] Geographical errors have also been noted in this decade.[7]

Livy's most regrettable failures in the political sphere are twofold. First, his blind patriotism makes for a less sympathetic insight into the Carthaginian viewpoint, especially in his analysis of the causes of the war. Secondly, there is his inability to appreciate the extent to which his Senatorial sources had denigrated the popular commanders.[8] In general, too, his portrait of Senatorial activity is over-idealised. He pays insufficient attention to the rivalries within the Senate, and its harmonious, intrepid patriotism is overdrawn.[9] On the other hand, he is to be commended for his clear picture of Senatorial administration, and for the voluminous detail with which he records the year-by-year appointments of officials.

---

[1] Above, 147 and 149, n. 2.   [2] Above, 144f.
[3] Above, 147, n. 4.   [4] Above, 159ff.
[5] Above, 158f.   [6] Above, 157f.
[7] Above, 154ff.   [8] Above, 167.
[9] Above, 166f.

Above all, it is through Livy that we win a thorough appreciation of the political and moral attributes which enabled the Roman character and the Roman constitution to weather the crises of the early years of the war, to retain the loyalty of most of her Italian allies, and to bring the war to a victorious conclusion.

Finally, the fourth and fifth decades may be analysed together. Some two-thirds of the narrative is here concerned with events in Greece and Asia, and for these the historian has followed Polybius alone. It is a paradoxical but demonstrably true fact that here, where Livy is content merely to transcribe from the Greek historian, and does not in the selection and organisation of his material take pains commensurate with those of earlier decades, the results are historically more valuable. For his importance for the Second Macedonian War and for the war with Antiochus, let the most eminent authority speak: 'This translation or rather adaptation of Polybius by Livy—vastly superior to his performance as regards the First Macedonian War—is of outstanding importance. Despite its great deficiencies and although it abounds in mis-statements, many of which are tendentious, it remains—except, of course, for the actual fragments of Polybius—the main source for the history of Rome's first two great wars in the East.'[1] Subsequently Livy's narrative becomes even more important, for Polybius' extant extracts diminish in number and extent; Books XXXVIII–XLV of Livy, narrating the events before the Third Macedonian War and the war itself, are indispensable.

What are the deficiencies mentioned in the above quotation? Livy's adaptation of Polybius is by no means free of simple mistranslations.[2] His account of the military operations suffers from over-simplification or

[1] M. Holleaux, *CAH* VIII, 138.
[2] Above, 143 f.

over-dramatisation, as in his version of the battles at Cynoscephalae, Thermopylae, and Magnesia.[1] The same point can be made of his siege descriptions.[2] His analyses of diplomatic exchanges omit or over-simplify important policy statements,[3] and he has made additions to Polybius' details of treaty stipulations from less reputable sources.[4] Above all, there is the deliberate suppression of acts and attitudes which put Roman armies and leaders in an unpleasant light.[5] Such defects of detail, however, only occasionally detract from the value of the general picture of Greek and Asian events of 200–167 B.C.

Interspersed with this detailed narrative of Eastern affairs are the briefer sections on events in Italy and the Western Mediterranean. Unfortunately, there was no Polybius to whom Livy could turn for authoritative guidance here. His account of the campaigns against the Gallic tribes of Northern Italy, the Boii, Insubres, and Cenomani (which preoccupied Rome until 191), and of the subsequent struggles with the Ligurians and Istrians, is wholly dependent on late annalistic sources who had only the barest documentary detail on which to base their narratives. The result is the usual annalistic compound of fictitious detail and contamination. For example, the Carthaginian Hamilcar, who acted as leader of the combined Gallic forces, is said by Livy to have been killed in the fighting of 200 B.C., when the Roman force was led by L. Furius Purpurio; three years later, he is again reported killed in fighting against Cornelius Cethegus, and Livy reports an alternative tradition which claims that he appeared in Cethegus' triumph.[6] Clearly the earlier battle has been filled out with detail from the later. Other pitched battles are reported without distinctive

[1] Above, 161, 201 and 162, n. 1.
[2] E.g. Ambracia; above, 158.   [3] Above, 210ff.
[4] Above, 150, n. 3.   [5] Above, 151f.
[6] XXXI, 21, 18; XXXII, 30, 12; XXXIII, 23, 5. Livy characteristically does not try to establish which version is correct.

detail and with stereotyped vocabulary; virtually the only credence which can be attached to them lies in the bare detail of commanders' names and such other facts as appeared in the *annales maximi* and in Senatorial documents.

A similar estimate can be made of Livy's report of operations in Spain, where a large-scale revolt had spread from the south in 197. There is however one exceptional section—a long account of the operations of 195 when Cato as consul led the Roman forces.[1] Livy may have used Cato's account here, or alternatively he has got it at second hand from a late annalist. There is welcome precision of topographical detail and tactics in the description of operations, and information on diplomatic activities. For the rest, the Spanish campaigning is delineated as unrewardingly as the Italian. Of both it may be said that there is ninety per cent fabrication without the saving merit of imagination; and Livy's inability to distinguish one engagement from another has resulted in the inevitable 'doublets'.[2]

There remains the central question of the depiction of Roman administration. Here the merits and defects are similar to those of the third decade. There is the very useful detailed framework of yearly appointments, deriving indirectly from the *annales maximi*. There is the regular *exposé* of Senatorial business, from which a clear picture emerges of the changes in diplomatic usage which follow upon Rome's Eastern expansion. But there is also the inevitably idealised portrait of Senatorial activity, with the excision of all discreditable elements.[3] And though there is some indication of internal dissensions within the Senate at the time of the trials of the Scipios,[4] insufficient attention has been paid to this factional manipulation of power in the other books of these decades.[5]

[1] xxxiv, 9–21.   [2] Above, 148.   [3] Above, 152.
[4] xxxviii, 43 (M. Fulvius and M. Aemilius); 54 (Cato and Africanus); 54, 7 (L. Furius Purpurio and Cn. Manlius). See also xxxix, 38–9.
[5] For a general survey see H. H. Scullard, *Roman Politics*, chs. vi–xii.

Systematic research on the *Ab Urbe Condita* has converged from widely differing viewpoints. German scholarship in particular has wielded the scalpel deftly in its division of Livian studies into various categories. For some, Livy is nothing more than a source-problem—a 'scissors and paste' historian ineptly gumming together items from different authorities. To others on the contrary he appears as a cunning manipulator of Rome's traditions, furthering the aims of a calculating Princeps. For others, who sedulously trace an intimate relationship between his compositional method and that of certain Hellenistic historians, he is pre-eminently a literary artist. There is an urgent need to reconcile these conflicting claims, to assess the relative importance of these facets in the pattern of the whole work.

Our most certain approach has been *to examine those sections of the Ab Urbe Condita for which the source used is extant*. This procedure demonstrates the fallacies resultant upon approaching the historian from one aspect. Livy is not a 'scissors and paste' historian, for his humanitarian sympathy, his patriotism, his fundamental religious feeling, and his overwhelmingly moral preoccupations powerfully affect his presentation. He is not an Augustan in any significantly political sense. Nor is he chiefly a descriptive writer, subordinating the historian's duties to more congenial literary aims. His central importance is as the historian of Ciceronian theory, seeking to encase truthful history in a worthy literary setting. His performance as historian is outshone by his literary virtuosity; but this should not blind us to the fact that he, no less than Cicero, regards history as the 'testis temporum, lux veritatis, vita memoriae, magistra vitae'.[1]

[1] Cic. *De Or.* II, 36.

SELECT BIBLIOGRAPHY

ADCOCK, F· E. In *CAH*, vol. VII (Cambridge, 1929).

ALY, W. *Livius und Ennius* (Leipzig, 1936).

ANDERSON, W. B. Livy IX³ (Cambridge, 1928).

BALSDON, J. P. V. D. 'Some Questions about Historical Writing in the Second Century B.C.', *CQ* (1953), 158–64.

—— 'Rome and Macedon, 205–200 B.C.', *JRS* (1954), 30–42.

BAYET, J. Budé edition, Livy I (Paris, 1940).

BELOCH, K. J. *Römische Geschichte bis zum Beginn der punischen Kriege* (Berlin, 1926).

BENECKE, P. V. M. In *CAH*, vol. VIII (Cambridge, 1930).

BIKERMAN, F. 'La lettre de Mithridate dans les Histoires de Salluste', *REG* (1946), 131ff.

BORNECQUE, H. *Tite-Live* (Paris, 1933).

BOUGERY, A. 'Tite-Live et le passage des Alpes par Hannibal', *Rev. Phil.* (1938), 120–32.

BRODRIBB, R. A. 'Verse in Livy', *CR* (1910), 13–15.

BRUNS, I. *Die Persönlichkeit in der Geschichtsschreibung der Alten* (Berlin, 1898).

BURCK, E. *Die Erzählungskunst des T. Livius* (Berlin, 1934).

—— *Einführung in die dritte Dekade des Livius* (Heidelberg, 1950).

BURY, J. B. *The Ancient Greek Historians* (London, 1909).

CAMPBELL, S. G. Livy XXVII⁶ (Cambridge, 1937).

CANTER, H. V. 'Rhetorical Elements in Livy's Direct Speeches', *AJP* (1917), 125–51; also *AJP* (1918), 44–64.

CAPES, W. W. *Livy* (London, 1879).

CATIN, L. *En lisant Tite-Live* (Paris, 1944).

CAVAIGNAC, E. 'Quelques remarques sur l'historicité de Tite-Live, XXXI–XLV', *Rev. Phil.* (1915), 5–23.

CICHORIUS, C. 'Ein neuer Historiker und die Anfänge von Livius' schriftstellerischer Tätigkeit', *Römische Studien* (Leipzig, 1922), 261–9.

CONWAY, R. S. Livy II (Cambridge, 1901).

CRAKE, J. E. A. 'The Annals of the Pontifex Maximus', *CP* (1940), 375–86.

CURCIO, G. 'La filosofia della storia nell'opera di Tito Livio', *Riv. IGI* (1917), 77–85.

D'ALTON, J. F. *Roman Literary Theory and Criticism* (London, 1931).

DEFOURNY, P. 'Histoire et éloquence d'après Cicéron', *Ét. Class.* (1953), 156–66.

DE SANCTIS, G. *Storia dei Romani* I–IV, I (Turin, 1907–23).

—— 'Livio e la storia della storiografia romana', in *Problemi di storia antica* (Bari, 1932), 225–47.

DESSAU, H. 'Die Vorrede des Livius', *Festschrift O. Hirschfeld* (Berlin, 1903), 461 ff.

—— 'Livius und Augustus', *Hermes* (1906), 142 ff.

DIMSDALE, M. Livy XXI (Cambridge, 1894).

DUNBABIN, R. L. 'Verses in Livy', *CR* (1911), 104–6.

DUTOIT, E. 'Quelques généralisations de portée psychologique et morale dans l'histoire romaine de Tite-Live', *REL* (1942), 98–105.

—— 'Silences dans l'œuvre de Tite-Live', in *Mélanges J. Marouzeau* (Paris, 1948).

ENGELBRECHT, A. 'Ein vermeintliches Zeugnis des Seneca über des Livius' philosophische Schriftstellerei', *Wien. Stud.* (1904), 62 ff.

ERKELL, H. *Augustus, Felicitas, Fortuna* (Göteborg, 1952).

FERRERO, L. 'Attualità e tradizione nella praefatio Liviana', *RFIC* (1949), 1–47.

FRACCARO, P. 'The History of Rome in the Regal Period', *JRS* (1957), 59–65.

FRANK, T. In *CAH*, vol. VIII (Cambridge, 1930).

GAGÉ, J. 'La "rogatio Petillia" et le procès de P. Scipion', *Rev. Phil.* (1953), 34–64.

GELZER, M. 'Römische Politik bei Fabius Pictor', *Hermes* (1933), 129 ff.

—— 'Der Anfang römischer Geschichtsschreibung', *Hermes* (1934), 46–55.

—— 'Die Unterdrückung der Bacchanalen bei Livius', *Hermes* (1936), 275–87.

—— 'Nochmals über den Anfang der römischer Geschichtsschreibung', *Hermes* (1954), 342–8.

GIARRATANO, C. *Tito Livio*[2] (Rome, 1943).

GRIES, K. *Constancy in Livy's Latinity* (New York, 1947).

—— 'Livy's Use of Dramatic Speech', *AJP* (1949), 118 ff.

GRIFFITH, G. T. 'The Greek Historians', in *Fifty Years of Classical Scholarship* (Oxford, 1954), 150–92.

HALLWARD, B. L. In *CAH*, vol. VIII (Cambridge, 1930).

HEINZE, R. *Die augusteische Kultur*[2] (Leipzig, 1933).

—— *Virgils epische Technik*[3] (Leipzig, 1957).

HELLMANN, F. *Livius-Interpretationen* (Berlin, 1939).

HESSELBARTH, H. *Historisch-kritische Untersuchungen zur dritten Dekade des Livius* (Lippstadt, 1889).

HOCH, H. *Die Darstellung der politischen Sendung Roms bei Livius* (Frankfurt, 1951).

HOFFMANN, W. *Livius und der zweite punische Krieg* (Leipzig, 1942).

HOLLEAUX, M. In *CAH*, vol. VIII (Cambridge, 1930).

—— 'Notes sur Tite-Live', *Rev. Phil.* (1931), 5–19, 193–208.

JACOBY, F. *Die Fragmente der griechischen Historiker* (Berlin, 1923–30; Leiden, 1940–50).

JONES, H. S. In *CAH*, vol. VII (Cambridge, 1929).

JUMEAU, R. 'Tite-Live et l'historiographie hellénistique', *REA* (1936), 63–8.

—— 'Remarques sur la structure de l'exposé livien', *Rev. Phil.* (1939), 21–43.

KAHRSTEDT, U. *Die Annalistik von Livius, B. xxxi–xlv* (Berlin, 1913).

—— (Melzer–Kahrstedt), *Geschichte der Karthager* III (Berlin, 1913).

KAJANTO, I. *God and Fate in Livy* (Turku, 1957).

KLINGNER, F. *Römische Geisteswelt* (Leipzig, 1943), esp. 426ff.

—— In *Gnomon* (1935), 575ff. (review of E. Burck, *Die Erzählungskunst des T. Livius*).

KLOTZ, A. In Pauly–Wissowa, *RE* XIII, 816–52, *s.v.* 'Livius'.

—— *Livius und seine Vorgänger* (Leipzig–Berlin, 1940–1).

—— 'Zu den Quellen der vierten und fünften Dekade des Livius', *Hermes* (1915), 481–536.

—— 'Zu den Periochae des Livius', *Philologus* (1936), 67–88.

—— 'Livius' Darstellung des zweiten Samniterkrieges', *Mnem.* (1938), 87–102.

—— 'Caesar und Livius', *RhM* (1953), 62–7.

KROLL, W. *Studien zum Verständnis der römischen Literatur* (Stuttgart, 1924), 331ff.

LAISTNER, M. L. W. *The Greater Roman Historians* (Berkeley, 1947).

LAMBERT, A. *Die indirekte Rede als künstlerisches Stilmittel des Livius* (Zürich, 1946).

LAST, H. In *CAH*, vol. VII (Cambridge, 1929).

LATTE, K. 'Livy's Patavinitas', *CP* (1940), 56–60.

LENCHANTIN, M. DE G. *Le storie di Livio come opera d'arte* (Pavia, 1942).

LITCHFIELD, H. W. 'National Exempla Virtutis in Roman Literature', *HSCP* (1914), 1–71.

LÖFSTEDT, E. *Syntactica* II (Lund, 1933), 294ff.

MCDONALD, A. H. 'Rome and the Italian Confederation, 200–186 B.C.', *JRS* (1944), 11–33.

—— 'The Roman Historians', in *Fifty Years of Classical Scholarship* (Oxford, 1954), 384–412.

—— 'The Style of Livy', *JRS* (1957), 155–72.

MAROUZEAU, J. 'Pour mieux comprendre les textes latins', *Rev. Phil.* (1921), esp. 165–6.

MARTIN, J. M. K. 'Livy and Romance', *GR* (1942), 124–9.

MICHAEL, W. *De ratione qua Livius in tertia Decade opere Polybiano usus sit* (Diss. Bonn, 1867).

MOMIGLIANO, A. 'Camillus and Concord', *CQ* (1942), 111–20.

—— In *JRS* (1945), 142–4 (review of P. Zancan, *Tivo Livio saggio storico*, and of Budé Livy 1, ed. Bayet).

—— 'Perizonius, Niebuhr, and the Character of Early Tradition', *JRS* (1957), 104–14.

MÜLLER, M. Livy 1 (Leipzig, 1875).

NISARD, D. *Les quatre grands historiens latins* (Paris, 1874).

NISSEN, H. *Kritische Untersuchungen über die Quellen der vierten und fünften Dekade des Livius* (Berlin, 1868).

NORDEN, E. *Die antike Kunstprosa* 1 (Leipzig, 1915), esp. 234–9.

OGILVIE, R. M. 'Livy, Licinius Macer and the *Libri Lintei*', *JRS* (1958), 40–6.

OTTO, W. F. Pauly–Wissowa, *RE* VI, 2048, *s.v.* 'Fatum'.

PAIS, E. *Storia di Roma*[3] (Rome, 1926), esp. 55 ff.

PALMER, L. R. *The Latin Language* (London, 1954).

PERROCHAT, P. *Les modèles grecs de Salluste* (Paris, 1949).

RAMBAUD, M. *Cicéron et l'histoire romaine* (Paris, 1953).

RIEMANN, O. *Études sur la langue et la grammaire de Tite-Live*[2] (Paris, 1885).

ROSTAGNI, A. *Da Livio a Virgilio et da Virgilio a Livio* (Padova, 1942).

DE SAINT-DENIS, E. 'Les énumérations de prodiges dans l'œuvre de Tite-Live', *Rev. Phil.* (1942), 126–42.

SCHANZ, M. (Schanz–Hosius), *Geschichte der römischen Literatur* 1[4] (München, 1927).

SCHULTEN, A. In *CAH*, vol. VIII (Cambridge, 1930).

SCOTT, K. 'Identification of Augustus with Romulus', *TAPA* (1925), 82 ff.

SCULLARD, H. H. *Scipio Africanus in the Second Punic War* (Cambridge, 1930).

—— *A History of the Roman World, 753–146 B.C.*[2] (London, 1951).

—— *Roman Politics, 220–150 B.C.* (Oxford, 1951).

SOLTAU, W. *Livius' Geschichtswerk, seine Composition und seine Quellen* (Leipzig, 1897).

STACEY, S. G. 'Die Entwickelung des livianischen Stiles', *Arch. f. lat. Lex.* 10 (1898), 17 ff.

STEELE, R. B. 'The Historical Attitude of Livy', *AJP* (1904), 15–44.

STEELE, R. B. *Case Usage in Livy: Genitive, Accusative, Ablative* (Leipzig, 1910, 1912, 1913).

STÜBLER, G. *Die Religiosität des Livius* (Stuttgart–Berlin, 1941).

SYME, R. *The Roman Revolution* (Oxford, 1939).

—— *Tacitus* (Oxford, 1958).

—— In *JRS* (1945), 104–8 (review of W. Hoffmann, *Livius und der zweite punische Krieg*).

TAINE, H. *Essai sur Tite-Live*[8] (Paris, 1910).

TAYLOR, L. R. 'Livy and the name Augustus', *CR* (1918), 158–61.

TIERNEY, J. J. 'The *Senatus Consultum de Bacchanalibus*', *Proc. Irish Acad.* LI, C, 5 (1947), 89–117.

ULLMAN, B. L. 'History and Tragedy', *TAPA* (1942), 25–53.

ULLMANN, R. 'Les clausules métriques dans les discours de Salluste, Tite-Live, Tacite', *Symb. Osl.* Fasc. 3 (1925), 65–75.

—— *La Technique des discours dans Salluste, Tite-Live, et Tacite* (Oslo, 1927).

—— *Étude sur le style des discours de Tite-Live* (Oslo, 1929).

WALBANK, F. W. 'Tragic History—a Reconsideration', *Bull. Inst. Class. Stud. London* (1955), 4ff.

—— *A Historical Commentary on Polybius* I (Oxford, 1957).

WALSH, P. G. 'The Literary Techniques of Livy,' *RhM* (1954), 97–114.

—— 'Livy's Preface and the Distortion of History', *AJP* (1955), 369–83.

—— 'The Negligent Historian: Howlers in Livy', *GR* (1958), 83–8.

—— 'Livy and Stoicism', *AJP* (1958), 355–75.

—— In *JRS* (1958), 192–3 (review of I. Kajanto, *God and Fate in Livy*).

WEBER, W. *Princeps: Studien zur Geschichte des Augustus* I (Stuttgart, 1936).

WEISSENBORN, W. In Weissenborn–Müller's edition of Livy I, *Einl.* (Berlin, 1885).

WHATMOUGH, J. 'Quemadmodum Pollio reprehendit in Livio Patavinitatem', *HSCP* (1933), 95–130.

WITTE, K. 'Über die Form der Darstellung in Livius' Geschichtswerk', *RhM* (1910), 270–305, 359–419.

ZANCAN, P. *Tito Livio: saggio storico* (Milan, 1940).

ZIMMERER, M. *Der Annalist Q. Claudius Quadrigarius* (Diss. Munich, 1937).

INDEX

ablative case in Livy, 262 f.
Abydus, 178 f., 193 ff., 196, 210 f.
Academics, 47, 51
accusative case in Livy, 261
Achaeans, 130, 169
Acilius (annalist), 29, 120
Acilius Glabrio, M'. (cos. 191), 171, 176, 207, 225
Actium, 4, 11, 12 n. 1, 14, 17
Ad Herennium, treatise, 220, 238
adnominatio, 240, 258
Aegina, 26
Aelius Tubero, Q. (annalist), 115 ff., 123, 139, 278
Aemilii, 166
Aemilius Lepidus, M. (cos. I 187), 107, 196, 210 f., 286 n. 4
Aemilius Paulus, L. (cos. I 219), 72, 104, 118, 166, 223, 231
Aemilius Paulus, L. (cos. I 182), 7, 90, 128, 227
Aeneas, 2, 94
Aeneid, the, 61, 178, 256
Aenus, 152
Aequi, 52 f., 59, 73 n. 2, 79, 147, 169, 182, 279 f.
Aetolians, 74, 108, 143, 152, 187, 206 f., 211, 233, 238
Africa, 95, 97–9, 128, 130–2, 178, 281
Africans, 41 n. 3
Alba Longa, 171, 257 f.
Albans, 224
Alcibiades, 41
Alexander the Great, 22, 24, 40, 65, 86, 88, 137, 157
Alexandria, 17, 148
Allia, the, 171
Allucius, 94
Alorcus, 193, 196
Alps, the, 154 ff., 183
Ambracia, 158, 203
Amphilochia, 189
amplificatio, 224
ἀναγνώρισις, 118
anaphora, 239, 243, 258

Ancus Marcius, 276
Anicius, 75
annales maximi, 110 f., 114, 116 n. 1, 120, 122, 150, 275, 286
annalistic presentation, 174 f.
annalists, 146, 158, 165, 279, 282, 285
Antenor, 2
Antiochus III of Syria, 7, 84, 93, 96, 100, 104, 150, 176, 181, 188, 199, 207, 232 f., 235, 238, 244, 284
antithesis, 239 f., 243
Antium, 58
Antonius, M. (cos. 99), 32
Antony, Mark, 2, 4, 17
Anxur, 73, 195 n. 3
Aous, the, 205
Apennines, 147
Apollonia, 107
apostrophe, 241
Appian, 115, 122, 201
Aquilii, the, 116
Aratus, 130
Arausio, 155
archaisms, 259
Archimedes, 79, 102
Ardea, 214, 216
Aristaenus, 222
Aristotle, 23, 25, 130, 220, 224, 242
Arpi, 105
Arrian, 22
Arruns, 118
Asconius, 2 n. 1
Asia, 7, 76, 95, 133, 284
Astapa, 194
Athene, 25 n. 1, 108
Athenian plague, 182
Athens, 3, 56, 148, 189, 192
Attalus I of Pergamum, 107 f., 148, 149 n. 1, 189, 210 f.
Attalus II, 152, 234, 238
Attica, 148
'Augustan' historiography, 10, 61, 271
Augustus, 6, 8 ff., 83, 113, 271, *and see under* Octavian
augustus, 15 f.

293

Bacchanalia, the, 61, 223
Badius, 200
Baecula, 154
Balbus, 4, 50, 60
ballad theory, 276
battle-accounts, literary treatment of, 197 ff.
Bellona, 170, 175
Bithynia, 84
Boeotia, 57 n. 3, 181
Boii, 285
Brachyllas, 101, 190
Britons, 41 n. 3
Brutus, *see under* Junius

Cadiz, 18 n. 2
Caecilius Metellus, Q. (cos. 206), 224
Caecilius Metellus, Q. (cos. 143), 15
Caenina, 195
Caesar, *see under* Julius
Caligula, 153
Callisthenes, 24, 33
Calpurnius Piso, L. (annalist), 115, 119, 128, 132, 142 n. 2
Camillus, *see under* Furius
Campanians, 109, 237, 280
Cannae, 54, 63 f., 78, 86, 96, 102–4, 127, 131, 162, 171, 181, 229
Capua, 78, 105, 173, 238
Carthage, 6 f., 76, 112, 118, 122, 135, 196, 282
Carthaginians, 87, 103, 108, 131, 145, 160, 181, 183, 258
Casilinum, 78, 101, 106
Cassander, 209
Cassius Longinus, C. (conspirator), 12, 163
Catiline, 104
Cato, *see under* Porcius
Caudium, 55, 68, 156, 160 n. 1, 204, 281
Celts, 28 n. 1, 41 n. 3, 160
Cenomani, 285
Ceres, 112 n. 2
Cerrinus Vibellius, 71 n. 1
characterisation, 82 ff., 228, 244
chiasmus, 240, 258
Chiomara, 76, 213 f.
chronology, 143, 145 f., 148 f.
Chrysippus, 53
Cians, 211

Cicero, 4, 11, 20 f., 23, 27–9, 32 ff., 38 f., 42, 45, 47 f., 50, 57, 59 f., 85, 112 n. 1, 113, 119, 130, 132, 136, 139, 173, 177, 206, 220 f., 235, 245 ff., 249, 262, 267, 269, 272, 278 n. 3
Cincinnatus, *see under* Quinctius
Cincius (Augustan antiquary), 117
Cincius Alimentus, L. (annalist), 28, 127 f.
Cirta, 230
Cisalpine Gaul, 271
Cissus, 199 n. 2, 252 f.
Claudia gens, 89, 92, 164
Claudius (emperor), 12, 18 n. 2, 219
Claudius, Appius (decemvir), 76, 89, 214 f., 225, 228
Claudius Asellus, 71 n. 1
Claudius Caecus, Appius (cos. I 307), 170, 175, 228
Claudius Marcellus, M. (cos. I 222), 36, 55, 63, 71 f., 78, 85 f., 101 ff., 106, 125, 127 n. 2, 229
Claudius Nero, C. (cos. 207), 102, 161, 202
Claudius Pulcher, Appius (cos. 185), 167, 209
Claudius Quadrigarius, Q. (annalist), 71, 111 n. 3, 115 ff., 145, 148, 151, 187
clementia, 66, 73 ff., 86, 92, 97, 151
Cleon, 68, 105
Cleonymus, 41
Cleopatra, 4, 17
Clitarchus, 24, 30, 42
Clodius Licinus, 128
Cloelia, 213
Clusium, 67
Coelius Antipater, L. (historian), 30, 42, 124 ff., 130 ff., 140, 147 f., 154, 156 n. 3, 158, 160 n. 3, 254, 282
Collatia, 216
Collatinus, *see under* Tarquinius
colloquialisms, 259 f.
Commentarii, Caesar's, 136, 203
concordia, 66, 68 f., 164
conference-scenes, 205 ff.
congeries verborum, 240, 243, 258
conjunctions in Livy, 263 f.
Corcyraeans, 225 n. 1
Corinth, 181, 205
Corinthian Games, 171, 184, 205

Corinthians, 225 n. 1
Coriolanus, *see under* Marcius
Cornelii, 166
Cornelius (Patavian augur), 64
Cornelius Cethegus, M. (cos. 204), 161, 285
Cornelius Cossus, A., 14 f., 113
Cornelius Nepos, 117
Cornelius Scipio, P. (cos. 218), 72, 103, 223, 225 n. 1, 232, 239
Cornelius Scipio Aemilianus, P., 7, 128 f.
Cornelius Scipio Africanus, P., 16, 55, 74, 76 f., 85–8, 93 ff., 109, 132, 133 nn. 1 and 2, 143, 145, 178, 188, 192, 202, 203, 214, 225, 228, 232 f., 235 f., 240 f., 286 n. 4
Cornelius Scipio Asiaticus, L., 86, 99
Crassus, *see under* Licinius
Cremera, 279 n. 4
Cremonis iugum, 155
Cremutius Cordus, 12
Cresimus, 119 n. 2
Crispinus, *see under* Quinctius
Croesus, 208
crowd-scenes, 206 ff.
Cumae, 63
Curiatii, 213
Cybele, 187
Cynoscephalae, 120, 151, 161, 186, 199, 285

dactylic rhythms, 253 ff.
Dasius Altinius, 105
dative case in Livy, 262
Decemvirs, 117
Decii, 88, 213
Decius Mus, P. (cos. 340), 229
Decius Mus, P. (cos. 312), 89 n. 1, 228
Demaratus, 208
Demetrius of Macedon, 101, 107, 205 f., 226, 235, 242
Demetrius of Phalerum, 25
Demosthenes, 45, 83, 245
dialogue-scenes, 208 ff.
Dido, 17
dignitas, 66, 78 ff.
Diodorus Siculus, 22, 115, 116 n. 1, 149, 161, 210, 278–80
Dionysius of Halicarnassus, 91, 115, 116 n. 1, 118, 123, 164, 170, 179, 183, 206, 228, 230 f., 278, 279

disciplina, 66, 70 f.
Dolopes, 189
doublets, 147 f., 286
dramatic devices, 201 ff.
Duillius, M., 92, 164
Durance, the, 156
Duris, 24 ff., 33, 42, 275
Dyrrachium, 7

Egeria, 48
Egyptians, 41 n. 3
ἔκπληξις, 177, 202 n. 3
Elea, 188
elogium, 85, 100
ἐνάργεια, 181, 183 ff., 190, 237
Ennius, 16, 136 f., 172, 249, 254, 256 f.
Ephorus, 22 f., 41, 130, 138
Epicureans, 47, 51, 56
Epirus, 188, 201
Etruria, 61, 154
Etruscans, 7, 84 n. 3, 108 f., 195, 276 f., 280
Euboea, 181, 188
Eumenes, 84, 232, 234, 238
exaggeratio, 241
exclamatio, 241

Fabia gens, 89, 166, 279 n. 4
Fabius Ambustus, 214
Fabius Maximus Cunctator, Q., 59, 71 f., 85 f., 88, 93, 95, 101, 105 f., 167, 176, 200 f., 223, 231
Fabius Pictor, Q., 28, 36, 89, 115, 117 ff., 124, 127 f., 130–2, 142, 152, 156 n. 3
Fabius Rullianus, Q., 71, 89 n. 1, 176, 225
Falerii, 75
Fasti Capitolini, 278
Fasti Triumphales, 111 n. 1
fatum, 53 ff.
fictio personarum, 241
Fidenae, 195, 279 f.
fides, 66 ff.
First Triumvirate, 117
Flaccus, *see under* Valerius
Flamininus, *see under* Quinctius
Flaminius, C. (cos. I 223), 58, 68, 106, 131, 167
Flavius, Cn., 119
foedus Cassianum, 279 n. 2
fortuna, 55 ff., 103

fortuna populi Romani, 58 f.
Fronto, 121
frugalitas, 66, 77, 92
Fulvius Nobilior, M. (cos. 189), 233,
    286 n. 4
Furii, 93
Furius Camillus, M., 16 f., 54, 58, 71,
    72 n. 5, 73, 75, 76 n. 1, 85, 92, 109,
    122, 146, 153, 195 f., 200, 222, 228,
    258, 280
Furius Crassipes, M. (praetor 187), 75
Furius Purpurio, L. (cos. 196), 285,
    286 n. 4

Gabii, 179
Gallograecia, 120, 187
Gaul, 130
Gauls, 7, 41 n. 3, 67, 108, 146, 171, 280
genitive case in Livy, 261 f.
Genucius, L., 52
genus deliberativum, 220 ff.
genus demonstrativum, 220, 227
genus iudiciale, 220, 225 f.
geography, weaknesses of, 153 ff.
Germanicus, 83
Germans, 41, 108, 136
gerund in Livy, 267
Glabrio, *see under* Acilius
Gracchi, 279
Gracchus Cloelius, 79
gravitas, 66, 78 ff., 101
Greece, 7, 83, 125, 128, 133, 148, 150,
    206, 284
Greek constructions in Livy, 261 f.,
    267
Greek drama, influence of, 83
Greeks, 108, 171, 184
Grenoble, 155

Hamilcar, 285
Hannibal, 7, 41 n. 5, 71 f., 78, 85 f.,
    88, 96, 100, 102 ff., 106, 109, 113,
    124, 127 f., 131, 147, 154 ff., 173,
    196, 202, 223, 225, 228, 232 f., 244,
    258
Hannibalic War, 7, 34, 38 n. 3, 61, 71,
    85, 93, 100, 105, 117, 122, 128, 130,
    152, 154, 165-7, 222, 272, 281
Hanno, 196
Hasdrubal Barca, 98, 162
Hasdrubal Gisgo, 87, 96 f., 99, 230
Hecataeus, 30

Hellenistic historiography, 22 ff., 122,
    130 f., 161, 177 ff., 191, 212 ff., 274,
    276
Henna, 36, 73
Heraclea, 193
Heraclia, 215
Hercules, 11, 104, 252 n. 1, 257
Hermes, statues of, 27
Hernici, 52, 279 f.
Herodotus, 21, 24, 48 n. 1, 114, 208,
    219
Hiero, 86, 144, 215
Hieronymus of Cardia, 22, 27
Hieronymus of Syracuse, 86 f., 215
Hippocratic theory, 23
historia, 43, 45, 137, 197, 217, 246 f.,
    254, 273
homoioteleuton, 240
Horace, 10 ff., 61, 257 f.
Horatii, 213
Horatius Cocles, 212 f., 256, 277
hortatio, 225
Hostilius Mancinus, C. (cos. 137),
    160 n. 1
'human' interest, anecdotes of, 212 ff.
hyperbole, 200 f.

Iasos, 24
Icilius, L., 215, 228
Ilipa, 154, 162
Illyrian War, Third, 75
Ilorci, 99, 154, 192
incrementum, 241
Indibilis, 74
indirect characterisation, 82 ff.
Insubres, 160, 285
interrogatio, 241 f., 243
irony, 240 f.
Isère, the, 155
isocolon, 239 f., 258
Isocrates, 22 f., 26, 29, 32 f., 219, 247,
    272 f.
Istrians, 285
ius gentium, 67

Janus, temple of, 8 n. 1, 10, 14
Jerome, Saint, 1, 2 n. 1, 3, 19
Jugurtha, 6
Julius Caesar, C., 7, 12, 28, 33, 37 f.,
    43, 47, 57, 73, 100, 136, 163, 203,
    245 ff., 262
Junius Brutus, L. (cos. 509), 70

Junius Brutus, M. (conspirator), 12, 163, 269, 272
Juno, 131
Juno Moneta, temple of, 111
Jupiter, 131, 170, 176
Jupiter Feretrius, temple of, 113

Kingsley, Charles, 36

Lacinium, 113, 124
Laelius, C., 192
Lampsacus, 188
Lars Porsena, 213, 277
Latins, 92, 224, 279, 280
Lentulus, L., 55
Leon, 238
Leontini, 36, 102
Leuctra, 24
lex Canuleia, 69, 123
lex Hortensia, 276 n. 3
lex Ogulnia, 165
lex Oppia, 86 n. 3, 228, 232, 242
lex Terentilia, 165
libertas, 164
libri lintei, 111 f., 116 n. 1, 122, 147, 277 f.
Licinian Rogations, 214, 278 n. 3
Licinius Calvus, C., 123
Licinius Crassus, M. (cos. 30), 15
Licinius Crassus, P. (cos. 205), 106
Licinius Crassus, P. (cos. 171), 169
Licinius Macer, C. (annalist), 112, 115
Lidice, 172
Ligarius, Q., 123
Ligurians, 109, 162, 285
Ligustinus, Sp., 216
Little St Bernard, 155
Livia gens, 152
Livius Andronicus, 236
Livius Drusus, M. (trib. 91), 163
Livius Macatus, C., 126, 153
Livius Salinator, M. (cos. I 219), 153, 161, 167
Locri, 74, 97, 202, 225
Lucretia, 13, 76, 91, 214, 216 f.
Lucretius, Sp., 216
Lucretius, T. (poet), 257
Lucullus, 136
Ludi Saeculares, 13
Lysias, 83 n. 2
Lysimachia, 188, 232

Macedon, 40, 76
Macedonians, 65, 143, 151, 157, 182 n. 1, 188, 198, 211
Macedonian War, First, 281 f., 284
Macedonian War, Second, 38 n. 3, 284
Macedonian War, Third, 7, 284
Maelius, Sp., 92
Magius, L., 9
Magnesia, 150, 162 n. 1, 285
Mago, 160 f.
Mancinus, *see under* Hostilius
Mandonius, 74
Manlius Capitolinus, M. (cos. 392), 60, 229, 251
Manlius Torquatus, T. (cos. I 347), 54, 71, 79, 151, 187, 200
Manlius Torquatus, T. (cos. I 235), 91
Manlius Vulso, Cn. (cos. 189), 76, 86, 187, 225, 286 n. 4
Mantinea, 26
Marcellus, *see under* Claudius
Marcius Coriolanus, Cn., 91 f., 213, 279 n. 3
Marcius Rutulus, C. (cos. 357), 92
Marcius Septimus, L., 194 f.
Marius, C., 7
Maronea, 152, 209
Mars, 47
Masinissa, 77, 87, 96, 143, 188, 230, 239
Mastarna, 277
Megalesia, the, 144
Megalopolis, 128
Melian Dialogue, 208
Menander, 192
Menenius Agrippa, M., 77, 86 n. 1, 92
Messalla Corvinus, 2 n. 1, 19 n. 1
metaphor, 240
Metaurus, the, 144, 161, 167, 184
Metellus, *see under* Caecilius
Mettius Fufetius, 65, 183, 257
military history, 157 ff.
Minucius, L. (cos. 458), 90
Minucius Rufus, M. (cos. 221), 72, 86, 90, 166 f., 200 f.
mistranslations, 143 f.
Mithridates, 7
Mons Sacer, 180, 231
Mt Cenis, 155
Mt Genèvre, 155
moralistic history, 26 f., 66 ff., 88 ff.
Mucius Scaevola, C., 75, 76 n. 1, 212 f., 277

Munda, 7
Myonnesus, 199 n. 2, 252 f.

Nabis of Sparta, 207
Naevius (trib. 184), 149
Nearchus, 22
Nemesis, 122
neologism, 260
Nepete, 58
Nero (emperor), 2
New Carthage, 74, 94, 98 f., 145, 148, 173, 202 f.
New Comedy, 214
Nicaea, 79, 101, 150, 205, 212
Nicander, 207
Nicanor, 148
Nicias, 105
Nissen's Law, 142
Nola, 102, 127 n. 2
Numa Pompilius, 11, 16, 48, 175, 276
Numantia, 160 n. 1
Numidians, 108

Octavian, 3, 4 f., 10, 17 (*see also under* Augustus)
Olympiads, 146
Onomastus, 209
oratio obliqua, 169, 206, 211, 242, 265 f.
oratio recta, 211 f., 233, 242 ff.
Origines of Cato, 134 f.
Ovid, 12 f., 61, 175, 214

Pacuvius Calavius, 229 n. 2
Palaeopolis, 189
Panaetius, 27
Papirius Cursor, L. (cos. 326), 40, 71, 86, 88, 225
Papirius, Sp., 51 n. 3
Papirius Mugillanus, M., 70
Parthia, 8 n. 1
participles in Livy, 266 f.
patavinitas, 2, 45, 267 ff.
Patavium, 1 f., 5, 18 n. 2, 19, 37, 45, 272
patriotic history, 65 ff., 144 f., 151 f.
pax deorum, 59
pax Romana, 10
Peloponnesian War, 34, 105
Pergamum, 107
Pericles, 26, 85, 220
periochae, 7, 8 n. 1
periodic style, Livy's, 250 ff.

Peripatetics, 25
peripeteia, 202, 210, 213
Perizonius, 276 n. 1
Perseus, 7, 38 n. 3, 84, 205 f., 226, 234, 242
Phaeneas, 107, 211 f.
Pharnabazus, 41
Pharsalus, 123
Phaselis, 199 n. 2, 255 f.
Philinus, 130
Philip V of Macedon, 7, 68, 79, 87, 101, 106 f., 120, 148, 151, 162, 169, 178, 186, 196, 205, 209–12, 226, 234, 238
Philippi, 45
Philopoemen, 41, 188
Philus, 160 n. 1
Phoenice, treaty of, 150 n. 3
Phylarchus, 26, 41 n. 3, 42, 275
pietas, 49, 66 ff.
Piso, *see under* Calpurnius
πιθανότης, 190
Placentia, 269
Plato, 4
Plautus, 29
Pleminius, 74, 97, 225, 227
Pliny, elder, 9, 55
Pliny, younger, 113
pluperfect tense in episodes, 179
Plutarch, 22, 26, 64, 88, 106, 115, 213
poetic influences, 253 ff.
Pollio, Asinius, 2, 11 n. 5, 20, 43, 45, 136, 267 ff.
Polybius, 5, 20–3, 27–9, 33 f., 38, 40, 42, 48, 53 n. 2, 55, 57, 68, 72–4, 78 f., 82–4, 86 f., 95, 97–9, 103, 105, 112 f., 118, 120, 124 ff., 128 ff., 133, 135, 138–40, 142–6, 148 f., 151–8, 160–4, 168, 173, 178, 181, 183 f., 186 f., 189 f., 194 f., 196, 200, 203, 205–7, 209 f., 213, 221, 231 f., 234 f., 238, 243, 272, 280–2, 284 f.
Pompeius Magnus, Cn., 7 f., 12 f., 163, 272
Pompeius Sextus, 3
Pompeius Trogus, 243
pontifex maximus, 110
Popillius Laenas, M., 75
Porcius Cato, M. (cos. 195), 27, 29 f., 50, 85, 86 n. 3, 93, 120, 131 f., 134 f., 145, 149, 201, 222, 228, 232, 241 f., 276, 286

Posidonius, 4, 27, 28 n. 1, 41 n. 3, 49, 53, 62, 135
Postumius Albinus, A. (historian), 29
Postumius Albus, A., 146
Postumius Tempsanus, L., 148
Praenestini, 73
praesumptio, 241
praeteritio, 241
Preface, Livy's, 51, 66
prepositions in Livy, 263
prodigies, 62 ff.
Prometheus, 25 n. 1
Pronoia, 53
Propertius, 61, 256
provocatio, 89
prudentia, 66, 71 ff.
Prusias, 84, 104
psychological history, 168 ff., 191 f.
Ptolemy (geographer), 154
Ptolemy I, 22
Ptolemy V Epiphanes, 210
pudicitia, 66, 76 f., 213 f.
Punic War, First, 7
Punic War, Second, 36, 38, 85, 124
    (*see also under* Hannibalic War)
Punic War, Third, 87
Pydna, 128, 184
Pyrrhus, 88

Quinctii, 92
Quinctilius Varus, P. (praetor 203), 161
Quinctius Caeso, 123, 147, 165
Quinctius Capitolinus, T., 92, 164
Quinctius Cincinnatus, L., 70, 77, 92, 279 n. 3
Quinctius Flamininus, L., 239
Quinctius Flamininus, T., 74 f., 78 f., 92, 101, 107, 150 f., 171, 184, 205 f., 210 f., 239
Quintilian, 38, 219 f., 223, 235, 237 ff., 246, 253, 268 ff.

ratio in war, 66, 71 ff.
recitationes, 6
Regal period, 276 f.
Regillus, Lake, 146
religious views, Livy's, 46 ff.
Remus, 47, 118
reticentia, 241
Rhegium, 105
Rhodes, 3

Rhodians, 199, 210 f., 232
Romulus, 10 f., 16, 47, 75, 76 n. 1, 118, 170, 195, 224
Rutilius, 149

Sabines, 109, 224, 279
Sacred War, 24, 25 n. 1
Saguntines, 71, 227
Saguntum, 84, 105, 118, 124, 139, 143, 145, 154, 180, 193 f., 196
Sallust, 10, 18, 20, 28, 30, 36, 38, 41 n. 3, 42, 43 ff., 51, 57, 59, 80, 84 n. 2, 85, 104, 117 n. 2, 123, 163, 166, 219, 231, 243, 254, 259, 267
sambucae, 192
Samnites, 7, 68, 84 n. 3, 108 f., 189, 237, 281
Samnite Wars, 7, 38 n. 3, 78, 174, 280 f.
Samos, 24
σαφήνεια, 189 f.
Satricum, 73
Scipio, *see under* Cornelius
Scipios, trials of, 93, 97, 133, 286
Sempronius Asellio, 29 f.
Sempronius Atratinus, C., 90
Sempronius Gracchus, Ti. (cos. I 215), 54, 185
Sempronius Gracchus, Ti (cos. I 177), 100
Sempronius Longus, Ti. (cos. 218), 72, 90, 118, 127 n. 2
Sempronius Tuditanus, 254
Senate, Roman, 152, 165 f., 283, 286
senatus consulta, 112, 114
senatus consultum de Bacchanalibus, 112
Seneca, elder, 9
Seneca, younger, 38, 49, 219
sententiae in speeches, 242
Sentinum, 154
Sergius Fidenas, L. (cos. 437), 70
Sergius, M'., 70
Servian reforms, 277
Servilii, 90 f.
Servilius, M., 79 f.
Servilius Ahala, Q., 52
Servius (commentator), 57 n. 1
Servius Tullius, 54, 91, 277
Sicilians, 102
Sicily, 27, 36, 101 ff., 125, 128, 130, 132, 281
Sicyon, 169, 181
siege-descriptions, 191 ff.

Silanus, M., 99
Silenus, 124, 128, 130 f., 155, 156 n. 3
similes in speeches, 238
Sisenna, 30, 44, 136, 254
Smyrna, 188
Solon, 208
Sophocles, 118
Sophoniba, 77, 87, 132, 230
Spain, 8, 15, 96 n. 1, 98, 128, 130, 134, 145, 147, 154, 156, 173, 192 f., 196, 203, 281, 286
speeches, 219 ff.
spolia opima, 113
Statiellates, 75
Stoic influence, 4, 27, 49 ff., 94, 272
Stoics, 56 f.
Strabo, 154
Stratius, 152
Suetonius, 219
Sulla, Cornelius, 7, 136
Sullan annalists, 17 n. 1
Sulpicius Longus, C., 200
superbia, 55, 68
Sutrium, 58, 195
συμπάθεια, 177
συντομία, 187 ff., 190, 199
Syphax, 77, 87, 99, 230
Syracuse, 36, 86, 99, 102, 144, 158, 182, 192, 283

tabulae pontificum, 29, 30, 35, 62, 110
Tacitus, 8, 11 f., 36, 38 f., 41 n. 3, 50 f., 79, 83, 110 n. 1, 163, 177, 208, 219, 228
Tanaquil, 118, 277
Tannetum, 154
Tarentum, 7, 74, 106, 126, 128, 131, 152, 173
Tarquinienses, 73
Tarquinii, the, 54, 216, 277
Tarquinius, L. (*magister equitum* to Cincinnatus), 77
Tarquinius, Sextus, 76, 179, 214, 216
Tarquinius Collatinus, L., 216
Tarquinius Superbus, L., 65, 91, 117, 179, 277
Tatius, Titus, 224
temeritas, 72
Teos, 186
Terentilius Harsa, C. (trib. 462), 164
Terentius Varro, C. (cos. 216), 72, 166 f., 231

Theano, 24
Themistocles, 85
Theopompus, 23, 30, 33, 130, 138, 247
Theoxena, 188
Thermopylae, 135, 154, 156, 201, 225, 285
Thermum, 154
Thessalians, 210
Thoas, 244
Thucydides, 21–3, 27 f., 34–6, 38, 40, 44, 68, 73, 83, 85, 105, 182, 208, 220 n. 2, 231
Thurian hostages, 74
Tiber, 77
Tiberius (emperor), 83
Tibullus, 257
Ticinus, the, 103
Timaeus, 24, 27, 30, 130, 132, 138
Timagenes, 117
Timasitheus, 64
Tolostobogii, 225
tractatio in speeches, 223
'tragic' historiography, 25 f., 41 f., 104, 218, 234
Transpadane Gaul, 1
Trasimene, Lake, 63, 68, 103, 127, 131, 144, 152, 160, 166 f., 170, 186
Trebia, the, 72, 118, 127, 160
Tricastini, 155
Tricorii, 155
Troy, 257
Tullia, 91
Tullius, Sextus (centurion), 227 n. 5
Tullus Hostilius, 171, 276
Tusculans, 73
Tusculum, 164
Twelve Tables, the, 69
Tyche, 56 ff., 129 f.

Umbria, 154
Umbrians, 7, 254

Valeria gens, 88 ff., 117, 121
Valerio-Horatian laws, 69, 278 n. 3
Valerius Antias (annalist), 30, 32, 42, 72, 89, 115 ff., 120 ff., 127 f., 133 ff., 139 f., 142, 144 f., 147 f., 149, 152, 231, 236
Valerius Corvus, M. (cos. 348), 89, 92, 225, 228
Valerius Flaccus, C. (*flamen Dialis*), 67

INDEX

Valerius Flaccus, L. (cos. 195), 86 n. 3,
   149, 201, 232
Valerius Laevinus, M. (cos. 210), 90
Valerius Publicola, P. (cos. 509), 77, 89
variatio, 134, 174
Varius, 12
Varro, 13, 47 f., 117
Veii, 17, 54, 75, 122, 193, 195, 222, 279
Vergil, 10 ff., 58, 61, 94, 102 f., 178,
   255, 256 f.
Verginia, 13, 76, 213–15, 225, 228
Verginius, A. (trib. 395), 147
Verginius, L. (trib. 449), 215
Verginius, L. (*tribunus militum consulari
   potestate* 402), 70
Veturia, 91

Vibius Virrius, 84, 238
Victumulae, 105, 195
virtus Romana, 66, 75
Vitellii, 116
Vocontii, 155
Volsci, 52, 59, 72 n. 5, 73, 90 f., 109,
   147, 182, 279 f.

Xanthippus, 71
Xenophon, 4, 22, 83, 157
Xerxes, 208

Zama, 103, 162 n. 1, 228
zeugma, 240
Zoippus, 215